Pressing Onward

David,
May we continue
to press onward
toward a brighter
future for our whole
community.

JP Cerdena

Pressing Onward

THE IMPERATIVE RESILIENCE OF LATINA MIGRANT MOTHERS

Jessica P. Cerdeña

UNIVERSITY OF CALIFORNIA PRESS

University of California Press
Oakland, California

Library of Congress Cataloging-in-Publication Data
Names: Cerdeña, Jessica P., 1991– author.
Title: Pressing onward : the imperative resilience of Latina migrant
   mothers / Jessica P. Cerdeña.
Description: Oakland, California : University of California Press, [2023] |
   Includes bibliographical references and index.
Identifiers: LCCN 2022044584 (print) | LCCN 2022044585 (ebook) |
   ISBN 9780520394001 (hardcover) | ISBN 9780520394018 (paperback) |
   ISBN 9780520394032 (ebook)
Subjects: LCSH: Women immigrants—Connecticut—New Haven—
   Social conditions—21st century. | Latin Americans—Connecticut—
   New Haven—Social conditions—21st century.
Classification: LCC JV6347 .C47 2023 (print) | LCC JV6347 (ebook) |
   DDC 305.489746/8—dc23/eng/20221109
LC record available at https://lccn.loc.gov/2022044584
LC ebook record available at https://lccn.loc.gov/2022044585

Manufactured in the United States of America

30 29 28 27 26 25 24 23
10 9 8 7 6 5 4 3 2 1

Contents

Acknowledgments   vii

Preface   xi

Introduction: On Love Alone   1

1. Leaving   17

2. Moving   41

3. Arriving   64

4. Mothering   111

5. Surviving   144

    Conclusion: Onward   179

Appendix A. Methods   183

Appendix B. Ethnographic Tables   185

*Appendix C. Organizations for Immigration and
Health Policy Reform and Activism*   193

References   195

Index   219

Acknowledgments

This book is for the women who opened their hearts and minds to me during a time of strain and isolation to share how they press onward both for themselves and for the future of their communities. This work has further convinced me of the power of community to help a person *salir adelante*, or get ahead, and it would not have been possible without my own academic mentors, family, and friends—or "chosen family."

I first thank Dr. Marcia C. Inhorn for believing in me even when I did not believe in myself, for pushing me to achieve more than I thought possible in my nascent academic career, and for serving as a surrogate mother to me—caring for my personal well-being and family—as well as a stand-in grandmother for my sons, Nahuel and Mayku. She has truly changed my life for the better. I am also grateful to Dr. Helena Hansen for her invaluable guidance, making time to coach me at coffee shops or after conference presentations, and for blazing the path of an MD/PhD woman of color balancing clinical expertise with significant research and community engagement. I must also give thanks to Dr. Lance Gravlee, whose invaluable wisdom, humor, and friendship have enhanced my methodological and leadership skills, advanced my understanding of the complex entanglements between race and medicine, and encouraged me to present my authentic self in academic spaces—an ongoing challenge for a not-quite-White girl with a repressed Jersey accent. I am also deeply indebted to Dr. Richard G. Bribiescas, who served as my first mentor at Yale, tethering me to the anthropology department while I drank from the firehose of anatomy, physiology, and biochemistry during my first two years of medical school. Rick's support of my student activism for racial justice and intersectional equity in his role as deputy provost for diversity, his immense achievement and challenging life history, and his ability to conjure a metaphor for *everything* continue to inspire me toward social change and accessible scholarship.

Several other faculty in the anthropology department have provided both intellectual and institutional guidance, helping me refine my contributions and easing my path toward a dual degree. They include Dr. Claudia Valeggia, Dr. Catherine Panter-Brick, Dr. David Watts, Dr. Erik Harms, and Dr. Doug Rogers. I thank them all for helping me become the scholar I am today. I also owe immeasurable thanks to the members of the Medical Anthropology Working Group (also known as MAWGies or "Marcians") for reading and critiquing my writing over the years and further refining my perspective: They include Dr. Sarah Brothers, Dr. Kristen McLean, Dr. Hatice (Nilay) Erten, Dr. Aalyia Sadruddin, Dr. Gabriela Morales, Dr. Haesoo Park, Dr. Elizabeth (Lizzy) Berk, and Rachel Farell.

This research relied on the support of several undergraduate research assistants, including Geraldo Salcedo, Victoria Vera, Moises Cosme, Daniel Guerra, Nicholas Ruiz-Huidobro Magdits, Jean Tobar, Sandra Amézcua Rocha, Lily Lawler, and Hannah Kiburz. This team undertook immense labors of interview transcription and translation and supported me in scheduling interviews, archival work, media analysis, and review of demographic data.

My advancement along this path would not have been possible without the support of the Yale MD/PhD program administration, particularly Dr. Barbara Kazmierczak, Cheryl DeFilippo, Alexandra Mauzerall, Dr. Reiko Fitzsimonds, and Dr. Faye Rogers. Thank you all for believing in me and for helping to reshape the path toward the MD/PhD in anthropology.

Similarly, I am greatly indebted to my funders, including the National Institutes of Health Medical Scientist Training Program, the National

Science Foundation, the Wenner-Gren Foundation, and the Robert Wood Johnson Health Policy Research Scholars program.

I owe the most to my family for their unfailing support along the way. Thank you to my husband, Ignacio, who met me as a twenty-two-year-old medical student and committed to loving me throughout my extended training and beyond. Thank you to my older son, Nahuel, whose curiosity and wonder at the world continually drive me to look at my surroundings in a new light. Thank you to my younger son, Mayku, whose imminent birth accelerated the pace of developing this manuscript, and whose un-failing smile reminds me to express gratitude. Both Ignacio and my chil-dren have deepened my heart and expanded my capacity to love. Thank you to my mother-in-law, María Eugenia, for her saintly patience and dedication to caring for Nahuel and Mayku while I worked away at this research. I also thank my father-in-law, Fernando, and my cousins, aunts, and uncles, for trusting me along this journey—and occasionally prema-turely promoting me to Dr. Cerdeña; I especially thank my cousin Alex, who never saw his name in a playbill after I transitioned from my first (more exciting) career in child acting, but who nevertheless has supported me with inexhaustible enthusiasm. Finally, thank you to my parents, Julia and David, and my brother, Chris, for challenging me, telling me, "If you don't like something about the world, go fix it," and celebrating each of my painfully nerdy milestones.

I also thank my "chosen family," the individuals who have shown me unconditional love and support throughout this challenging career. These include John Schmidt, Robert Rock, Sydney Green, Luisa Rivera, Alyssa Mitson-Salazar, the community of Saint Joseph of Arimathea and my pas-tors Father Matthew and Mother Cheryl, and my Health Policy Research Scholars family (also known as the "GOO"), particularly Dr. Marie Plai-sime, Dr. Mya Roberson, Dr. Rebekah Cross, Dr. Yaminette Diaz-Linhart, Dr. Laurent Guerrera, Dr. Marcela Nava, Dr. Arjee Restar, Katherine (Katie) Gutierrez, and Deanna Barath. Likewise, I am deeply grateful to my various communities, including the Yale Student National Medi-cal Association/Latino Medical Student Association; NextYSM and the Committee for Diversity, Inclusion, and Social Justice (CDISJ); HAVEN Free Clinic; Unidad Latina en Acción; and the broader network of Latinx leaders in New Haven. Thank you all for welcoming me, nourishing my spirit, and inspiring me.

I am honored to work with the University of California Press. Thank you to Kate Marshall for shepherding me through the editorial process and to Chad Attenborough for supporting me during production. Thank you, also, to Dr. Emily Daniels for developmental editing and to Jennifer Hammer at NYU Press for invaluable feedback that enhanced this book.

Finally, thank you to my interlocutors for your *confianza* (trust or confidence) in me, for sharing your stories, and for teaching me even more profoundly how to mother amid challenging circumstances.

Preface

In Criscuolo Park, where the Quinnipiac and Mill Rivers pour out into Long Island Sound, I sat on a small pier, hugging my knees to my chest. I had seen local teens hang out here, laughing and sharing Coke or flavored cigarettes. Once I saw a young man lean his bike against the wooden ramp and sit cross-legged in the middle of the pier, losing himself in meditation.

Despite its lack of conventional beauty—the vista marred by oil tankers and interstate traffic—the pier invites reflection. The Quinnipiac River once served as the lifeblood of the Algonquian-speaking tribes that lived on and nurtured the lands of southern Connecticut. Although these people called themselves Eansketambawg, meaning "We, the original surface-dwelling People," European colonists named them the Quinnipiac(k), using the Algonquian name for the "long flowing river" (Ouinni-pe-oghq) and "long water land" (Quinni-pe-auke) that together formed the area around what we now call New Haven. Today the river flows alongside the Fair Haven neighborhood, which for generations has been a home for migrants from eastern and southern Europe, the southern United States, and Latin America. Latinxs (people with Latin American heritage, of any gender) in the neighborhood, particularly those with Indigenous heritage, have assumed the responsibility of caring for these lands and waterways. As I sat there, I remembered the words of a local Totonac activist, Adriana Rodriguez, who publicly criticized immigration enforcement, saying, "My people have moved across these lands for tens of thousands of years. I don't believe in borders."

I tucked my chin between my knees, warming myself against the uncommonly damp and chilly August afternoon. Just then, a flicker of orange caught my eye. I watched as a stunningly painted monarch butterfly fluttered down, settling and stretching its wings along the wooden rail of the pier. As she slowly opened and closed her wings, alternately resting and flexing them, I found myself curious. Where had she come from? Had she made a temporary home here in New Haven, growing fat on the milkweed some neighbors planted to nourish her? Was she following her southing instincts, escaping the unseasonably cold and heavy rains of New Hampshire or Maine, her body programmed to seek the land of her great-grandparents?

I was resting on the pier to reflect on the event I had just held in the park. A handful of the women who had shared their stories in my study—referred to as interlocutors to represent their role as people who speak between communities in anthropology—had joined me to share a meal, discuss their experiences in the study, and focus my interpretations. I had bounced chubby babies that had been in their mothers' bellies when we had last met. I had shared information about state-based rental assistance and subsidies for women to launch their own home daycare businesses.

Shy, and with little to say about the research, Nieve, from Quito, Ecuador, now twenty years old, lit up when she heard about the daycare program. "Now that she's a little bit older," Nieve said, holding her five-month-old daughter, who was wrapped in a fluffy pink jacket and staring at me with stern dark brown eyes, "I want to go back to work, but I also don't want to leave her. This would be perfect."

When Nieve and I had spoken almost a year earlier, she had told me she dreamed of starting a business to support her mother, her three younger siblings, and her baby. Her husband worked for a construction company, and his work was intermittent; they relied on her income as a fast-food worker to meet their expenses. Early in the pandemic, her husband lost his job, and though Nieve wanted to keep working, she feared the risks of contracting COVID-19 while newly pregnant. I had helped her connect with financial relief and community support organizations and facilitated her enrollment in the free prenatal program Me and My Baby, funded and run by Yale–New Haven Health. Since then Nieve's attitude had changed. A year earlier, she had seemed anxious, stalked by unpaid bills and mounting debt, fearful of giving birth during the peak of the pandemic and about exposing her undocumented status. She clung to her dreams of saving money to support her daughter's education and start a business but admitted that they felt impossible. "I work so hard, but it's not enough," Nieve had told me. "My baby gives me hope. I just want to do everything for her. I want the best for her."

Now, with her well-fed, observant daughter resting on her hip, Nieve mapped out the steps toward the future she had long imagined.

"So, with the money from the state, I can run a daycare from my home and keep my daughter with me?" Nieve asked. I reassured her and reviewed the details of the program. She applied and began the process of obtaining the necessary licensing.

Later that afternoon, as I studied the monarch butterfly on the pier, I thought about Nieve, who had left behind the life she knew in Ecuador, seeking economic security and work opportunities. Her mother and grandmother had scraped by selling vegetables at local markets, but the increasing cost of living had made it impossible for the family to survive on that income. Nieve, her mother, and her siblings came to New Haven, where jobs for Spanish speakers were abundant. Now presented with an excellent job opportunity, Nieve thought not of herself, but of her daughter.

Like Nieve, monarch butterflies sense when their homes can no longer provide for their needs. They pick up and leave, abandoning everything familiar to them. As they fatten on nectar while wintering in Mexico, they slow their metabolism to save energy for breeding. Tens of thousands of monarchs converge on the forests, sustaining themselves on limited supplies of flowers and milkweed. Theirs is a one-way journey. It is their grandchildren or great-grandchildren who will return to their homelands, when the milkweed flowers again. Nieve imagines someday her family will return to Ecuador, but not yet. For now, she focuses on preparing for her daughter's future, first by achieving financial security, then increasing her savings, and finally investing in her daughter's education. Nieve's dreams for her daughter, perhaps like her grandmother's dreams for her, will serve as the compass for the coming generations.

Meanwhile, in Criscuolo Park, a gust of wind off the water blew the monarch off the ledge. She quickly recovered, shaking her wings as if to brush off the blow. Then she took off, alighting on the grassy weeds at the entrance to the community garden in the southeast corner of the park.

Delicate yet determined, monarchs overcome formidable barriers. Ecologists could tell the story of the monarchs as one of suffering and loss. The species has plummeted toward extinction, its population reduced by 80 percent over recent decades. Deforestation and urbanization have depleted the monarchs' food resources in their homelands, and climate change has created severe temperature changes and violent storms that kill off many migrating butterflies.

Viewed in another light, however, monarchs seem strikingly resilient. Despite the storms and spring freezes that threaten their futures, monarchs bounce back, reviving themselves for their journey back home. They ingest substances from the milkweed plants that are toxic to other species to protect themselves from predation. These are not coquettish cowards who flaunt their magnificent colors and retreat at the slightest challenge: monarchs are powerful and persistent.

Medical anthropologists have often treated Latin American migrants as sufferers: possessors of broken bodies, stigmatized biologies, and burdens of stress that hold them back. This book tells a different story. Centered on the women who hold their children as the guiding stars of their lives, this ethnography recounts the powerful ways Latin American migrant mothers have pressed onward amid trauma, legal violence, and economic fallout arising from the COVID-19 pandemic and the hostile Trump presidential administration. Whether gliding or roosting, frantically flapping or harvesting, these monarch-like mothers engage intergenerational wisdom and cognitive survival tactics to enact what I call *imperative resilience*, or a necessary resistance to oppression. This book details the imperative resilience of these migrant mothers, highlighting their sacrifices, journeys, and future trajectories. Despite their precarity, I seek to illuminate their daring and devotion as well.

Introduction

ON LOVE ALONE

I met one of my interlocutors, Célia, and her new baby for a postpartum and life history interview at their apartment complex in East Haven, Connecticut, before COVID-19 restrictions precluded in-person interviews. As I entered the building, kicking freshly mown grass from my shoes, I noticed that the mailbox for her apartment was scribbled with different versions of her surname and her husband's. The uncommonness of multiple surnames in the United States often provokes confusion in bureaucratic settings like medical registration or mail delivery.

I tapped the apartment door, clutching a gift bag. Almost immediately, Marcelina, Célia's sister-in-law, opened the door and ushered me in, her face glistening with sweat and her hair swept into a ponytail. "Thank you, you are too kind," she said, setting the bag on the countertop and returning to the stove, where she was prepping two meals at once. "Célia will be out in a minute."

A little boy with short, dark hair sat on a potty chair in the living room watching Nick Jr. in Spanish. His shirt, printed with the characters of *Paw Patrol*, rode up to reveal a round belly curving over his squatting legs.

After a minute, Célia appeared, wearing red plaid flannel pajamas with a thick elastic band across her belly. She smiled softly, her face heavy with fatigue. "How's the baby?" she asked Marcelina.

"Sleeping," Marcelina answered, adjusting saucepans on the stove. "He'll probably want his milk soon."

I peered into the bassinet to see a wrinkly face framed by downy black hair. The baby's fists stretched toward his face as he wriggled in his white swaddle blanket.

I reached into the gift bag and handed out the diapers, fruit, and slippers I had brought. Célia thanked me and called to her older son, Alonso, offering him an apple. Alonso rushed over, pants at his ankles, as Marcelina hurried to yank them up over his bottom. He grabbed an apple and took a too-big bite, smiling at me.

Célia and I sat at the small round table in the kitchen and began to talk. She shared the story of her migration, her adjustment to the New Haven area, and her baby's birth. Back in Ecuador, she had studied to be an accountant, earning a certification equivalent to that of a US certified public accountant. She took a job as a bookkeeper at a large company. Despite working over sixty hours a week, Célia could barely pay her mortgage and other household expenses. Then their first baby was born, and her husband lost his job.

"Our country only offers jobs to young people," Célia told me. "They want you to be young, but also to have work experience. It's very contradictory. At forty, you're already old.... They'd prefer a twenty- or twenty-five-year-old. If you can find a job, the options are limited. You have to take jobs that demand a lot of time for little pay. It's not worth the sacrifice of so many hours away from home, away from your son or your wife, when your salary barely covers your expenses. You cannot even look for a job, thinking, well, with two jobs, I could help my family, because the first job demands that you work all day, ten to twelve hours."

"They want you to have a bachelor's degree to wash dishes," Marcelina added, rolling her eyes.

Célia continued, "You face a tough decision. You think, I'm going to be away from my country, my family, everything I know. Here, I am with them, but I can't feed them. We cannot live on love alone."

Célia was among the fortunate few I interviewed who was able to obtain a family tourist visa to join her husband, who had already migrated, in the United States. She came with Alonso, then eight months old.

"We told her to be careful," Marcelina said. "In Ecuador at the time, children were being kidnapped. So, we said to her, 'Don't let your guard down. If you have to lose the suitcase, drop it, but don't let go of the baby for any reason.'"

Abruptly, Gabriel, the newborn, let out a high-pitched yell. "It's okay, *mi amor*, we'll solve it together," Marcelina crooned. She jiggled Gabriel in her arms and passed him to Célia, who snuggled him to her breast to nurse.

When Célia and Alonso arrived in the United States, Célia took a job cleaning houses while her husband worked in construction. "Here, the work is harder, but you get paid enough to get by," Célia told me. "I got used to it. I like to work. I would finish at three or four in the afternoon and come home to serve my husband and my son soup for dinner, to prepare his lunch for the next day. In my country, I could never see my baby."

Everything changed when the pandemic hit in March 2020. Célia stopped working to avoid exposure while pregnant and to take care of her son. Meanwhile, her husband was laid off for several weeks from his construction job. When he resumed work, the entire family feared he would bring the virus home. "At first, it was very drastic," Marcelina said. "He would come home and undress at the door. Even the baby panicked, and if his father tried to hug him, he'd yell, 'No!'"

"It was pretty traumatic," Célia commented. Yet the family planned how to get through their difficulties. "I talked with my husband about how we could cut back our expenses and ease our stress," Célia said. "When you have children, you have to be calm for them—not act tense or fight. This is how we *seguir adelante* [press onward]."

FROM INTERGENERATIONAL TRAUMA TO PRESSING ONWARD

Célia narrates the challenges of living amid state failure and her strategies to adapt and *seguir adelante*. Her story is both exceptional and ordinary: her experiences of undercompensated work and insecurity in Ecuador resonated throughout my interviews with other women, and yet her advantage in arriving in the United States on a tourist visa was a privilege few others shared.

Célia's story exemplifies many ways in which my research surprised me. I had planned to study intergenerational trauma, a phenomenon I had observed at the local free clinic among migrant mothers seeking support for depression, who worried that their traumatic histories were affecting their children. Célia did not report any of the experiences of migration-related trauma that my study attempted to assess. Her symptoms—which scored 5 out of a possible 80—did not meet the clinical criteria for post-traumatic stress disorder (PTSD), but rather reflected her precarity as an undocumented migrant woman from an unstable situation in her home country. Célia disclosed unwanted memories of stressful experiences, primarily recalling poverty and attendant violence in Ecuador. These memories often resurge as she watches Spanish news. Célia also reported hypervigilance and mistrust of others as a mother of two young children living unauthorized in an unfamiliar country.

Célia also narrated some powerful ways of adapting to her circumstances. When the family's income in Ecuador could no longer cover their expenses, Célia made the difficult decision to leave and resettle in New Haven. To make ends meet, Célia told me, she and Marcelina occasionally cooked and sold typical Ecuadorian dishes, including *humitas* (steamed corn cakes), for extra income. When the pandemic challenged their finances, she sought support from local diaper and food banks, including the migrant mutual aid organization Semilla Collective.

Célia's story relates both the personal impact of the pandemic—including her small son's fear of contracting the virus from her husband—and the economic fallout. Because of the pandemic, the women I interviewed juggled job loss, reduced pay, the illness and death of friends and family, remote schooling for their children, mask mandates, and the inability to access pandemic relief benefits like expanded unemployment benefits or economic stimulus checks.

METHODOLOGICAL APPROACH

This book relies on person-centered ethnography to capture the experiences of migrant mothers. Person-centered ethnography shows how individuals are situated in social, material, and symbolic contexts. In medical anthropology, this methodology permits interrogation of the ways that historical, political, social, and cultural contexts constitute human behavior, psychology, and biology (Bernard and Gravlee 2014). Specifically, I conducted in-depth, semistructured interviews with sixty-five women between January 2019 and May 2021. These interviews covered the topics of sociodemographics, migration histories, experiences of social adversity and adaptation in the United States, health and reproductive histories, attitudes toward parenting and motherhood, and responses to the COVID-19 pandemic. I completed follow-up interviews with twelve women and life history interviews with three. Follow-up interviews with postpartum women addressed birth experiences, with particular attention to COVID-19 restrictions, parenthood, infant care, and social support. Life history interviews had an open-ended format and often included experiences of childhood, especially parent-child relationships, education, labor, social relationships and romantic partnership, migration experiences, and motherhood.

Because of the pandemic, I conducted most of my interviews (94 percent) over the phone. This necessity led me to revise my assumptions about going "into the field." On the one hand, connections and audio quality sometimes fell short, and I could not offer the same affirmation and encouragement through nonverbal cues that I might have done in person. On the other hand, rather than meeting women in a sterile conference room at a prenatal clinic, I could talk to them at home, amid their busy lives. Often, one of my interlocutors would pause to handle a hot pan on the stove or to settle a screeching toddler. Once or twice I asked for patience so that I could nurse my own baby or run interference before he slathered a plate of rice and beans all over the wall. The flexibility of phone calls also allowed interviews to pause and resume, or to take place at atypical hours, in the early morning or the evening. Particularly long interviews sometimes spanned living rooms, cars, and socially distanced outdoor strolls as my interlocutors fit conversations with me around their commitments to family and personal well-being. Discussions about financial stress often led to late-night messages in which I helped women connect with food banks, nonprofit organizations, and mutual aid funds. In many ways, I feel I grew to know my interlocutors more deeply than I might have had I spoken with them only during their clinic visits. (For more details on methodology, please see the appendix.)

To foreground the narratives of my interlocutors, I have employed the techniques of oral history interviews and archival research to describe patterns of Latin American migration to New Haven and consequent shifts in social and political relations. I conducted oral history interviews with thirteen individuals, including journalists, politicians, activists, and community leaders with ties to the Latinx population of New Haven. I corroborated information from these oral histories through archival and demographic research. I also interviewed three key staff members at the prenatal clinic from which I recruited interlocutors, the Women's Center of Yale–New Haven Hospital.

Because I began this research with an interest in intergenerational trauma, backed by clinical experience, I carried out surveys of migration-related trauma and trauma symptoms, using the instrument proposed by Keller et al. (2017) and the PTSD Checklist for the DSM-5 (Weathers et al. 2013). I had also originally intended to collect epigenetic and neuro-endocrine biomarkers, aiming to assess correlations between traumatic experience, subjective narratives, psychopathology, and biological variation. Limitations on in-person research precluded the collection of hair and saliva samples, so I relied on ethnographic interviews and surveys to evaluate these relationships. Ultimately I found that the rigid instruments I had chosen could not capture the imprints of traumatic experience the way ethnographic narrative could. Similarly, I completed the Edinburgh Postnatal Depression Scale with postpartum women, and I note the ways that a focus on biomedical symptoms neglects the interconnectedness of social experience and psychology.

THE ETHICS OF STUDYING INEQUITY

Shortly after arriving at Yale University as a medical student, I came to resent the physical and imagined boundaries my colleagues constructed to separate themselves from "the community." Many of my peers, despite having lived in New Haven for years or even decades, could not name the city's neighborhoods and knew little about local politics or history. Before beginning my research, I became involved in activism for immigrant and worker rights and for racial justice, and I joined a faith network well beyond the Yale catchment. I soon came to share the distaste my activist peers swallowed down every time they heard the carillon-neurs clang the bells from the top of Harkness Tower: that sense that Yale owned New Haven and considered its residents as invited guests, rather than the other way around. When I decided to break with disciplinary convention and carry out my fieldwork in my own city, I confronted the challenging dynamics of using my Yale title—and benefiting from univer-sity resources—while seeking to collaborate with my neighbors outside the university. I continued to straddle this divide throughout the research.

Prior to the pandemic, I used my position as a medical student (I was then an MD/PhD student in medical anthropology) to connect with clinics where pregnant women from Latin America—particularly undocumented women—often sought care. Based on its volume of patients and its pro-vision of free prenatal care for eligible women through the Me and My Baby program, I decided to work primarily through the Women's Center of Yale–New Haven Health. Collaborating with clinical site directors and providers, I identified potentially eligible patients and recruited women in waiting rooms or exam rooms prior to their appointments or imme-diately afterward. If the patient had a long-standing relationship with a clinician—for instance, if she had seen the same provider throughout her pregnancy—I asked the provider to present the study and introduce me in the last few minutes of the visit. If the patient was new to the practice, I often wore my anthropologist's hat to ease anxiety, turn the attention to her social concerns and her experience of pregnancy, and to help her navigate the visit as she desired.

When pandemic restrictions limited face-to-face contact, I shifted my approach. I included flyers for my research study in the welcome packet for new patients. Providers notified patients that they might be contacted about the study and, unless women declined contact at that time, my re-search assistants or I would call to assess their interest and schedule a phone interview for those who wished to participate.

To protect confidentiality, I have used pseudonyms for all migrant mothers, their children, and clinic staff quoted here. In rare instances when I became concerned that a woman could be identified by elements of her story, I have adjusted details while preserving the main features of her narrative. Those interviewed for oral histories granted permission for me to use their real names.

Although anthropologists often offer small tokens of appreciation to their interlocutors, it was important to me to ensure that their participation in this study, and their involvement with a Yale affiliate, yielded greater material benefit. Each woman received a $100 gift card for participation in the initial interview, which took place during her pregnancy. Those who participated in follow-up interviews received an additional $50 gift card. At one point, financial delays resulted in slower disbursement of gift cards, and those affected received an additional $10. At the conclusion of the study, as discussed in the preface, several women joined a gathering to share results, at which they received a meal and gift bags containing personal care items, masks, hand sanitizer, formula, and lactation snacks; many women gave their children *las dos*, meaning both breast milk and formula. On top of that, I did everything I could to use my experience in medicine, at Yale, and in New Haven to connect women with resources. I notified providers or the nurse manager about concerning symptoms women reported to me. I contacted the clinic social worker, the Special Supplemental Nutrition Program for Women, Infants, and Children (WIC) office, or the Head Start coordinator about extreme financial distress, nutritional needs, pending evictions, workplace abuse, or unsafe housing. I identified food and diaper banks and occasionally hand-delivered donated goods.

These efforts do not begin to represent the reparations owed to oppressed communities in New Haven and elsewhere, nor do they truly mitigate the historical and ongoing harms perpetrated by Yale against the city's residents. If anything, I learned how the promise of compensation—and delays due to bureaucratic hurdles within the university finance system—can further erode trust among marginalized communities. This reparative work is ongoing and will require visionary policy reform, beginning with local investment and powerful institutions like Yale holding themselves accountable to justice.

MY SOCIAL POSITION AND POWER, OR POSITIONALITY

Although I first approached this project as a clinician, its subject echoes my family history. My maternal grandmother is Chilean. My great-grandfather was Mapuche, an Indigenous man from rural southern Chile, who married a Yugoslavian émigré in Santiago and moved to the United States. My grandmother, like many Latinxs with strong European heritage, identified more strongly with her Slavic background—evidence of the pervasive anti-Indigenous racism in the Americas. Although it was his second language, my great-grandfather primarily spoke Spanish, but he spoke a broken Serbo-Croatian-Slovenian with my great-grandmother. My grandmother, who never fully learned Spanish, married an Italian man, and his mother and sisters inculcated her into New York Italian traditions, effectively overshadowing her Chilean culture. Even now, despite their dark features and high cheekbones, my aunts and uncles often choose not to identify as Latinx; in fact, some actively resist the label, enchanted by the racist mirage of assimilationism and Whiteness.

I am Indigenous, but I am not an Indigenous scholar. I have no attachment to the Mapuche who are claiming territorial autonomy and protesting economic inequality. Apart from a DNA test, a family tree, and my solidarity, I have no current ties with these communities. I am affected by historical and cultural loss. At the same time, my heritage makes this project more personal.

During my oral qualifying exams for the dissertation that produced this book, I discussed the types of trauma Latin American migrants confront when relocating to the United States. One of my examiners listened intently, then furrowed their brow. "I am not convinced that these types of experiences constitute trauma," they said.

I froze. I felt as if this person had balled up my exam and lodged it deep in my throat. *What do you mean?* I wanted to ask. I felt hot tears fill my sinuses. I muddled through an answer, sputtering out words like *precarity* and *violence*, interspersed with a few statistics. I received the word that I had passed, accepted the congratulations, and went to my car to cry. Those words felt visceral. They undermined the premise of my work, my observations as a clinical student, and as I later understood, the new meanings I had pieced together about my family.

In the following weeks, I thought more about my grandmother. She grew up poor in Hell's Kitchen. Her father, though kind, struggled to express himself, and their time together was largely wordless. Poverty strained her parents' marriage: though they barely spoke the same language, they argued constantly. When I asked her about my great-grandmother, all I

heard was, "She was mean." My grandmother cared for her younger siblings, all while enduring the emotional abuse of her mother and the silence of her father. She developed "manic depression," now called bipolar
disorder, and has endured multiple psychiatric hospitalizations.

It is not possible to attribute my grandmother's mental illness entirely
to her socioeconomic circumstances and her status as the child of immigrants. But as I listened to her narrate her life, it seemed likely that
the poverty and isolation her family endured contributed to the development—or exacerbation—of her bipolar disorder. Through the lens of
intergenerational trauma, I see a woman who developed mental illness
after confronting her mother's verbal abuse and her father's withdrawal
after displacement from his community's ancestral lands. Hearing from
a trusted mentor that the experiences of Latin American migrants do not
qualify as trauma called into question my family's history.

Again, I do not claim to be part of the community featured in this research. Unlike many of my interlocutors, I have light skin, US citizenship,
and unaccented, native proficiency in English. At the same time, my ethnic ties to my interlocutors and my narrative relationship to my research
have compelled me to constantly examine the origins of my claims to
knowledge; like all knowledge, mine is situated (Haraway 1988).

This project further draws from practices of collective ethnography
(Clerke and Hopwood 2014; Lahelma et al. 2006). To assist me in data collection and analysis, I employed nine undergraduate students, all but one
of whom identified as Latinx/e/o/a. Each represented different dimensions of *Latinidad*, phenotypically, socially, economically, and across diverse intersections of gender and sexuality. As part of their involvement in
the project, each assistant agreed to engage their own positionality as they
shared field notes and contributed to the collection, interpretation, and
analysis of data. As such, I include—with permission—quotes from field
notes made by my research assistants that informed this ethnography.

Importantly, this is not a decolonized study—not even close. Although
the idea for this project emerged from community concerns, this work
exhibits many of the pitfalls of colonialist anthropology, White academia,
and my education at predominantly White institutions. I have attempted
to democratize this study by engaging my interlocutors and oral history
narrators in my interpretations of the data and plans for dissemination,

and by working with undergraduate research assistants who hail from similar communities. At the same time, I acknowledge these ongoing power hierarchies and seek to disrupt them.

THE IMPERATIVE RESILIENCE OF MIGRANT MOTHERS

This book attempts to evaluate the experience of migrant motherhood, demonstrating the powerful ways women cope with histories of trauma and ongoing structural adversity. In asking how Latin American migrant women accommodate traumatic histories and motherhood, especially during the COVID-19 pandemic, I found that they devise and deploy sophisticated means of moving beyond their painful pasts and resisting the violence of the present. By carefully selecting life partners who advance their own strategic goals or relying on the strength of their mothers and grandmothers in moments of doubt, these women show "resilience" because there is no other choice. I call this *imperative resilience.*

My use of the term *resilience* departs from circulating definitions of the term in the fields of public health and social science (and in common dialogue) as "grit," or healthy functioning, or maintaining a positive trajectory amid difficult circumstances. If I had written this book in Spanish, I would have used the word *resistencia,* which can mean both "resilience" and "resistance," the latter of which more accurately describes the rational actions of the women I met. Here, I attempt to reclaim the word *resilience* to mean strategic resistance to oppressive structures, rather than inherent or learned toughness, positive psychology, or unexpected achievement in the face of adversity.

Although this work examines many aspects of social suffering, it is not a "pornography of pain." Like the historian Carolyn Dean (2003), I do not believe it is necessary for those with greater social, cultural, political, and financial capital to experience symbolic proximity to "sufferers" in order to engage in moral action. Instead, I characterize the strategies women employ in response to structural—and global—disadvantage, and the ways policies can foster reproductive and mental health equity.

I met women in some of the most challenging moments of their lives, as they tightened their budgets and sheltered their families from a deadly virus while repressing experiences of trauma and loss. They continued to pay their bills, feed their small children fruits and vegetables, nurse and bathe newborns, and avert detection of symptoms of mental distress on clinical screenings. With limited social support and next to no public aid, these women invested their cognitive, emotional, and somatic resources to ensure that their children would have choices they never had. Imagine what might happen if women could store this energy as surplus—if they could rely on their spirituality, their intimate relationships, and their matrilineal bonds for fulfillment and self-confidence rather than survival.

Public health experts urged individual citizens to take responsibility—by masking, distancing, and getting vaccinated—for "flattening the curve" of COVID-19 infections. But to build a truly healthy society, we must also flatten inequality so that each person can live to their fullest potential. To this end, I spoke to community health workers, community organizations, clinicians, social workers, and policymakers. As a physician-anthropologist, I aim to connect the sectors holding the power to enact structural reform with those that directly influence the health and social conditions of migrants. I hope that by reading this book, clinical workers can enhance their structural competency, or recognize how socioeconomic, political, and cultural forces shape health outcomes (Metzl and Hansen 2014). This way, scholars and healthcare workers can support structural interventions like immigration reform—rather than behavioral modification or individual therapies—to improve migrant well-being, and students can dream bigger than I can to fight oppression with liberation.

MY INTERLOCUTORS

The women who shared their lives with me hailed from diverse areas in New Haven County. Although a plurality lived in New Haven—particularly the Fair Haven and Hill neighborhoods—others built their lives in West Haven, East Haven, Branford, Hamden, and Waterbury. The average age of women was around thirty-one years old, and the length of time they had spent in the United States varied from two months to twenty-four years, with an average stay of about 8 years. With few exceptions, women lived in rented homes, either apartments or townhouses; some who had migrated alone rented rooms in apartments or trailer homes with extended family or friends. Forty-three of the women already had children, ranging from infants to late teenagers. Twenty percent of mothers had children they had left behind in their home countries. More than half subjectively reported living in poverty—or nearly evading poverty—while the remainder identified as middle class. Most women were out of work because of the pandemic. Those with jobs worked in food service, health or childcare, housekeeping, or factories and distribution centers. I discuss further the economic and social effects of the COVID-19 pandemic in chapter 5.

MONARCH BUTTERFLIES: A METAPHOR FOR MIGRATION AND ADAPTATION

In his poetic, autobiographical novel *On Earth We're Briefly Gorgeous*, Ocean Vuong compares the sacrificial move his mother made moving from Vietnam to the United States to the migratory patterns of monarch butterflies. He writes, "Female monarchs lay eggs along the route. Every history has more than one thread, each thread a story of division. The journey takes four thousand eight hundred and thirty miles, more than the length of this country. The monarchs that fly south will not make it back north. Each departure, then, is final. Only their children return; only the future revisits the past" (Vuong 2019, 8).

I employ this image of the monarch butterfly to evoke the lives of the mothers in this study. Monarchs metamorphose from wriggle caterpillars into winged creatures that are beautiful, delicate, and capable of extraordinary feats. This metamorphosis represents both "post-traumatic growth" (Tedeschi and Calhoun 1996) and adaptation amid constraint.

Most of my interlocutors planned to stay in the United States indefinitely. Only eight (12 percent) had considered returning to their home countries. The permanence of the monarch's migration characterizes the transgenerational histories of most women. Their children do not experience either the robust social support or the unrelenting insecurity of their home countries. They build lives for themselves as children of immigrants, with the cultural loss, the liminality, the feeling of being *ni de aquí, ni de allá* (neither from here nor from there), and the tenacity such an identity requires.

Ultimately, I hope that this image of elegance and strength will prevail over any pitiable accounts of suffering experienced by women in this study. These women are much more than their worst moments. The creativity, fortitude, and patience so many demonstrate enables them not only to survive amid trauma and structural vulnerability but also to soar.

OVERVIEW OF THE BOOK

Chapter 1 examines the impacts of state failure in Latin America—violence perpetrated by governments that has sown conflict and inequality. I consider how, despite advances, social programs in Latin America fail to meet the needs of regular citizens, and how corrupt and amoral law-enforcement agents undermine trust in government. As members of a civically stripped underclass flee to the United States, they become part of a new underclass of "illegal," exploitable laborers. These conditions of structural vulnerability—an adverse position in power hierarchies that constrain life prospects—lead to the production of fear, racism, and economic oppression that replicate conditions in migrants' home countries.

Chapter 2 examines the violence of migration, particularly border crossings. Departure or displacement from a country of origin and relocation in a destination country can lead to migration-related trauma, which conditions migrants' physical and mental health. Contrary to "push-pull" theories of migration, the decision to migrate is influenced mainly by personal and situational factors. Women in this study gave various reasons for migrating—including economic precarity, personal experiences of violence, family reunification, and curiosity or rebellion. In the process, they frequently encountered gender-based and legal violence. An overemphasis on political and economic drivers to the neglect of individual subjectivity risks pathologizing migrant actors.

Chapter 3 first examines the demographic category of *Latinx*, considering the heterogeneity of the US Latinx population, the inherent contradictions in this construction of a pan-ethnic whole—specifically the erasure of Black and Indigenous identities—and the politicization of the term in response to demographic trends. Engaging the positionalities of my interlocutors, my research assistants, and myself, I demonstrate the utility and limitations of the Latinx category and its construction as a "race" in addition to an "ethnicity," as determined by the U.S. Census Bureau. I recount the previously unnarrated history of Latin American migration to New Haven, Connecticut, between 1930 and 2020, drawing from oral history interviews, archival research, and census data. This community, particularly in the predominantly Latinx Fair Haven neighborhood, has achieved significant gains with respect to housing, urban safety, health equity (including COVID-19 vaccine outreach), environmental issues, immigration, and economic development.

Chapter 4 examines the racialization of Latina birth and motherhood in prenatal care, by which some women are empowered to reproduce while others are discouraged. I detail and critique a privately funded prenatal care program for uninsured, low-income mothers, emphasizing how institutional barriers may deprive women of their right to care. I revisit Célia's story, considering how her traumatic birth experience situates her as a poor but "hardy" Latina woman. Acknowledging such racism and trauma, I describe the ways women harness intrinsic and community resources to press onward, or *seguir adelante*. Imperative resilience encompasses multiple techniques, including strategic coupling (securing relationships with men to build social and financial capital), intergenerational fortitude (the transmission of wisdom and values through matrilineages), and spirituality (deriving support through direct, individual communion with God).

Chapter 5 examines the racially and genetically based COVID-19 health inequities propagated through popular media and scientific discourse, identifying structural factors that increase the risks of exposure and the consequences of the disease for Latina migrant mothers. The embodied effects of the COVID-19 pandemic on these mothers disrupt their lives through infection with the virus, grief over the illness and death of loved ones, and economic loss. Returning to issues of racialized health, I discuss women's beliefs surrounding racial disparities in COVID-19 infection, emphasizing the contrast between individualistic (and genetic) explanations and sociostructural attributions to racial inequities in COVID-19. I then review and reconsider attitudes toward vaccination, including the notion of "vaccine hesitancy," engaging anthropological frameworks of belief. I conclude with policy recommendations, developed in partnership with my interlocutors, to improve the social conditions of migrant women.

Departing from anthropological accounts that focus on migrant social suffering, this ethnography narrates the trauma and adversity of Latina migrant mothers while highlighting their strengths and showing how their vision of their children's future enables them to press onward.

1 Leaving

"Miss, I'm very sorry," Lidia halted, her voice lacking the easy confidence of our earlier conversation. "I'm worried that my details could be... exposed,... and the truth is... very concerning. Above all for the safety of my family."

I reassured Lidia that her information would remain confidential and that she was welcome to share no more than she felt comfortable doing.

"In Honduras, my husband was a doctor. He worked for the Ministry of Health and for the attorney general's office. He was the coroner in the area where we lived," Lidia began tentatively. "What happened is that, about a year ago, my husband began receiving anonymous letters at our door. After a couple of months, my husband moved us to a town about twenty or thirty minutes away, saying it was so I could be closer to my work.

"But we were only there about a month when he tells me, 'Look, my assignment has been changed, and we need to move to the city.' The city was about six or seven hours away, and I asked myself, How could it be that we just unpacked the last box from our move a few days ago, and now we have to move again? My husband said again that it was due to his job. So we moved and found a new school for my son.

"After about four or five months, I noticed my husband acting more strangely. He never said anything to me, but I could tell, and I would ask him about it, but he would never say anything. Until one morning, before going to work, he woke me up and said, 'Look I need to talk to you.'

"He begins to tell me about months of letters threatening him, his job, and our family. I asked him, 'How come you haven't told me anything?' and he just said, 'I didn't want to worry you.' So, when those letters kept arriving at our home—even after we had moved to another town—he thought it would be best for us to move to a more distant city, and he had arranged for us both to keep our jobs there.

"That morning, he had found my car with the entire passenger side beaten in. The doors were sunk in, and it was badly destroyed. And he had found a note that said, 'As much as you want to hide, we know where you are—and we know where your wife and son are.'

"So we had to move again. My husband has family in rural La Paz, so we went to visit them. And when we came back, there was another note, saying that no matter how hard we tried, we would not be able to escape them, they would always find us.

"We didn't know what to do. We had already changed addresses a number of times and they had still found us. So, we had to report to the authorities.

"The police said they were going to protect us. They said they would assign us security, that they would stand outside the house for us. But it never happened. We never saw any movement from the police. No one was outside the house. No one knocked on our door to say, 'We're here in case of any suspicious activity.' I mean nothing, nothing, *nothing*.

"We had a tourist visa [for the US] that we'd received three years prior, by the grace of God. We had no choice but to leave. We took one suitcase each. I didn't even say goodbye to my parents."

Lidia and her family stayed with a relative for a few months while they settled in New Haven. Her husband took a job in landscaping to support them. "The truth is, it has been quite tiring. I mean, it was quite a drastic change. It was a tremendous change for, for all three of us. In Honduras, my husband was a professional, a doctor. And now what does he do? He had to learn to use tools.... He came across people from our own country or from neighboring countries who—because he does not have the experi-ence—have treated him very badly. The changes in his body, in his face, in his hands have been . . ." Lidia's voice trailed off.

"He says, 'This is just what it is. It is nice to learn a little of everything, because we do not know when it might be useful, not only for us, but to be able to help others.' And yet he comes home and plays with my son and my son says, 'Daddy, your hands hurt me.' And my husband says, 'Well, yes, look: My hands are hurt.' And my son tells him, 'Yes, but don't touch me with your hands, you're hurting me!'"

Lidia's family had applied for political asylum, but according to their lawyer, their case was complicated because they had overstayed their tour-ist visas. Because of the COVID-19 pandemic, their case had not yet been processed when we spoke. "We move around with the greatest caution," Lidia said. "Because we're already here, illegal, you know?"

THE "NEW" VIOLENCE OF LATIN AMERICA

Lidia's story exposes the impact of sociopolitical violence in Latin Amer-ica. Although some migrants leave their home countries voluntarily, out of a sense of adventure or to seek better opportunities, migration often results from the failure of the state to protect its citizens. In these cases, migration may be a life-or-death decision. In this chapter, I discuss the forms of state failure and violence in Latin America that compel hundreds of thousands to flee each year.

Latin American history is pierced by violence. From colonization, African enslavement, and Indigenous genocide in the fifteenth through eighteenth centuries, to political conflicts and brutal dictatorships amid state modernization in the nineteenth and twentieth centuries, and social strife arising from state destabilization in the contemporary period, each era of Latin American history features acts of inhumanity perpetrated by dominant social and political groups against subordinate ones. While this history of violence affects individuals and communities through historic and transgenerational trauma, it is the current sociopolitical upheaval—including assaults and homicides as well as weak social safety nets—that most directly informs decisions to migrate. This "new" violence reflects social disruption and the ways gestures toward democratization have failed to meet the needs of citizens (Pearce 2010).

Contemporary violence in Latin America erupts from a confluence of factors, including social inequality, poverty, drug trafficking, and judicial weaknesses and corruption. This violence reinforces existing social orders, maintaining the elevated status of wealthy, land-owning men.

Although many consider state failure to be defined by civil war and the disintegration of state institutions, in Latin America it is characterized by postauthoritarian, nominally democratic but dysfunctional state institutions that citizens do not consider legitimate. Systemic flaws in the region include unreliable electoral politics, lack of government accountability, economic inequality, and social exclusion, which in turn lead to violence. State failure undermines citizenship and the foundations of democracy through its inability to uphold the rule of law and protect citizens. When the state loses its grip on the use of legitimate force, "drug lords, violent political entrepreneurs and gangs of disenchanted youths rule supreme" (Koonings and Kruijt 2004, 2). This failure breeds fear, violence, and distrust, shattering the social fabric and affecting citizens' physical and mental health.

THE VIOLENCE OF SOCIAL INEQUALITY

The violence engendered by social inequality forces families without political or economic power into a permanent underclass. While social inequality is an inevitable feature of market economies, extreme forms of inequality may be maintained and legitimized through constraint of citizens' rights, specifically resistance to policies of economic redistribution, social integration, and welfare (Oxhorn 2001; Marshall and Bottomore 1987).

Many migrant women related their frustrations at the high cost of education and inadequate wages in their home countries. Priscila, a thirty-eight-year-old woman from Tlaxcala, Mexico, told me: "I finished studying, but in my country, you sometimes have to pay to get a job. For instance, for me to get a job as a math teacher in a rural area, I had to pay 20,000 pesos [$1,000]. And even then, I could only get a part-time job. I didn't have any connections."

Almudena, from the same region, said her father sold land to raise the thousands of dollars needed to pay for her teaching examinations, internship, and union dues. "He was so angry when I left [for the States], because he had sacrificed so much for my career. But what could I do? I could barely meet my expenses with what they paid me."

Célia lamented that in Ecuador, "everything is expensive. Let's say a father in a family earns $400 a month, working from 8 A.M. to 8 P.M. You have to pay electricity, which is $50 to $100 a month. Then groceries are maybe $150. And that doesn't include fruits and vegetables! We lived on the coast, where there were plenty of melons, grapes, apples, things like that, but we couldn't afford them. You can only buy the most basic foods, like lentils and beans. And then, of course, you have to pay the mortgage. Even with two salaries, it was not enough to support ourselves, let alone our son."

Ysabel, a graduate of nursing school in El Salvador, said that the only job she could get paid $80 a month. "On $80 a month, no one can survive," she told me.

These women describe what the economist John Roemer (1998) defines as "inequality of opportunity," by which "circumstances," including race, gender, and family background, outweigh "efforts," like educational attainment and labor, as determinants of economic advantage. This perversion of the neoliberal emphasis on individual responsibility calls for public action. An assessment of inequality of opportunity in six Latin American countries found that between one-quarter and one-half of inequality in economic consumption is due to differential circumstances. Indigenous- and African-descended groups experience the greatest opportunity deprivation (Ferreira and Gignoux 2011).

Gender inequality merits particular attention in Latin America, given the pervasive and harmful gender stereotypes persisting from the colonial era. My conversation with Ascención, a thirty-two-year-old mestiza woman from Chiquimilla, Guatemala, revealed how gender inequality continues to constrain the lives of women.

ASCENCIÓN: In Guatemala, you get used to the economic failure. Sometimes my children would go without eating because there was not enough money.

JES: So, you had trouble finding work?

ASCENCIÓN: Yes, it is difficult to find work there. There's work, but they'll only hire men. Eventually you get used to it. And so, in order to push my children forward in life [*sacar a mis hijos adelante*], I came [to the United States].

Because access to and control over resources varies by gender, household income is not always pooled among members (Braunstein and Seguino 2018). In Latin America, despite relative gender parity in educational attainment, women's economic advancement lags behind men's. Women are less likely to participate in the labor force, largely because of biases regarding women's capabilities and enduring perceptions that women should disproportionately shoulder household responsibilities. Reducing household income inequality, through policies such as public investment and increased minimum wages, improves gender equity. However, except in Chile, social spending programs are limited (Grugel and Riggirozzi 2012).

Advances in social programs—as seen in Ecuador, Bolivia, and Argentina, for instance—were brought about by force. Powerful social uprisings, particularly among women, labor organizations, and Indigenous groups, forced state actors to respond to demands for higher public spending on education and worker protections. Protests against water privatization in Bolivia crushed the reelection hopes of Gonzalo Sánchez de Lozada, leading to the ascent of Evo Morales, the Indigenous leader of the union of coca producers. In Ecuador, Indigenous movements ousted two presidential administrations, eventually electing Rafael Correa, who increased spending on hospitals, roads, and schools (Becker 2013). Following the 2001 economic collapse in Argentina, working-class activists achieved an increased minimum wage for nonunionized workers, expansion of health benefits, and universal financial support for families with children (Grugel and Riggirozzi 2012). Still, leftist social organizations have decried the inadequacy of these reforms, indicating the futility of ambitious social welfare agendas that lack the support of the conventional oligarchy (Becker 2013; Solimano 2004). When women—particularly single or divorced women—fail to earn enough to meet their financial needs, or to obtain adequate benefit from social programs, migration becomes more appealing. At the same time, the family separation imposed by migration contradicts prevailing gender ideologies, forcing women to compromise their long-held values and redefine their roles as daughters, mothers, and female kin in order to achieve security (Abrego 2014).

The criminalization of drug production and commerce, supported by US administrations, has promoted infighting among subordinate social classes. Violence enacted by gang leaders—and abetted by law enforcement authorities—permits social control over common citizens. Gang leaders intimidate communities into complying with their territorial control, and the economic advantages of gang-organized robbery and drug trafficking drive young people to crime (Strocka 2006). The inability of the state to contain criminal violence—or, in some cases, its complicity— as well as the failure to prevent citizens from taking justice into their own hands attests that these so-called social or interpersonal forms of violence have a political dimension (Cruz 2016).

Social inequality and criminal violence in Latin America have been fomented by US interventionism, particularly economic, political, and militaristic incursions. US promotion of neoliberal economic policies, including free-trade agreements like NAFTA, and the southward expansion of the "War on Drugs" have resulted in displacement and dispossession as well as dangerous practices of drug trafficking (A. Green 2007; Corva 2008; Holmes 2013; Public Citizen 2016). Drug enforcement and border control policies have created the potential for multibillion-dollar enterprises for smuggling drugs, weapons, and people. The lucrative nature of these enterprises contributes to political and judicial corruption.

THE POLICE AS INSTRUMENTS OF STRUCTURAL VIOLENCE

Lidia's family's decision to migrate in the face of the failure of the police to protect them demonstrates how institutionalized or structural violence drives migration (Galtung 1975). However, police forces also enact violence to preserve social hierarchies. A study of 234 migrants from Central

America found that just 25 percent had reported experiences of threats or violence to the authorities, and of those, only 11 percent described police intervention as effective (Keller et al. 2017).

Structural violence reflects gender as well as class differences. Elvira, a thirty-five-year-old woman from the Dominican Republic, described to me how the police protected her cousin's abusive husband. "In my country, justice is not like what it is here," she said. "He was a man. He was a lawyer. He had connections. So, no, they did nothing."

Elvira's somber testimonial signals how the criminal justice system serves to preserve the social and political capital of dominant groups, in this case, educated and well-connected men.

Juana, a twenty-six-year-old from Zacatlán, Mexico, related how her sexual assault was dismissed by the local police force. "I would walk twenty or twenty-five minutes to school, and for some reason, I had this feeling of needing to look back... like a voice said, '*Bebita,* over here.' I turned around and saw a man following me. I wanted to start running, but it was too late, and he attacked me.

"He took a razor and held it to my neck, yanking my hair. I couldn't even scream. I was so afraid he would kill me. Then he pushed me to the ground and got on top of me. I thought he would rape me. I was shaking. But just then a *combi* [city bus] came by, and he ran off.

"I left to make a claim to the police, but in Mexico, the laws are not very good. I talked with the police, but they didn't believe me. They thought I might be making it up because I had no evidence. Still, they promised me that plainclothes officers would stand guard outside the school, but they were never there. So, nothing was done.

"This is why I am so afraid to go back. I could never forgive myself if something happened to my daughter. It is very unsafe, what with the violence, the robberies, the kidnappings. And the police refuse to do their job. They're bought, they're sold."

In her ethnographic research with Mexican migrant women, the sociologist Gloria González-López learned that women consider such intimidation and aggression as *robo*, or theft—of a woman's body, her innocence, and her social belonging—abetted by patriarchal gender arrangements and state inattention. Women can either surrender through silence or coercive marriage, or resist through migration (González-López 2007).

Ascención shared her own views of police corruption. "You can file a complaint, but they don't do anything. Sometimes you can try to pay them if you have money. If you don't, they pretend they don't know anything."

These women's stories represent examples of state failure through the weaknesses of the criminal justice system. Fourteen women of my interviewees (22 percent) related experiences in which the police ignored their reports or failed to enact justice. Through such inaction, the police act as agents of the oligarchy. Underclass citizens may then take drastic measures to enact justice for their communities. Juana explained, "There's no law to help people. People have to do justice by their own hands." She went on, "There was a man in a village near mine who had raped a girl, but he was never arrested, and he went on to hurt others. The town got together and lynched him. They tied him up and beat him. They demanded justice because the law did nothing. Your courage and anger rise up when you see that the police don't do their job."

STATE FAILURE AS A DRIVER OF MIGRATION

The impunity of the powerful, and the insecurity it engenders in the less powerful, keeps Juana and women like her in the United States, despite immense challenges. Eight women (12 percent) cited civil unrest and violence in their home countries as reasons for staying in the United States. Lidia detailed the pain of thrusting her four-year-old son into a strange country: "It's totally different—the language, the customs—it's impossible. Even my son felt it, because he keeps saying, '*Mami*, I want to go back to my old life. When are we going to see my *ita* [*abuelita*, grandma]? What about Luna and Sol [the family puppies]? I want to bring them because if not, they won't remember me anymore.'

"It's so stressful for him to speak English. He asks me, 'But *mami*, why can't I speak English?' And to everyone on the street, or at Walmart or the grocery store or the laundromat, he asks 'Do you speak Spanish? Do you speak Spanish?' He wants to play and interact with others, but he can't. It's so difficult."

The decision to migrate is fraught with danger, destabilization, and isolation. Yet the advantages to life in the United States outweigh the struggles of migration and resettlement. "This is a country of opportunities," Célia told me. "Here, you can apply for daycare, which is very expensive in my country. We have security. We have a stable environment."

Juana said: "There are so many privileges of this country. There are good opportunities to study, good schools, good jobs. I could never risk my children suffering the insecurity and violence if we were to go back. No, I'm not going to leave and return where things are not right."

In short, state failure not only drives transnational migration but also sustains it. A state's inability—or deliberate failure—to provide adequate protection and assistance as well as full citizenship rights to all undermines peace and stability (Deng 2004). The production and maintenance of an underclass in Latin America stripped of civic entitlements spawns a new underclass of "illegals" in the United States who serve as a cheap and exploitable labor force (L. Green 2011).

STRUCTURAL VULNERABILITY

I met Teresa at the Yale–New Haven Hospital Women's Center, a reproductive health clinic, prior to the COVID-19 shutdowns. Her eyes crinkled at the corners when she smiled and her dark hair fell neatly at her back, against her black jacket and white scarf. Teresa explained how, five years earlier, she had obtained a tourist visa for the United States. "I introduced myself with my cousin, who helped me because he had a stable job with a good income," Teresa explained. "We acted as if we were a couple. Thank God, they gave me the visa. Now, I had the opportunity to come, and I accepted, with pains in my soul for leaving my mother and daughter. I made the decision so as not to see her suffer: I would suffer so she wouldn't have to."

When Teresa departed Ecuador at the age of twenty-four, she left her three-year-old daughter in the care of her mother. She hoped, "with God's blessing," she would obtain papers for her mother and daughter to live with her. "I've always been a tough woman, a *luchadora* [fighter]. I was nervous because I didn't know the language. It was so hard to leave everything in my country, to be alone, not knowing anyone or being able to count on anyone. I thought, I'm going to get lost out here, but then again, I've always been curious, and I knew I could move on."

Teresa met her partner on Facebook while she was living in Ecuador and quickly merged her life with his on moving to the United States. "We had never met in person. I didn't really know who he was. You know how some people appear to be one way on Facebook and then they can turn out to be totally different." At first, their relationship was "beautiful." Then he became possessive and controlling. "I think part of the problem was alcohol," Teresa said. "He would go out drinking and come home and humiliate me, even beat me."

"Once [my husband] hit me when we were out in public, and someone called the police. I was so afraid of what they might do to me. But they made him take anger management classes and he's been a lot better since.

"I think the pregnancy is the news that changed everything," Teresa continued. "At first, when I found out, I was a sea of tears. I did not want to have his baby. What if he kept mistreating me? What life was I going to have? I came here with the purpose of making life better for my mother and daughter, and this pregnancy was now an obstacle. I thought about aborting. I wanted to die sometimes. I just didn't want to exist anymore."

Things changed for Teresa when she sought advice from her brother in Ecuador, who helped her open up to her mother and daughter. They took the news well, and Teresa felt encouraged. Teresa told me that her father physically abused her mother, even threatening her with guns, knives, and machetes. Their shared history of violence bonded her with her mother, who remained determined and independent.

"Thank God, now with the blessing of the baby, my partner has changed a little," she said. "He hasn't yelled at me or humiliated me. He's more passive. He doesn't go out anymore, doesn't drink. He went through his classes and asked for my forgiveness. This baby we're having has made him behave better and take responsibility. And my daughter is happy that she is going to have a little brother. She has even picked out some names for him—she's very smart. Seeing her reaction helped my resolve."

Given her emotional migration and experiences with intimate partner violence, I asked Teresa to tell me more about how she handles difficulties in her life. "I try not to think about it," she told me. "I let time pass until I forget. Hardly anyone supports me. I encourage myself to *salir adelante* [press onward, or get ahead]. I keep fighting. I get closer and closer to the goals I have set for my life. I will fight harder and harder to get a good job, save money, and get papers for my mother and daughter."

Teresa's narrative illustrates both the particular susceptibilities of women migrants and her powerful resolve. Her selection of a partner, a US citizen who she believed would help her establish a new life, exhibits a pattern I term *strategic coupling*, by which women engage in intimate or legal relationships with men in order to access social, political, and financial capital. Teresa's marriage promised social integration in New Haven and the possibility of legal US residence. After just three months, however, the power imbalances in her relationship degenerated into abuse. Though she did not say so explicitly, I understood that she had avoided reporting this abuse to the police out of fear of deportation.

Despite these adversities, Teresa engaged in cognitive strategies of avoidance and problem solving, an approach I call "imperative resilience." Teresa counts her mother among her inspirations and seeks to emulate her in her relationships with her children. I name this transmission of qualities of strength and adaptability from parent to child "intergenerational fortitude."

Teresa's capacity to press onward does not negate her hardships. Her position as an undocumented, abused, Spanish-speaking Latina woman exacerbates what medical anthropologists refer to as her *structural vulnerability*—a heightened risk for adverse health outcomes because of her low status in socioeconomic, political, and cultural hierarchies (Bourgois et al. 2017). Experiences of "illegality," racism (both interpersonal and institutional), and poverty shape migrant women's embodied experiences.

"ILLEGALITY"

Aihwa Ong and colleagues describe the process of crossing the border, either by plane or on foot, and taking up a new life in the United States as a dynamic and often brutal process of "self-making and being made" in relation to the state (Ong et al. 1996, 737). Undocumented status, or "illegality," represents a specific type of power inequity. Because undocumented migrants must constitute themselves as citizens in the sense of belonging to the national population and territory while recognizing their racial, cultural, and economic exclusion from hegemonic White social structures, they are motivated to hide markers of this stigmatized status (Gonzales 2016).

In conversations about immigration and health policy, US-born people often ask me why migrants do not just "wait in line" for admission into the United States. This question reveals a lack of understanding of the restrictiveness of US immigration policy.

Consider my family's case. My husband's uncle José traveled from Peru to Mexico in the early 1980s and crossed the border into the United States, wearing the full suit and tie his mother insisted would protect him from arrest. In 1986, President Ronald Reagan signed into law the Immigration Control and Reform Act, which legalized nearly all undocumented immigrants who had arrived prior to 1982, including José. When my husband's family migrated from Peru in the early 1990s to evade widespread terrorism and an economic downturn, José was able to sponsor my in-laws, my husband, and his twin brother for permanent residence. The process took twelve years. Had it taken just two months longer, my husband and brother-in-law would no longer have qualified as minors through their dependence on my father-in-law, José's brother. After obtaining residence in 2011, my husband, a student, waited ten years before he could afford to pay the fees for the US naturalization application and biometric assessments. He became a citizen in 2021, nearly thirty years after migrating. Lawful migration requires patience and fortunate circumstances.

Many migrant women I met lived in a state of "liminal legality" (Menjívar 2006). These included those who qualified for Deferred Action for Childhood Arrivals (DACA), temporary protective status (TPS), and asylum court hearings. As the Trump administration attempted to end the DACA program and TPS for migrants from El Salvador and Nicaragua, and as the pandemic postponed many immigration court dates, the political situation of these women grew even more precarious.

"'Illegality," a status that applies to nearly eleven million Americans, determines social opportunities and access to services (Lopez, Passel, and Cohn 2021). The anthropologist Sarah Willen encourages us to think beyond illegality as a "juridical and political status" or "sociopolitical condition" to understand more deeply the ways in which it "generates particular modes of being-in-the-world" (Willen 2007, 11). This notion of illegality—and its defining features of exclusion—also influences health (Willen 2012b; Quesada 2011, 2012).

Under harsher immigration enforcement regimes, migrants experience worse health and more mental distress, and migrant parents are less likely to seek the health benefits for their US-born children for which the children are eligible by virtue of their US citizenship. Fear of deportation—or of losing a caregiver to deportation—is associated with inadequate prenatal care for pregnant women and higher rates of depression, anxiety, emotional distress, and hypervigilance in children (Rhodes et al. 2014; Rubio-Hernandez and Ayón 2016).

Jackelín, from Guatemala, shared with me her experiences of fear and distress and her transition to a more confident outlook. "Before, I was scared. I learned to drive, and when a police car passed by, I would start shaking because I thought they would stop me or give me a ticket. But I realized that they only look for people who do something wrong. On the contrary, people like me are victims—the police can protect us. That helped ease my mind. Now, I feel safer if I see a police car. I trust that they are here to protect us from any problem, as long as we don't harm anyone."

"I'm worth just as much as people who have papers," Jackelín tells me, her voice triumphant. "I have rights. No one has the right to harm me just because I am not a [legal] resident here." Many women shared Jackelín's attitude: Though they harbored fears of deportation, they generally believed they were safe as long as they stayed out of trouble. Camila, a thirty-six-year-old woman from Puebla, Mexico, explains these contradictory beliefs.

JES: Are you afraid of getting into trouble because of your legal status?

CAMILA: Yes. Sometimes yes.

JES: Are you afraid that the police will find you?

CAMILA: Well, no. I don't know, I mean, I'm not doing anything wrong. Sure, I am here in a different situation [being undocumented], but I don't worry that I'm doing something I am not supposed to.

Although many women felt they were not at risk of imminent deportation as long as they complied with local laws, this compliance involves many sacrifices and compromises, including spending more time at home, avoiding driving, and restricting their social networks to people of *con-*

fianza, or trust. Maribel, a thirty-three-year-old from Cuenca, Ecuador, advises her son to avoid close friendships: "I'll be talking to my son, and he'll say something like, 'They're my friends, they're my friends.' And I sit him down and say, *'Mijo,* they *tell* you they're your friends, but they're really just your schoolmates. Right? You don't know who their parents are, where they come from. I mean, you have to get along with your classmates, sure, but you don't have to get close to them, because you don't know the environment people live in.'"

Maribel relies on her family for social support, engaging in friendships as a performative obligation for social integration. She goes to birthday celebrations or other gatherings with colleagues but does not consider them true friends. In this way, Maribel's illegality structures her social world.

Illegality also strains relationships among members of mixed-status families. Nikki, a thirty-four-year-old DACA immigrant from Jamaica, describes her resentment toward her US citizen brother for flouting the law when she felt she needed to toe the line. "You know, I think one of the things that just bothered me and made me constantly upset with my brother was like, 'You are an American. The things that you are afforded in this country, I am not.' He never had to go through the poverty that I went through. I just thought he took so many things for granted."

Undocumented members of mixed-status families often feel like they are stuck in quicksand: One false move, and their lives—and the lives of their families—are at risk. By contrast, family members who are citizens may experience survivor's guilt and additional burdens of representing the family in bureaucratic settings (Castañeda 2019).

If mixed status can drive wedges between family members, it can also forge bonds between those with a shared interest in protection. Susana, a thirty-year-old Ecuadorian who herself benefited from DACA, told me how she and her citizen siblings had insulated their undocumented mother until she was able to adjust her status. "I was afraid, knowing my mother was illegal," Susana tells me. "My brother, my sister, and I had to protect her." This meant assuming the responsibilities of driving, earning enough to support their mother, and communicating with landlords, healthcare providers, and other official figures.

The women in this study who adjusted their status mostly did so by marrying US citizens. Only two successfully applied for and received asylum. In their study of Central American migrants, the physician and human rights expert Allen Keller and his colleagues found that 70 percent of their study participants met the criteria for asylum (Keller et al. 2017). Yet just 300,000 of the world's 26.4 million refugees (about 1 percent) originate from Latin America; most are from the Middle East. Many Latin American migrants were thus grasping at an elusive hope of obtaining legal status.

RACISM

"Have you experienced discrimination?" I asked Nikki.

"Oh, I could write a book," she answered in an exasperated tone. "I had this one client one time who said, 'I've been so nice to *your kind.*' Yeah, there was that. And then I had one other client call me a Black N-word bitch. Yep, I remember that. I think I also remember one of my teachers from high school saying, 'Oh, you're pretty for a Black girl.' There was that.

"There's also a lot of 'Oh, you're not like the others. You know, you're so articulate.' Those are ... pretty much textbook stuff. Oh, also! Once, I used to nanny for a little bit, and I went to pick up one of the little kids from a party, and the host of the party offered me watermelon. And I said, 'No, thank you.' And she said, 'Oh, I thought you people liked watermelon.' That one I'll never, never forget. That was probably three years ago. I also really try to avoid police confrontation."

Nikki self-identifies as Jamaican, as a dark-skinned Latina, and as an immigrant. But in the US, everyone treats her as Black. She describes the culture shock of moving as a teenager from Jamaica—where everyone looked like her—to Florida. "My dad moved us to what had to have been one of the Whitest neighborhoods around, basically. We were the only Black family in that entire section. Mmm-hmm. But now, I realize, you know, part of it was the fact that that area was very Republican. My sisters and I did okay. My brother did not do well at all."

Nikki's younger brother, Dante, had a tendency to flout rules—a behavior Nikki mentioned she resented because of her own precarious immigration status—and had frequent run-ins with the police. "So my dad was a truck driver. He was always away. And my stepmom was like a low-level accountant for a furniture store. So she was never really home," Nikki told me. "I was the oldest one, and I took care of my younger siblings. Dante was three and a half, four years younger to me, and I think he struggled because he didn't really have a father figure at home. We see that a lot with families who have an absent father figure. Shit hit the fan, you know. My brother got into a lot of trouble."

She described how Dante would fire at birds with his slingshot or take mail from other people's mailboxes, behaviors that caught the attention of the police. "[Stealing mail is] a federal offense," Nikki said. "And when you're the only minority family in the neighborhood, it really freaks you out. I remember one time it was like two o'clock in the morning, and the police were knocking on my bedroom window because they were bringing my brother home. He had been out riding his bicycle in the middle of the night because he was bored, you know? He was just a kid like that. But then it becomes this big thing in the neighborhood, like, 'Oh, of course, there's trouble at the Campbell house.'"

Dante was not the only Black man in her family who endured additional scrutiny from law enforcement. "My dad was arrested in Florida," Nikki told me. "They stopped him for like a taillight, or something. And they said that he had weed in the car, but he didn't. And the police were just like, 'Well, we know how you Jamaicans are.' My dad also had a registered firearm, but he didn't have it on him, and they targeted him for that, too. Thankfully, they let him go home later that night."

Given her personal and familial experiences with racism, Nikki hoped for better for the daughter she was expecting. "My hope is that she won't have to go through the same struggles that I've gone through. You know, she'll clearly be seen as a Black woman. But I hope that there'll be a little bit more respect and more equality, hmm? That her life will be just a little bit easier. A more level playing field."

Nikki's embodied expression of *Latinidad* distinguishes her from many of my Indigenous and mestiza interlocutors. She confronts criminalization both for her skin tone and for her liminal immigration status (Ramos 2020).

However, many Latinas confront a different experience of racialization. They may recognize unequal treatment but feel unsure what to attribute it to: Is it my accent? My inability to speak English? My race? My immigration status? Much of this confusion results from the ambiguities surrounding the racial classification of Latinx identity (see chapter 3). Many of my interlocutors struggled to assign themselves to conventional racial categories. Common responses to my question about racial self-identification included the following:

JACKELÍN: I think I'm mixed race. I have difficulty with that question when asked. I don't know how to answer.

CAMILA: I don't know my race. I know I'm not White.

RAQUEL: I don't really feel like I have any race because I don't identify by a race—I don't know how to describe myself. If you ask me, actually, when I fill out a hospital form and they ask for race, it concerns me. Why treat me differently if I'm Black, White, colored, Indigenous . . . right? I mean, I guess, historically, I would be mestiza because Chileans were colonized by the Spaniards. We're Indigenous mixed with Spanish, meaning mestizos, but I don't consider myself any of that, actually.

MILDRED: I don't know. Well, I've always identified myself as Hispanic, I don't know. I guess just Hispanic.

ELMIRA: I don't know whether to say I'm Hispanic or Black, maybe. I know I'm Hispanic. Maybe mixed race.

LEOCADIA: Well, I'm Brown. Not Black, not super Brown, or White. I guess like a mix.

NOELIA: I think I should be White because I'm Hispanic . . . um, yeah. White, I think.

LIDIA: I don't really understand the question. Mmm . . . maybe mestiza?

CINTIA: I'm Latina. I don't know. I don't really know what to say, because I don't consider myself White. I don't consider myself Black. I don't consider myself. . . . To me, I'm just Latina. I don't like to talk about it. Whether you are Brown, whether you are White, to me, we are all the same.

CARLA: I don't know, because usually I'd just say Latina or Puerto Rican. It's not like there's a color palette. But yeah, I usually choose White.

GLADYS: My race? You mean, not Latina? Mmm . . . I guess I'm White, then.

JENIFER: Ummm . . . I think I'm the second thing you said [mestiza].

AMALIA: Aren't I just Hispanic?

MELIZA: We're supposed to be American Indians, right?

ROSA: I don't know, I'm just Hispanic.

DEBORA: Well, brown? Light brown, I guess.

DELIA: I don't know [my race]. It is most likely mixed.

INÉS: I wouldn't know how to say... What is mestiza, again? I think I'm Indigenous, or mixed. Something in between.

This dilemma of self-classification calls to mind the sociologist Laura E. Gómez's argument for the treatment of Latinx as a distinct racial identity, noting the contradictions between racial categories Latinxs choose and the ones ascribed to them by others (Gómez 2020, 3). The US racial classification system differs significantly from those of other countries in Latin America. For instance, in Brazil, residents can self-identify as *branco* (White), *pardo* (Brown), *preto* (Black), *amarelo* ("yellow"), and *indígena* (Indigenous) (Instituto Brasileiro de Geografía e Estatística 2011, 34–35).

Many of my interlocutors blamed their experiences of discrimination on their perceived social class or level of English proficiency. Susana, a young Ecuadorian woman who spoke both English and Spanish fluently, related how a medical assistant insulted her intelligence, presuming she did not understand. "So, it happened right here [in the clinic]," Susana told me. "There was a Hispanic woman who was going to draw my blood. And she told me, in Spanish, to hold my arm a certain way. And mind you, I understand both English and Spanish. And so I did what she said, and then she goes, 'Oh no, move it like that.' I wasn't really sure what she meant for me to do. So, then she says to her friend, in English, 'Oh these girls don't understand anything.' And I got so pissed off! I told her, 'I understand what you're saying.' It was just crazy: I was being discriminated against for being Hispanic by a Hispanic woman."

Ysabel, who does not speak any English, commented, "Oh yeah, some people are racists. They'll see I don't speak English, I try to ask some questions, and they don't want to help. They get angry, like we're bothering them or something. They don't even try to help us."

Although the use of English has become routinized in commercial spaces, the United States has no official language. Collectively, Americans speak more than 350 languages, the most common of which, after English, is Spanish. However, mounting anti-Latinx prejudice, stoked by the Trump administration, has revived a movement to formalize English as the official mode of communication (King 2017).

The perception that an individual is Latinx confers stereotypes about language ability and social position. Raquel, who also speaks English well, told me how she went to the post office to mail a package to her sister and was called a "freeloader." "The man saw that I was pregnant and thought I had just come here to have my baby and take advantage. But this pregnancy wasn't in my plans! I'd had two losses—I didn't think my womb could carry a baby. It was a total surprise, for me and for my husband."

Raquel, usually patient and calm in our conversations, sounded frustrated. "People think that everyone who comes here wants to have children, or what do I know, to get more benefits. But it was not like that in my case. I have many, many plans. I have an incredible desire to keep working. I didn't come to this country trying to profit off anything."

In her historical and sociological analysis of Black reproduction, Dorothy Roberts observes that White women are celebrated for giving birth, whereas Black women are stigmatized and thought to transmit their "inferiority" and "deviance" to their children (Roberts 1999). Drawing parallels to the Brown, migrant body, Roberts's analysis suggests that migrant pregnancy may likewise be criticized, criminalized, and discouraged to prevent the transmission of undesirable traits like "freeloading." Racialized experiences vary with intersections of phenotype (or skin color), language ability, and documentation status.

POVERTY

Raquel's urgent desire to distance herself from the "freeloader" label emerges in response to long-standing stereotypes of migrants as parasites who give birth to "anchor babies" in order to circumvent immigration laws and obtain government aid (Chavez 2013, 176). This characterization represents an "abjectification" of migrant women, a form of repulsion and expulsion that establishes them as "Other" (Butler 1997; Gonzales and Chavez 2012). Many women internalize these racist stereotypes in order to distinguish themselves from undeserving, exploitive migrants. Most of my interlocutors emphasized their commitment to participating in the labor force, supporting themselves, and not taking welfare. Several condemned other migrants who abused social services, particularly during the pandemic.

Raquel told me, "When I lost my job in New York, we went looking for food. So my husband and I both lined up at a food bank, to make sure we got enough, given that there were two of us. But I saw people who lined up, got their food, went home, and then came back! I mean, there were women and children there—couldn't these people stand to consider those who really needed the help?"

One form of aid that many women were ready to accept without shame was healthcare. Nearly all women received some form of healthcare assistance, whether from private programs available through Yale–New Haven Health or public health insurance.

Priscila, a Mexican woman who had lived in the United States for fifteen years, distinguished healthcare support from other forms of welfare. "For example, I'm pregnant right now, right? The only thing that I have ever asked for during all my pregnancies is medical support, because it is very expensive. But from there on out, nothing else. But there are other people who ask for food, who want help to pay the rent... they ask for help to pay their bills, electricity. All kinds of things. And I say, I mean, if the baby is mine and I wanted to have a child, and I choose to keep it, it's my responsibility." Priscila sounded harsh and indignant, echoing points one might hear on conservative talk shows. She went on: "If I were in my country, the government would not give me anything. Here, you get pregnant, and they give you financial aid. Here, there are various [medical] programs to help pregnant women, and to that, I say, okay, sure. But some people take too much advantage."

Priscila defines pregnancy as a form of social labor that merits support. She distinguishes this from financial support after a baby's birth. The entitlement of pregnant women to healthcare is common to different global settings. In her study of the perceived morality of providing healthcare to unauthorized migrants living in Tel Aviv, Israel, the medical anthropologist Sarah Willen found that migrants mostly believed the government should pay for prenatal and delivery care (Willen 2012a). Willen attributes this belief to values of social reciprocity by which migrants view their care as compensation for their contributions to society.

Priscila also acknowledges, however, that she sought medical aid for her husband when he developed cancer. "I got support because it was cancer, and I was the only one who was providing for my household. My husband was ill for three years in his battle with cancer. Between bringing him to the hospital, I could not work as much. I even sent my children to live with their grandmother [in Mexico], but I still had to send them money."

Again, Priscila distinguishes her situation from those who "take too much advantage." "So yeah, I was the only breadwinner, I had to pay my bills, my rent, everything, all while supporting my husband in his illness. And so, yeah, I got help. But it really bothers me that other people think that they're in the same situation and take too much advantage."

Priscila considers herself exceptional: she narrates her receipt of medical aid for her husband's cancer in the context of her roles as a worker, mother, and sole breadwinner for her family. She believes she is entitled to healthcare support because of her participation in the labor market. As the medical anthropologist Alyshia Gálvez notes, this attitude "reinforces neoliberal models of citizenship that offer only a narrow spectrum of rights in exchange for labor" (Gálvez 2011, 43).

Foucault dissects the power architectures of healthcare and social welfare by noting the distinction made between "the good poor and the bad poor" (1980, 185). The "good," or working, poor may be ill or infirm but are seen as deserving of therapeutic intervention or material assistance so that they can be transformed into a useful source of labor. By contrast, the "bad" poor are seen as willfully idle and thieving (Foucault 1980). Priscila constitutes herself as one of the "good poor," whose prenatal care and other medical assistance enables her to contribute to society. Part of her self-conception as exceptional relates to the absence of universal healthcare in the United States and the high costs of medical care. "I applied for nothing but medical support, which is the most, the most important," Priscila said. "Why? Because if I work, my children will have enough to eat. It is my business; it is my responsibility—it is not anyone's responsibility. No one came and said, 'Hey, you know, have a son, and I'll help you support him.' No."

This "bootstrap" mentality must also be understood in the context of threatened changes to "public charge" rules under the Trump administration. In 2019, the Department of Homeland Security issued a correction to the Inadmissibility on Public Charge Grounds for denying applications for legal residence. Under the revised rule, any migrant who received public benefits for more than twelve months in any thirty-six-month period was considered a likely "charge" on the federal government and thereby unworthy of citizenship or permanent residence. The rule was revoked in March 2021.

As Gálvez notes, many migrants pay a "sweat equity," often paying income taxes, property taxes, and sales taxes while receiving few benefits in return (Gálvez 2011, 43). The medical anthropologist Seth Holmes found that many of the migrant farmworkers he worked alongside fully recognized the injustice of paying federal taxes, effectively sustaining the Social Security program, while failing to benefit from government aid (Holmes 2013, 188–89).

Nikki identified this unfairness when complaining about her ineligibility for state medical insurance under DACA. "I work. I pay taxes. I've been here since I was eleven years old. And yet I don't qualify for HUSKY [Connecticut Medicaid]. In Connecticut, you can only get insurance for your pregnancy. I got it just for being pregnant with my son and then for six weeks afterward—that's it!" Nikki believes that her "sweat equity"—along with her long-standing presence in the United States—should entitle her to Medicaid.

Regardless of their relationship to systems of social support, many women reported intense economic anxiety, particularly during the COVID-19 pandemic. They also commonly reported dependence on partners or other family members for income, a situation that intensified their sense of financial insecurity. Célia, for instance, said that her greatest source of stress is finances. "I worry that my husband will suddenly be without a job, because he supports the house," she told me. "For instance, the week I was hospitalized [for delivery complications], he asked for the whole week off to help me. But now that means he didn't work for a week, so we might not have enough for the rent. I mean, I really needed him with me, to help me, but I worry so much about how it will affect our finances."

Roughly half of my interlocutors told me that their money runs out by the end of the month, meaning they have little money in reserve for situations like work slowdowns (e.g., seasonal fluctuations in landscaping work), illness, or other emergencies. As a result, they have to cut back on food quality, "luxuries" like cable and internet, and *remesas* or remittances sent to support family members in their home countries.

"My partner always says, 'You have to cover as much of your legs as you can with as far as the blanket reaches,'" says Yaiza, a thirty-six-year-old from Ecuador. "You have to live half-comfortable to have your food to live on."

The interlocking oppressions of illegality, racism, and poverty constrain life prospects for many migrant women. Yet strategies of coping, and harnessing intrinsic and community resources, permit them to *seguir* (or *salir*) *adelante.*

CONCLUSION

State failure and the multiple forms of violence it produces drive migration from Latin America to the United States. This failure creates inequalities of opportunity by which personal characteristics like race, gender, and family social status outweigh the economic advantages gained through education and labor. Despite efforts to expand social welfare programs in Latin America throughout the 1990s and 2000s, ongoing protests by Indigenous, women, and labor activists reveal the deficiencies of these attempts. Moreover, weaknesses of the criminal justice system—particularly neglect and corruption among law-enforcement agents—reinforce structural violence and perpetuate physical violence throughout the region. Conditions of state failure result from global economic and political forces, particularly US intervention in Latin America.

Those who leave their home countries in response to state failure face social insecurity and economic exploitation. Such inequalities of opportunity persist, and perhaps worsen, on migration to the United States. Structural vulnerability—stemming from migration enforcement, racism, and economic inequality—renders migrant women susceptible to abuse and mental distress. Yet their imperative resilience empowers them to advance toward their goals.

2　Moving

Anahi

"We came through the desert," Anahi, a forty-year-old woman from Guatemala, told me. "There were no houses, no food, no water. We had to buy food at the border and load it into our backpacks for the journey. We spent eight days walking through the desert, carrying water, food, and whatever else we could bring. There was nothing there, only thorny plants and sand. Everything is dry. There is no water in the ground.

"When immigration tried to find us, we would hide on the ground in ditches or under the bare pines. Sometimes we would fall asleep for a while. We walked at night, on our hands and feet, because it was so hot. When the heat was too much, we would lie among the trees waiting for the temperature to drop so we could continue the next day. In areas where immigration security was too tight, the coyote would tell us we couldn't pass—we'd have to get out of there. We walked for far too long...

"Eventually, we ran out of food and water. We entered into Arizona and passed through a ranch with animals and horses. We were so thirsty, we had to drink from the animal troughs.

"We huddled in a car toward Kansas, but it was snowing heavily, and the car crashed and flipped over. We ran through the snow, and each got lost in the darkness of the night. A policeman eventually caught me and another traveler. He said had we been four or five people, he would have arrested us. But instead, he let us go, and we continued on to where we had family in New Haven."

Caridad

"We were three or four women and thirteen men in the group," Caridad, said a thirty-four-year-old from Peru. "If we had to run, we women knew we'd be left behind." Caridad spent three months traveling from Peru to the Mexican border. She had to pay off multiple soldiers and border guards to arrive safely.

"They gave us a backpack with water, some fruit, and some canned food. The water was so heavy, I didn't want to carry it. And the canned food was awful—it weighed so much, didn't give much energy, and made us sick. Two of the women became very ill, vomiting everything they took in, and they had to turn back.

"On the second or third day, I couldn't carry it all anymore, and I left almost everything behind. Another Peruvian man in the group helped me carry my gallon of water. Despite all that, I became very dizzy. The man took out some oranges and pressed them to my lips. He told me I needed to go to the river to drink some water. I couldn't walk, and so he carried me on his shoulders and brought me water from the river. We had to hide in holes in the ground from the immigration planes overhead.

"When border patrol found us, the man and I managed to hide in some bushes. But they caught the only other woman—the niece of another traveler—and sent her back to Mexico. The uncle crossed back to find her and try again.

"Then it was just twelve men and me. I tried to lead. I thought, 'If they start running, where will that leave me?'"

After several more weeks of travel, Caridad arrived in New Haven. "It's safer here—in Peru, they'll shut the lights out on the bus and steal the necklace right off your neck. It happened to me, gave me a huge red mark," Caridad explained. "Here in New Haven, you can carry your purse to the store without worry.

"Plus, in the summer it smells like the ocean," she adds, a smile radiating through her voice.

PAINFUL PASSAGES: MIGRATION-RELATED TRAUMA

The Sonoran Desert, where many Latin American migrants attempt to cross into the United States, is an arid region covering approximately one hundred thousand square miles in southwestern Arizona and southeastern California, as well as most of Baja California and the western half of the state of Sonora, Mexico. It is the hottest North American desert, with limited rainfall and accordingly inhospitable terrain. According to Humane Borders, Inc. , as of November 2021, 3,790 migrants have been found dead in the desert in Arizona alone. This number excludes those whose bodies were too decomposed to be recognized (Humane Borders 2022; Prendergast and Devoid 2021). The migrant body count measures the effectiveness of a policy called "prevention through deterrence," which seeks to inhibit border crossings by making them more hazardous. Selective placement of border patrol agents forces migrants to take longer, more dangerous paths across the Sonoran Desert, subjecting them to harsh conditions that can lead to dehydration and death (De León 2015). The crisis will only worsen as climate change causes longer and more intense summer heat.

The plight of migrants in the desert evokes that of the monarch butterfly. Southerly winds funnel monarchs into a central flyway over Texas, crowding them together along their journey of more than three thousand miles. As climate change and urbanization lead to unendurable travel temperatures and declines in their food supply, monarchs face the risk of death from heat and starvation just like overexposed humans passing through the desert.

Anahi and Caridad's stories attest to the physical toll of migrating across the Sonoran Desert. These women endured dehydration, exposure, and the precarities of being a woman in groups of mostly men. Both women were lucky: they arrived at their destination safely without encountering immigration authorities. Less fortunate migrants may make multiple attempts to cross after environmental hazards and immigration authorities force them back.

Latin American migrants face dangers such as thievery, kidnapping, extortion, and dehydration. Women are also at greater risk of rape, assault, trafficking, and forced prostitution. After settling in the United States, many of these women experience intimate partner violence, as their social positions make them vulnerable to abuse. Over 75 percent of Latin American migrant women living in the United States report histories of trauma (Fortuna, Porche, and Alegria 2008; Mendenhall 2012; Vogt 2018).

Perreira and Ornelas (2013) refer to harrowing migration experiences as "painful passages." In their study of 281individuals, they found that 29 percent of foreign-born adolescents and 34 percent of foreign-born parents living in the United States had experienced trauma during migration. Of those with traumatic histories, 9 percent of adolescents and 21 percent of their parents were at risk for post-traumatic stress disorder (PTSD). Coinciding global and local sociopolitical forces—including economic factors, government structures, and "legal violence"—that shape migration experiences also affect health outcomes (Castañeda et al. 2015; Menjívar and Abrego 2012).

Trauma often involves a close encounter with physical violence or death (Herman 1997). However, trauma also encompasses the emotional response to such experiences, the psychic scars left by tragic and painful events (Fassin and Rechtman 2009). Trauma is therefore "a clinical and social event" (Panter-Brick et al. 2015, 822–23), in which individuals' subjective memories of trauma shape, or rupture, their sense of coherence in their lives and may lead to symptoms of mental illness. Migrants, including voluntary migrants as well as refugees and asylum seekers, are especially susceptible to trauma and its aftermath. A study of seven thousand refugees seeking resettlement in Europe and North America found the prevalence of PTSD among them to be roughly ten times higher than among the age-matched general population of the destination countries (Fazel, Wheeler, and Danesh 2005; Schouler-Ocak 2015). *Migration-related trauma*, a term referring to trauma surrounding departure or displacement from a country of origin and relocation in a destination country, applies to the experiences of many of my interlocutors (Wiese 2010; Perreira and Ornelas 2013).

BORDER CROSSING

Imagine: you're a twenty-year-old woman and you decide to leave home. There is nothing for you there: no job, no money, a hungry family, and threats of robbery and rape looming every time you leave the house. You tell only two people, maybe your parents, maybe your siblings, that you are leaving. You do not want anyone to know about your departure because you might not make it, or your family could be kidnapped or threatened if they knew you were headed north. You catch a bus through the countryside—or if you're lucky, a flight to the border. From there, you meet up with a dozen or so travelers—mostly men—and a guide (coyote) who is so young that he has just the shadow of a mustache at the corners of his lips. Friends have warned you that the men might rape you, but you decide that crossing the border is worth the risk. You wait for night-fall, then take your backpack, holding a gallon of water, and set out on foot across the desert. If you're lucky, your crossing takes three nights, or maybe five, sheltering during the day's blistering heat amid the sparse trees or in the ditches. Then, one night, you see lights flashing. The boy guide yells, "Run!" and everyone scatters. You try to keep up but eventually give in and surrender yourself to the immigration authorities. They take your prints and toss you into a cell with thirty others, with one toilet in the corner. La Migra (the immigration agency) either lets you out with a court date—if you are savvy enough to request asylum or are carrying a baby on your back—or dumps you back in Mexico so you can try again.

Here I examine the specific traumas that migrants encounter through experiences like this. I consider specifically the effects of gender-based violence and the "legal violence" of immigration enforcement as factors in health outcomes.

Gender-Based Violence

"There were several people," Jackelín told me. "We had to follow one person, and then another, and then another. I think there were, like, three or four guides. One of the guides was a man who was about fifty years old. He told me that I . . . that I should stay and live with him. That he was going to give me everything. That he already had a wife, but he wanted to pay me to be his *mujer* [woman]. I said no, that I had no intention of doing that.

"He pushed me to have sex with him. He told me, 'If you don't accept, I'm going to leave you out in the dirt.' And he said, 'You have no one, you have no one here, and now you're in another country, so you can't do anything.' I was afraid inside, but I told him that he had no right to harm me. He laughed and said, 'Oh yeah? How can you prove it? Who do you think is going to look out for you?' I answered, 'My family that I have there [in the United States].' And so he said, 'What can your family do? Your family is there, and you are here. You are in my hands.'

"After that, he started treating me badly. He no longer paid attention to me. He would leave me behind and wouldn't wait for me. At one point when we were walking, a very big thorn—as big as a nail or a screw—got in my shoe and cut up my foot. But the man was already so upset with me, he refused to wait for me. I was scared that he would leave me there, lost, in the desert.

"I did get lost once. The guide, he left me and two others behind, and so we spent the night alone. I don't know if you've heard of those animals, they're like big dogs, they call them coyotes. They are huge, and they eat people. We slept under the trees, and we could hear the coyotes coming closer, shrieking, and howling. We had no idea whether or not we would live. It was terrifying."

Although the guide never directly assaulted Jackelín, his threats, intimidation, and neglect after she rejected his advances rendered her journey far more precarious.

Fear of rape was among the most common concerns for women who crossed the border. In my interviews, I heard many variations of the same dread.

PRISCILA: There were those rumors...that they touched women. There were also a lot of criminals and groups from other countries, they began to assault and abuse women. But you take the risk if you want a better life, the life you want to lead.

ADELINA: It was ugly, you know, traveling as a woman. The men are very macho. I was afraid of rape.

YSABEL: I thought our coyote would grab us when he was high on marijuana, because there were two of us women. I was so afraid he would rape me.

ALMUDENA: For women, it was more dangerous because they would abuse us. They assault and abuse you if you're a woman.

JEANETH: There are people who tell stories saying they were raped. Thank God that didn't happen to me.

MELIZA: I was afraid because they warned us there were people who would come and attack the group. There was a risk they would rape my sister and me, and the other women who were in the group.

JUANA: One, I was very afraid that I would be raped. Two, I was afraid I would not be able to survive the weather as we crossed. They were all men, and they were all ahead of me—it was very difficult to keep pace as a woman. So yes, I was very afraid those two things would happen to me. But then I had no other choice, I was already there, and I had to be strong, and now I have to wipe my tears and move on, because there was no other option. I had to give myself the courage, because it was only me. There was no one who took care of me. It was my turn to wipe my tears and continue praying to him and asking Diosito with all my heart to give me strength, fortitude, and keep moving forward.

Although none of the women with whom I spoke reported being sexually assaulted during their crossings, their narratives may omit such experiences as a result of feelings of shame and denial. Many, like Jackelín, were harassed, intimidated, and threatened with abandonment. These fears are not unfounded: up to 90 percent of women migrants suffer sexual violence. Likewise, threats of leaving women behind to cope alone in the desert have a ghastly basis in fact. In their study of bodies recovered along the migrant trail, the Binational Migration Institute found that women had 2.87 times greater odds of dying of exposure than men (Rubio-Goldsmith et al. 2006). The particular plight of women migrants often receives less attention in scholarly work on migration, perhaps because most individuals apprehended at the border are single men (Caldwell 2021).

Women's choices to migrate, intentionally facing the risks of rape and abandonment, highlight their agency. All my interlocutors recognized the risks: they undertook careful evaluations of their past and their possible future in their decision to engage in the violent process of migration.

How should we understand the role of threatened violence and the gender differential in risk? Gender-based violence is often invisible. Even penetrative sexual assault rarely leaves marks on the body. Despite the absence of visible scars, such violence persists into the futures of those who experience it. The anthropologist Carolyn Nordstrom notes that these forms of violence have a "tomorrow," leaving behind "shattered selves, confidences, futures" (Nordstrom 2004, 226). The most common trauma symptom reported by my interlocutors was the harboring of strong negative beliefs about the world, such as "No one can be trusted" and "The world is completely dangerous." These enduring attitudes shape the ways women relate to others and to their new environment.

The nature of these symptoms underscores the limitations of clinical instruments for assessing trauma. The tool I used, the PTSD Checklist for the DSM-5 (Weathers et al. 2013) or PCL-5, asked about the experience of sexual violence and threats of sexual violence separately, allowing me to account for the common experience of the fear of potential assault. However, my index of trauma symptoms did not fully capture the warlike mistrust of others and lingering fear many of my interlocutors carried.

After fearing sexual assault at the hands of her *polleros* (smugglers), confronting theft, and enduring two months in immigration detention, Almudena describes a psychological state akin to shell shock. "Some of these things hurt too much, you can never fully recover," Almudena said. "When I first got here, it was different, difficult. Why couldn't I just lead a happy life? I was filled with negativity, everything bothered me." She paused before continuing. "From there, you decide to pull away from people. I stopped talking with my cousins and my friends at work. It's like no one can understand what happened."

Such patterns of avoidance and mood change are characteristic of PTSD, yet Almudena's score on the PCL-5 was a 2 out of 80. The instrument failed to record her psychological sensitivity in the way deep ethnographic engagement did. After my semistructured interview with Almudena, we spoke about services that would benefit her, as well as the power of being heard.

"Humanity needs to know these stories, right? About us immigrant women?" Her tone became urgent. "People do not know. . . . It is honestly incredible that this is happening in humanity. Why build the walls, right?

Or the borders? Without these barriers, so many people would not expose their lives...because so many people have died right there in the desert. Why not just give us a permit so you can let us in to work?"

Almudena said I was the first person she had told about her experiences of near rape. The vulnerability and intimacy surrounding gender-based violence—and the fear of not being believed—fosters isolation, as Almudena acknowledges. As I heard such stories, my ethnographic engagement often took the form of care work, tuning my attention to the intimate needs of my interlocutors. Feminist anthropologists have commented on the profound care work they undertake with women survivors of sexual violence. Ethnographic research requires dedication to and solidarity with communities. In consequence, anthropologists often engage in translational aid, engaging their social capital as well-connected academics to persuade those in power to understand and act on the needs of their interlocutors (Backe 2020; D. Davis 2013; Craven et al. 2013; Anzaldúa 2012). As a medical student and ethnographer trained in psychoeducation and mental health first aid, as well as a Spanish speaker, I often found myself providing psychological support and helping connect women with clinical resources. When mental health concerns exceeded my capacity, I connected women with mental health support. When they confronted deprivation—or when their isolation prevented them from fulfilling their needs—I facilitated social services like mutual aid and nutritional support. In some cases, I and my father-in-law—who works for a nonprofit organization engaged in social services for Latinx communities in Connecticut—delivered boxes of donated food to women experiencing intense social and economic stress.

Cages and Hieleras: Conditions in Immigration Detention

"When I crossed the border, immigration authorities caught me," nineteen-year-old Ysabel recounts. "I had arrived in Arizona, but they took me to Texas. I was there for a whole week. Being in jail was horrible. There were no windows, no way to look outside. If it was night or day, I didn't know. And the food was terrible.

"They told me it was called *la hielera* [the icebox], the place where they locked me up. It was freezing. They gave us these aluminum blankets, which helped a bit but not much. It was so cold; I got a bad nosebleed: A lot of blood came out and I couldn't get it to stop. They just gave me some ice and some kind of pill to make me stop bleeding.

"There were like thirty or forty of us locked in the cell—I didn't count. The bathroom was disgusting, open in the cell covered by just a few bricks. It smelled awful. I had no freedom to move about, I was locked in there the whole time. Some of the guards would intentionally wake us up when we were sleeping, banging on the doors. Some just walked around the cell to try to catch us doing something."

Almudena was detained by immigration authorities five times. On each occasion, she was booked, strip searched, and deposited at the border. "They would grab us, put handcuffs on our wrists, and ask us to remove our shoelaces, belts, and anything we carried. We had to let our hair down. If we wore rings or earrings, we also had to remove them. They separated the women from the men—they arrested so many of us. From there, we had to wait until it was our turn to give them our information. They took photos of us and fingerprinted us. And then they would just take us back to our cell until they let us leave. They would grab, like, fifteen people at once and just dump us at the border, leaving us."

Ascención recounted her imprisonment with her two children. "It was like a refrigerator, a *hielera*. The room felt very cold. They would wake you up and undress you. You couldn't even lie down, it was so crowded. They took away my oldest son, who was fourteen at the time, to be with the men. But he was a kid, not an adult! Eventually I had to sign some papers, and they sent me to a shelter where I could call my family."

THEORIES OF MIGRATION

Migrants are not naive about these perils. They take these risks consciously and intentionally. The question is, why?

Conventional theories of migration often refer to "push" and "pull" factors: economic disadvantage as an outward driver of emigration, and economic opportunity as a magnet for immigration. These views, informed by the work of the nineteenth-century German-English geographer Ernest Ravenstein (1885), are based on economic principles that assume human behavior to be based on rational choice, supply and demand, and maximization of profit (O'Reilly 2015). This neoclassical economic framing disregards the many factors that influence the incredibly disruptive act of migration. Among the women in this study, forty-six (71 percent) cited economic insecurity or opportunity as a reason for their migration, implying that the rest left for more personal reasons.

Newer theories of migration recognize many additional factors—including social networks and individual emotional experiences—that both facilitate and hinder migration (O'Reilly 2015). US migration experts note that push and pull factors are like the poles of a car battery, in that positive and negative forces are needed to initiate either ignition or migration. However, other variables determine who chooses to migrate and where they go.

For monarch butterflies, Ocean Vuong notes, "migration can be triggered by the angle of sunlight, indicating a change in season, temperature, plant life, and food supply" (Vuong 2019, 18). As with monarchs, a person's decision to migrate can certainly result from urgent deprivation, but it can also be deeply personal. Importantly, none of these motivations exists in isolation. As migration scholars note, multiple factors to converge to inform migration patterns.

REASONS FOR MIGRATING

"I Was Young": Migration as an Act of Rebellion

When Almudena left her home, she was driven by a strong desire for independence—strong enough for her to attempt the border crossing five times before succeeding.

"I finished my education when I was about twenty-two years old. I had a boyfriend that I knew for four years before coming here [to the United States]. So, well, he told me that he was coming here when I finished studying and then would come back to Mexico, but I finished studying, worked, and he didn't come back. So I decided to come here. I went to look for him, and I was surprised to find that he was already married. But by then I had already decided I was coming, and it had cost me so much to get here."

"To be honest, nothing was missing in my life," Almudena told me. "My parents weren't high-class, but we were middle-class, comfortable. I had finished studying, and all that was left was to work and enjoy life, right? But I couldn't do it. At that age, sometimes you get into a rebellious stage.... I never thought about the consequences. And yes, the desert is very dangerous, but at that age, you don't think about those risks."

Ana Paula, a forty-one-year-old from Ecuador who also migrated when she was twenty-two, echoed this thinking. "I was young, right? I didn't think much about coming." Although Ana Paula stated that her decision was partly motivated by the weak economy, really, she said, it was just about "getting out of the house."

"When I was back in Ecuador, I was working in a post office, but I was only making about $140 a month. As a high school graduation gift, my mom took me to visit my uncle here. I just fell in love with this country. And so I went back again a few years later. By that time, I was twenty-one, and I really wanted to be independent, but I knew I would never be able to because of my income. So, you know, I spoke to my parents, and I say, you know, 'I'll probably go there [to the States] and make some money, for like two years and then come back.' But those two years just became nineteen!"

Ana Paula said that her parents had stable jobs, their own home, and enough money to live comfortably. She originally planned to "just make money and probably go back and buy a house or a little farm, and a little car" so she could avoid "worrying about paying a lot of bills." However, after a year or two in the United States, she was inclined to stay. "It was easy to find a job and make money. I was going out and coming back at whatever time I wanted. I didn't have anybody telling me what to do. I kept telling myself 'Just one more year, one more year,' but I just fell in love with being here. It wasn't worth going back when I could have the things I wanted—a job, a place of my own, a car—here. I always tell my mom, if I had to do it all over again, I would."

Like many long-term US residents, Ana Paula spoke English comfortably, owned her own business, and cared for her children and her parents, whom she had persuaded to join her. She had rented the same home, with a backyard, for several years, so that it almost felt like her own. Ana Paula lived out her own version of the American dream.

This cluster of women who enacted migration as rebellion parallels findings by the anthropologist Leo Chavez in his study of Mexican migrants to San Diego. Many left "'for adventure' and to satisfy curiosity about what life is actually like in the United States" (Chavez 1992, 33). Yet this spirit of adventure often collapses under the weight of everyday violence and marginalization. As one of Chavez's interlocutors poignantly summarizes, "I came for adventure to the richest country, where we live like dogs" (1992, 34).

The stories told by Ana Paula and Almudena shed light on an often-unappreciated dimension of migration: choice. All migrants—including refugees—ultimately leave their home countries by choice. For many, that choice is forced by economic deprivation, war, natural disaster, or community violence; others make the move from a position of relative comfort. The medical anthropologist Alyshia Gálvez describes the Mexican women in her study as having "projects" to "improve" or "overcome" their life chances (*superándose*) (Gálvez 2011, 19). The social policy scholar Nando Sigona cautions against "constructing undocumented migrants as passive and agency-less subjects overdetermined by structural conditions" (Sigona 2012, 51). Experiences of migration vary according to intersectional social positions.

Monarch butterflies have a much greater chance of surviving the winter in a warmer climate. Yet it is not only the signal of changing temperatures that drives them south: even with relatively weak environmental cues, monarchs seem to have an internal timer, modulated by epigenetic signaling, that prompts them to move (D. Green and Kronforst 2019). Both intrinsic and extrinsic factors converge to drive migration; the relative strength of these factors varies by individual.

Family Reunification

A small number of interlocutors emphasized family reunification as the primary motivation for their decision to migrate. This rationale aligns closely with the priorities of US Immigration law over the past half century. The Immigration and Nationality Act of 1965, also called the Hart-Celler Act, abolished the prior quota system based on national origins, instead giving preference to family members of US citizens and permanent residents. This reform shifted the "color line" of immigration, leading to influxes of migrants from Latin America and Asia whose claims to Whiteness failed relative to those of their European Irish, Polish, and Italian predecessors. Through the Hart-Celler Act, many Latin Americans and Asians who had family members with established footholds on US soil, due to prior immigration waves that favored importation of cheap labor, now had a pathway to lawful migration. In her book *Fictive Kinship*, the sociologist Catherine Lee argues that US immigration policy has always promoted family reunification, even under draconian schemes like the Chinese Exclusion Act of 1882. All these regulations—like shifting from a quota-based system to one that values existing US families and highly skilled workers—devise criteria for "legitimate" families worthy of reunification and center those whose gender, class, and racial or ethnic characteristics align with "American" ideals (C. Lee 2013). In other words, framing certain immigrants as assimilable—or "like us"—constructs policies that either facilitate or hinder the process of becoming "American."

Marisol, a thirty-four-year-old from Michoacán, Mexico, describes how she came to the United States as a young teenager. "My mom was already here... with all her family and her siblings. My mom sent for me. I came here with other people who brought me here, but my mom paid." Her father had a good job working at a sugar and honey plant, but when friends told him of the higher wages they earned in the United States, he decided it would be best for the family to migrate.

Marisol's father obtained a work visa under which he was required to return to Mexico every six months, but her mother stayed on—undocumented—working in a factory. It was economic opportunity that spurred her parents to migrate; Marisol and her siblings came solely to be with their parents.

The immigration system is not intended to support women like Marisol. Migrants like her parents, who live in a state of liminal legality—eligible to obtain social security numbers and work permits but without the security of permanent residency or citizenship—are not meant to bring other family members into the United States. Yet the pull of familial support, often coupled with unfavorable socioeconomic conditions, encourages migrants to circumvent the official mechanisms of reunification (e.g., visa or residency sponsorship) to join their relatives.

For women from the Caribbean, transnational barriers are often more permeable than for Latin Americans from South America or the Northern Triangle of Central America. Puerto Ricans, as US citizens, are free to move between the island and the mainland. Dominicans and Jamaicans, because of geographic proximity and vast diasporic communities in hubs like New York City, often visit family in the United States as a rite of passage, and some then decide to migrate.

Antoinetta, a twenty-three-year-old from the Dominican Republic, visited her family multiple times on a tourist visa before deciding to settle in the United States. "We had so many family members who lived here—some in New York, in Boston. So many from my dad's side had lived here for a long time," Antoinetta said. For her, life in the United States was familiar. So when her partner moved to New Haven for work, it made sense for her to join him. "I hadn't planned on staying here, but my son's father asked me to stay. Now I want to stay here for the rest of my life. I want to become a citizen," Antoinetta told me.

Because of her regular family visits to the United States and the broad network of family support she enjoyed, Antoinetta adapted quickly. "I liked this country, how a person can become independent and get ahead. I can tell you that, overall, I haven't had a hard time here or anything." Having multiple relatives living as permanent residents or citizens gave Antoinetta a familiarity with social safety nets, like Medicaid (called HUSKY in Connecticut). She could also lean on a broad network of kin for support with childcare or unforeseen expenses. For her, the move to the United States was a matter of convenience, akin to a US-born college graduate moving from their college city back to their hometown for familial support.

Economic Precarity and Opportunity: When the Political Becomes Personal

In the conversation I describe in the introduction, Célia and Marcelina spoke at length about economic insecurity in Ecuador.

MARCELINA: There has always been insecurity. You have to be careful.

CÉLIA: Yes, mostly because there is no work. There, if you have it, it's always unstable—it's not a safe bet.

MARCELINA: The salaries are low.

CÉLIA: And, like we said, unreliable.

MARCELINA: You have to do a lot of work.

CÉLIA: It's a lot of pressure.

Their inability to earn enough to support their families, despite working long hours, prompted them to seek a better life in the United States. In many such instances, a partner or childless friend travels first, to test the waters and report back. Marcelina had migrated with her husband first to Spain and then to the United States. She was thrilled by the higher pay, multiple job opportunities, and networks of support for migrants in New Haven and urged Célia to join her. Célia's husband, Eduardo, who had lost his job around the time of the birth of their first child, migrated first. After three months of painful separation, Célia joined him.

CÉLIA: I came alone with my eight-month-old baby.

JES: How did you decide then, in November 2018, that it was time for you to leave?

MARCELINA: They wanted to take advantage of the coming holidays. He had a stable job and said to me, "Why don't we see if they can come now, and we can spend Christmas together?" He talked with Célia, and she said yes. They also missed each other.

Célia's decision to migrate—and the timing of her travel—stemmed from both economic disadvantage and the desire to reunite her family. Célia and her family were fortunate to receive tourist visas for their entry into the United States after paying a fee and completing an interview at the US consulate, during which authorities evaluated her family's assets, identification documents, and motivations for travel. Célia and her husband were determined to be able to offer legitimate reasons for visiting the United States and to be assessed as being at low risk of overstaying their visa, which allows a visit of up to 180 days. Many other migrants confront the riskier option of crossing the border.

Lucía, a forty-three-year-old from Tlaxcala, Mexico, said she left for the United States "to seek a better life."

"I was a single mother," she explained. "I worked alone; the dad wasn't in the picture. I was working as a kitchen assistant, making and selling food and so on. There's an expression, 'In life, when you don't have help, you just have to do it on your own.' You have to want to make things better for yourself."

For Lucía, single parenthood exacerbated the difficulties of limited job opportunities and low pay. She had dropped out of college in her second semester because she could no longer afford to attend; consequently, her only options for work were dishwashing, domestic help, or food service. When she had her daughter and her partner left her, Lucía struggled to meet her regular expenses. "The single woman must always fight harder," she told me.

Lucía spent $3,000 to hire a coyote to guide her across the border, a process that took a week. She hopes that her daughter and son—now thirteen and five years old—will finish their education, a goal she could not achieve, so that they can have a better future. When I spoke with Lucía, she was about four months pregnant and predicted she was having a second girl. "I want my children to study, especially the girls, so they can get ahead. I don't want them to depend on a man or anyone else. May they be strong women who ask for what they want, without relying on their husbands or family members or anyone else."

Célia and Lucía agreed on the importance of seeking better opportunities for their families. Although their experiences differed with respect to the financial and physical costs of migration, both were personally and economically motivated to make this sacrifice.

In a similar vein, Noelia, a forty-year-old from Chiapas, Mexico, recounted, "We couldn't find work. It was the economy. Sometimes we couldn't even buy our everyday food. And then, like twenty years ago, we had a daughter who died because we didn't have the money to take her to the doctor." Noelia and her husband had suspected their infant daughter was ill: she was not feeding well, she had lost weight, and yet her body seemed strangely swollen. She had also spiked a fever. Noelia and her husband had hoped she had an infection that would pass on its own. They knew they would not be able to afford the high fees that doctors would demand up front for treatment. Her baby died within a few weeks.

"I couldn't stay there after my daughter passed away," she told me. "I didn't want to be where I had those painful memories, knowing we couldn't save her. So we decided to come here."

For Noelia, poverty and economic inequality resulted in family tragedy. Although material deprivation certainly sparked the idea of migration, it was the emotional experience of losing her daughter that finally spurred her and her husband to act. Noelia's husband migrated first, landing a job in New Haven in construction, and Noelia paid $2,500 to a coyote to pass her from Chiapas to join him. She told no one she was leaving, fearing either that she would die in the desert or, if she did cross the border successfully, that gang members at home would presume her family had money and blackmail them. "When they know that someone comes here [the United States], they'll rob and steal from [their family]. They'll blackmail them, threatening to kill them if they don't pay up."

When she crossed the border, Noelia was the only woman in a group of sixteen. The men resented her, thinking that if they ran into immigration authorities, they would all be caught because she would be too slow to escape. "Thank God, I had a lot of help from the coyote," she told me. "He cared about me, told me it would be okay. He even gave me serums so that I wouldn't get too dehydrated. He was a very, very good person."

The fees Noelia and Lucía paid their coyotes were comparatively low: fees for my interlocutors ranged between $2,500 and $13,500, with an average of around $7,000. Lucía told me, "Now, the coyotes no longer work on their own, like they used to. Now, they're under the control of the gangs, the mafia. The gangs force the coyotes to smuggle people or drugs. They charge up to eight thousand, ten thousand dollars. That's why now it's so difficult to cross, because they have to pay the mafia so they can keep working."

Migration entails both personal upheaval and significant financial investment. Although a few women in this study decided to leave on the spur of the moment, most contemplated migration for months to years prior to acting.

The convergence of political, economic, and individual factors motivating migration echoes a common refrain in social science literature, of the political becoming personal, and vice versa. A focus on broader political and economic forces—as in conventional push-pull migration theory—overlooks the very personal effects of those forces and their influence on the decision to migrate. Conversely, inattention to structural factors can problematize or even pathologize individual choices, without recognizing the ways psychology and behavior respond to violent social architectures.

"They Just Kill": Personal Violence as a Force in Migration

It was difficult to hear Ysabel at first. She spoke softly and tentatively, and I had not yet upgraded my audio equipment to facilitate phone interviews. She initially offered two- to-three word replies to my questions, but as we eased into the conversation, she revealed more details of her story. "In my country, we lacked the money to buy food," Ysabel told me. "Since we worked in the field, we couldn't earn much."

Given this comment, I initially categorized Ysabel's motivation for migrating as strictly economic, but when I asked her whether violence was a concern, she said, "Yes, that too. These bad people came into our community. They killed people, just like that, without fear. We were afraid to walk down the street because they have no mercy, they just kill. I was so afraid. It was not easy to walk the streets."

Cañar, an Andean province in south-central Ecuador, has not escaped the gang-related violence and petty theft that characterize the region. The Overseas Security Advisory Council, in partnership with the US State Department, warns US travelers that the region is a "critical-threat location" because of limited judicial resources that permit homicides, armed assaults, robberies, sexual assaults, and home invasions (Overseas Security Advisory Council 2020). In addition, Indigenous resistance to territorial encroachment and neoliberal economic policies has resulted in violent clashes between Cañari communities and government officials. Ysabel, who grew up speaking Quechua and identifies as Indigenous, feared her life would be in danger if she returned to Ecuador.

Like so many others, Ysabel was motivated to migrate at least in part by economic reasons. However, it was her experience of "everyday violence" (Scheper-Hughes 1992) that ultimately drove her to leave. Violence, in its various configurations, is ubiquitous in Latin America because of economic inequality and state failure (see chapter 1). Yet the presence of violence in a region is often not enough to drive emigration: it is personal experiences of violence, such as the murders Ysabel witnessed in her community, that propel migrants to leave.

Like Ysabel, Verónica and her husband worked in the fields, in their case, in a rural village in the San Marcos region of Guatemala. They too lived in poverty: Verónica had only a sixth-grade education, which limited her job prospects. Given the village's proximity to the Mexican border, on known drug-trafficking routes, they were particularly susceptible to cartel violence.

VERÓNICA: My husband worked as a caretaker for a melon farm. There, as he was working, they shot him. And the threats kept coming. So, we had to leave.

JES: Oh wow, how horrible!

VERÓNICA: Yes, so with his being assaulted and the economic conditions in our country, there was no way we could stay there.

The success of the farm made it a target for control by opium growers. Although Verónica's husband did not own the farm, his role as a manager rendered him prey to extortion efforts by drug leaders. When Verónica and her husband realized that the threats would not let up, they decided to flee. Although Verónica had believed that her family's rural isolation—and their relative poverty—would shield them from attack, once the threats became personal, Verónica, her husband, and their nursing baby made the trek across the border.

For Ysabel and Verónica, community and national patterns of violence took a personal toll. Aida's experience of violence was highly individualized. "Yes, there was economic instability in my country," Aida said about her home in Honduras. "But that was only secondary. Really, it was because a man there was harassing and bothering me."

She told me how, beginning when she was sixteen years old, a man at church began stalking her. "I was a dancer at the church. He would always wait for me as I left. Then, at night, somehow, he would always find me. He told me I was pretty, that I had a good body. It made me feel so uncomfortable."

Aida shared her concerns with her mother, who did not know what to do. They both feared she would be raped, or even killed, but they knew the police would not take any action if she reported the man. "Of course, I've heard of cases when a woman has already been raped or killed, then the police will intervene, but by then, it's too late. I didn't want to happen to me what happens to so many girls there."

The stalking worsened over the next few years. When she narrowly escaped assault after the man cornered her, Aida decided she had to leave. "It's not safe there. Even with thousands of cops, you're not protected." She had been willing to endure the frustrations of working five days a week—and studying on the weekends—but still lacking the resources to support herself, her mother, and siblings. But when she experienced vicious *machismo* and gender-based violence firsthand, Aida decided to migrate. Despite this harassment, she says, "I'm also glad that I had the opportunity to search for new possibilities and create a new life here."

THE PRODUCTION OF ILLEGALITY

I conducted my fieldwork at a time when the system and conduct of immigration authorities came under intensive scrutiny. In the spring of 2018, the "zero tolerance" policy against irregular migration imposed by the Trump administration cruelly separated thousands of migrant children from their parents, hundreds of whom have not yet been reunited as of this writing (Buchanan, Wolgin, and Flores 2021). A number of Congressional representatives publicized evocative photos of detention conditions, including images of unbathed children on cots with tinfoil blankets, surrounded by chain-link cages.

The conditions in detention evoke Michel Foucault's analyses of the modern penal system, in particular the way judicial punishment lays hold on the soul (Foucault 1977). Ysabel experienced the physical discomforts of crowded conditions, rationing of food, freezing temperatures, and sleep deprivation, but this form of incarceration also has a cumulative, dehumanizing effect. Constant surveillance and the targeting of migrant bodies for disciplinary control grooms them for subservience, docility, and compliance as members of the American underclass.

Migrant bodies serve as locales of regulation, emphasizing the role of the state in defining legitimacy (Castañeda 2019). The Salvadoran sociologists Cecilia Menjívar and Leisy Abrego proposed the category of *legal violence* to describe the punitive and disciplinary functions of the law and the way it harms migrant bodies. They argue that immigration policies purposely construct the status of illegality (Menjívar and Abrego 2012).

In fact, US immigration policy has historically engaged racist, exclusionary practices that welcome migrants as cheap sources of labor while withholding state protection from them. The 1790 Naturalization Act required each naturalized citizen of the United States to be a "free white person" of "good moral character" (Treitler 2015). This orientation persisted with the Chinese Exclusion Act of 1882, which banned Chinese nationals from immigrating or claiming US citizenship, and the 1921 Emergency Quota Act, which set quotas for immigration from countries outside the Western hemisphere (Ngai 2014). By contrast, the Immigration Act of 1864 and the Mexican Farm Labor Agreement of 1942 (often known as the Bracero Agreement) provided for migrant labor to address US worker shortages on farms and in factories. US political leaders have continued to enact laws to allow US employers to access—and exploit—migrant workers while blocking pathways to full citizenship. In this way, immigration enforcement epitomizes racial capitalism: the subjugation of Brown, migrant bodies advances neoliberal interests. The Canadian activist and scholar Harsha Walia writes, "US border rule reveals seamless relations between the carceral administration of genocide and slavery at home and imperial counterinsurgency abroad, domestic neoliberal policies of welfare retrenchment and foreign policies of capitalist trade, and local and global regimes of race" (Walia 2021, 26).

US policy has carefully configured the category of illegality as a sociopolitical condition characterized by an unequal power relationship to the state (De Genova 2002). Unlike citizens and permanent residents, undocumented migrants cannot make claims to political or legal security, which compounds their social vulnerability. "If there were no borders, there would be no migration—just mobility" (De Genova 2017).

Moving from one's home country to the United States involves separation from familiar social groups and structures, and transition and incorporation into the new society. For many migrants, the latter process is incomplete: they are folded into the nation without becoming part of it and remain excluded and abjectified (Chavez 1992, 2013).

CONCLUSION

Migrants choose to relocate for many reasons, including economic precarity, violence, family reunification, and youthful rebellion. Stories like those of Anahi and Caridad convey migration-related trauma, highlighting the state-sanctioned and gender-based violence faced by women migrants. Through immigration enforcement and the concomitant production of illegality, migration becomes a social determinant of health. The accumulation of trauma and the deprivation of rights places the mental and physical health of migrants at risk. Although it is true that economic disadvantage and opportunity both push and pull migrants across borders, these forces resemble the signals of seasonal change that prompt monarch butterflies to embark on their migration. Migration must be understood in terms of agency—and constraints on that agency—taking into account the ways US immigration policy purposely generates categories of exclusion.

3 Arriving

When you cross the border from Mexico into the United States, you lose more than your political status as a recognized citizen in the country where you reside. You shed the identity that gives you a sense of value and belonging in your home country and become anonymized as an outsider, an "Other." Whether you are a Quechua-speaking rural Indigenous Ecuadorian, a Spanish-speaking mestizo Costa Rican, a Totonac-speaking coastal Mexican, a Creyol-speaking Black Haitian, or an Italian-speaking White Argentine, passing into the United States erases that particularity. In the United States, all people with Latin American heritage are racialized as Hispanic or Latino (or, in a gender-neutral form, Latinx).

WHAT IS LATINX?

Latinx is an inclusive, gender-neutral term for "Latinos/as," abbreviated from *Latinoamericanos*. It refers to individuals with origin in or heritage from Latin America, including those who trace their roots to Central and South America and the Caribbean. Descendants of Spanish settlers in what is now the southwestern United States—Hispanos, Tejanos, and

Californios—who became US residents after the Treaty of Guadalupe-Hidalgo in 1848 may also identify as Latinx (Haverluk 1997; Nostrand 2010). Constructions of the Latinx community must therefore attend to pluralities in racial identity, language, origin, and migration history (Silva, Paris, and Añez 2017).

Latinxs are the largest racial or ethnic group in the United States, numbering 60.6 million and constituting 18.5 percent of the population as of 2019 (U.S. Census Bureau 2020). By 2030, Latinxs are expected to constitute nearly 30 percent of the US population (Vespa, Medina, and Armstrong 2020). Latinxs are also the youngest racial or ethnic group in the United States: one-third of the nation's Latinxs are younger than eighteen years old (Noe-Bustamente and Flores 2019). At the same time, the category of "Latinx," or *Latinidad*, carries contradictions. The category has become politicized both within and beyond the community in ways that shape community organization and immigration enforcement. The features of *Latinidad* that bond those who identify with the label—shared language or linguistic origins, histories of colonization and migration or dispossession, and experiences of oppression—sow communities of Latinxs in patches throughout the country, including in New Haven, Connecticut.

LATINIDAD AS CONTRADICTION

"How have heterogeneous Latin American-origin groups come to be imagined—and to an extent imagine themselves—as part of a pan-ethnic whole?" the sociologist Michael Rodríguez-Muñiz asks in his book *Figures of the Future* (Rodríguez-Muñiz 2021, xvi). "What forces have been at play and what have been the consequences?"

As an exercise in positionality, I asked each of my research assistants to reflect on their intersectional relationships with the broad category of *Latinidad*. Their responses reflect the complex entanglements of race, politics, and gender in this category.

One student responded, "I identify as an Afro-Latino and, to tell you the truth, it has been very difficult trying to reconcile with my *Latinidad*. I did not always identify as Afro-Latino because for the longest [time]

I wasn't aware of such a label." The student went on to explain this history, and how common configurations of *Latinidad* excluded his family's Blackness. "My mom and grandma are both Afro-Boricua and I still, because of the way *Latinidad* is presented, did not associate them with being Black as a child. People have this image in their head of what a Latinx person is, and this image contributes to the erasure of Black and Indigenous Latinx folk.

"I identify as Afro-Latinx because to not do so would be an offense to my ancestors that were forcibly removed from Africa and brought to PR [Puerto Rico] as slaves. I know because of my proximity to Blackness that these ancestors exist and that I am a product of their exploitation. I honor them every day that I am alive because their blood runs through my veins."

The student's mood shifted from proud to solemn. "Identifying as an Afro-Latino has also been difficult for me, though, because I am fair-skinned as a result of my multiracial identity. Navigating identifying as Black and what that means for me is something I worked on for a very long time. Ultimately, *Latinidad* has really complicated the journey to embracing and understanding my identities. The struggle to get to where I am today, though, has made me very critical of *Latinidad*. I always fight for a more inclusive definition, and it made me realize how diverse *Latinidad* actually is."

This student's narrative reveals the tensions between *Latinidad* and racial identity, particularly articulations of Blackness. Early activists constructed *Hispanic/Latino* as a category distinct from Blackness. The historian Sonia Lee proposes the concept of *bifurcated racialization* to explain the way that Latinxs—particularly Puerto Ricans—imagined themselves as "exaggerated opposites" to Black Americans. Puerto Ricans imagined themselves as "patient," viewing Black activists instead as "militant" and more radical, and used this characterization to justify their interest in organizing separately from Black Americans (S. S.-H. Lee 2014, 14). This tension is particularly salient among the Puerto Rican community of New Haven, which was the first among Latinxs in New Haven to establish a cohesive social presence.

Another student echoed the assertion that *Latinidad* erases "Black and Indigenous Latinx folk," describing her experience as an Indigenous Mexican American. "Coming from an Indigenous migrant family means amazing things for me and complicates so much more. It's about learning what my migrant communities mean when they refer to 'their' Mexico while thinking about the Japóndarhu (lake region) and *chiquicaztle* (stinging medicinal herb) from 'my' Mexico and the nostalgia I get from eating tamales in East L.A. [Los Angeles] and New Haven," she reminisces.

"Part of my relationship to *Latinidad* and Indigeneity often meant feeling like an outsider with my peers. I did not feel comfortable enough to speak about things that were taboo with my 'real' Mexican friends and much less the greater American population. Sacred practices around health and grooming stayed within the family and our *compadres*. I remember feeling afraid that I would be bullied by others for sharing my stories about the *temazcal* (communal sweat bath) in Mexico and the way we re-create it in CA [California] alongside all 5 women in the household. I would keep quiet about my mom's healing abilities and the way I met so many other kids, because their families would bring them to our house for a *limpia* [cleanse] and *sobada* [healing massage]. My parents' native languages were also rarely heard in the household, until recently. We are now an outspoken quadrilingual household."

The student describes how she transitioned from feeling shame and isolation to pride, but not pride in her identity as Latina. "These experiences are continually being shaped and loved more outspokenly by all of our family. My perspectives on *Latinidad* are that *Latinidad* has never truly benefited my family and people like us. It cannot encompass (nor should it) the complexities and resistances to *Latinidad*. My family and I mainly use it in White spaces and White politics to refer to ourselves for outsiders. I think that is the best it gets." *Latinidad*, this student observes, is an imperfect category that cannot fully capture the richness of Indigeneity, including Indigenous languages, connection to the land, and spiritual practices.

Taking a more analytical tone, another student observed, "*Latinidad* and I have an extremely rocky relationship. I understand its purpose within the racial contexts of the US and its potential as an organizing political tool, but it also has a dark history as an agent of colonization. *Latinidad* works as an anti-imperial agent, but its conceptualization as a shared identity sinned in homogenizing populations. States like Mexico, Costa Rica, the Dominican Republic, Paraguay, etc. , used *Latinidad* as a neocolonizing tool to render populations as uniformly *mestize* or *mulate*. The dichotomy of population left out Indigenous and Black communities; states sometimes even forced miscegenation, committing terrible atrocities of sexual violence.

"Conversations of *Latinidad* center White, light-skin Latines of higher income countries without addressing the anti-Blackness and anti-Indigeneity of our '*raza*.' Yet, for simplification purposes, I still tick off the Latino box in the census. I am a person of contradiction."

Latinidad is, by nature, contradictory—politically useful, yet individually invalidating. As the philosopher Linda Martín Alcoff argues, *Latinidad* both "invokes histories of colonialism, slavery, and genocide" that may shortchange Black and Indigenous Latinx people and represents "a thorn in the side of 'manifest destiny,' 'leader of the free world,' and other such mythic narratives that legitimize US world dominance" (Alcoff 2000, 39). As such, *Latinidad* carries both pain and political power. Rodriguez-Muñiz echoes this sentiment—and those of the third student I quote—noting that articulations of *Latinidad* arise from "stratified colonial relations" that center particular "raced, gendered, classed, and sexual experiences" while marginalizing others (Rodriguez-Muñiz 2021, xvii).

I confronted the problematic aspects of *Latinidad* throughout my research. Well-intentioned scholars frequently asked me, "Why choose this population? Why all of Latin America? Why not just recent migrants?" The answer is that my interlocutors are connected by shared experiences of racialization and sexualization in the United States, even if some do not fully endorse the label of *Latina* or *Hispanic*.

THE POLITICIZATION OF *LATINIDAD*

Rodríguez-Muñiz further articulates the political aspects of conceptualizing a Latinx population. He notes that demographic groups do not simply exist: they are constructed and freighted with political judgments through what he calls *population politics*, observing how the state produces difference through its construction of demographic categories (Rodríguez-Muñiz 2021).

In my first-year university course Latino/a Experiences in the United

States, the professor instructed us to read works by the political scientist Samuel P. Huntington, who decades ago criticized Latinx communities for failing to adopt "American" norms. Huntington sided with many right-wing political commentators who advanced a narrative of a "Latino threat" and stoked fears about a *reconquista,* or reconquest of the American Southwest (Chavez 2013). The class—largely composed of first- and second-generation Mexican immigrants and a few others from South America and the Caribbean—revolted. Why should we accept the legitimization of anti-Latinx political vitriol? Assimilationism is racist! What does this mean for our group—all recipients of a scholarship named for a Puerto Rican university student?

Regardless of our viewpoint, the professor wanted to prepare us to meet the narrative of Latinxs as linguistically, culturally, and politically separatist. Violent media characterizations of Latinxs as "invaders" and racialized Others continue to inflame xenophobia and promote the abrogation of citizenship rights.

In his book *The Latino Threat,* the anthropologist Leo Chavez examines this fiction, noting the contested idea of citizenship. "A legalistic definition of citizen is not enough," Chavez argues. "Other meanings of citizenship— economic, social, cultural, and even emotional—are being presented in debates, marches, and public discourses focused on immigrants, their children, and the nation" (Chavez 2013, 13).

Conceptions of cultural citizenship cannot be divorced from processes of race making and enforcement of racial hierarchies in the United States, which have always privileged Whiteness. Notably, though the U.S. Census Bureau considers "Hispanic/Latino" an ethnicity, this position tends to pit Latinxs against Black Americans, encouraging the "dominant racial narrative that African Americans 'deserve' their place at the bottom of the hierarchy, while, in contrast, putting Latinos into the dominant ethnic narrative in which striving 'immigrants' overcome the odds to assimilate" (Gómez 2020, 15). Early Latinx migrants—particularly Puerto Ricans—defined themselves in contradistinction to Blackness, noting phenotypic differences such as softer hair and lighter skin (S. S.-H. Lee 2014). European heritage confers citizenship benefits to Latinxs who carry the "phenotypic passport" of fairer complexions and lighter eyes (Gonzales 2016). As with Italian, Irish, and Polish immigrants of the past

(Guglielmo 2004), the Latinx narrative of self is constructed as destined toward Whiteness.

Anti-Blackness and colorism pervade the experience of *Latinidad*, both in Latin America and in the United States. Some Dominicans walk in the shade to avoid darkening their skin, just as they undergo hair relaxation and keratin treatments to "correct" their *pelo negro* or *pelo malo* (Black or "bad" hair). These habits grew out of assertions of Dominican superiority over their Haitian neighbors. Latina women may receive directives from their mothers not to bring home a man "any darker than me," provoking scandal if they date darker Latinos or Black Americans.

Latinx imaginations as non-Black at worst and White at best find expression in attacks by Latinxs against Black people. George Zimmerman, who murdered seventeen-year-old Trayvon Martin on February 26, 2012, justifying his action with his role as neighborhood watch coordinator and his suspicion of Trayvon's hoodie, has a Peruvian mother and identifies as Hispanic on voter registration forms. Nikolas Cruz, who killed seventeen people and injured seventeen others in the 2018 shooting at Marjory Stoneman Douglas High School, grew up in an adoptive Latinx family and inveighed against Black, Latinx, and Jewish people. White supremacist organizations claimed him as their own despite his Spanish surname. *Latinidad* has always been constructed in tension with Blackness in politically exclusive and sometimes violent ways.

LATINX AS RACE (VERSUS ETHNICITY)

The Latinx narrative in the United States traces its origins to *mestizaje*, or racial miscegenation, reinforcing ties to Europeans (Wertsch 2007; Gómez 2020). The Spanish Empire in Latin America enforced a caste system based on ancestry and physical characteristics. Because Whiteness conferred advantages such as land ownership, it incentivized *blanqueamiento*, or "whitening," through race-selective marriage. Nations advanced the *blanqueamiento* agenda through policies to attract European migrants and obstruct movement from Asia or Africa (Gómez 2020). As a result, many Latin Americans (and Latinos) trace their lineages to the Iberian Peninsula through Spanish family crests and surnames, shoring up their claims to Whiteness, or near-Whiteness. In US census inventories, more than half of Latinxs assert they are White (Cohn, Brown, and Lopez 2021). This assertion matters little, however, in the American racial terrain. The sociologist Julie Dowling states that self-proclaimed "White" Latinxs "are not generally recognized as white by others. Hence, it becomes quite clear that they do not truly 'own' whiteness as it is not a valid social identification for them" (Dowling 2014, 133). Regardless of how they classify themselves, most Latinxs are viewed by White Americans as racialized minorities.

This distinction is central to my own delayed acceptance of my Latin American heritage. Growing up, I understood myself as culturally Italian and racially White. Then, when I was auditioning as a child actress, casting directors barred me from playing White characters, particularly in the summer, when my skin tanned to a deep brown. My talent manager instructed me to avoid sun exposure, to wear lighter-toned makeup, and to straighten my hair to increase my eligibility for White roles. My Cuban aunt urged the same, both punishing and teasing me with the name Negrita [Blackie] when I spent too much time playing on the beach. Despite my best attempts to conform, casting companies funneled me toward roles as the recovering offender living in a halfway house or the hypersexual teenage temptress, even asking me to provide voice-overs for darker-skinned cartoon characters and dolls. After I left acting, my college peers in the Midwest cemented my identity as not-quite-White with an exchange familiar to many:

THEM: Where are you from?

ME: I was born in New York.

THEM: No, where are you really from?

ME: I guess I grew up in New Jersey.

THEM: But where are your parents from?

ME: New York.

THEM: What about before that?

These encounters hindered my full acceptance into my majority White academic community. Then, when I was pulled over by police for the first time and saw my identity checked on the ticket as "Hispanic," I came to realize that, regardless of my self-conception, the world viewed me as Other.

A NOTE ON TERMINOLOGY

Over the past several decades, activists, scholars, and politicians have debated how to identify this growing population of migrants from Latin America and their descendants. The ambiguities and mounting controversies surrounding terms such as *Hispanic* and *Latino* underscore the need for careful use of terminology in describing this diverse population.

The 1975 Ad Hoc Committee on Racial and Ethnic Definitions, created under the Nixon administration, debated multiple terms for the purposes of census classification, and, despite a lack of consensus, settled on *Hispanic* (Fears 2003). Many activists rejected the term, pointing out its ties to colonization and Spanish imperialism. They favored *Latino*, which refers to Latin American geography and the Romance linguistic origins of the diaspora. *Latino* emerged as the preferred term for people of Latin American origin in the 1980s, largely in response to the perception of *Hispanic* as a bureaucratic label (Hayes-Bautista and Chapa 1987; del Olmo 1981, 1985). Beginning in the 1970s, the Federal Office of Management and Budget and had applied the term *Hispanic* to twelve million Americans of "Spanish origin or descent," and it first appeared on the US census in 1980. Aiming to promote equal opportunity, Congress resolved to include data collection on this population in future censuses (Alcoff 2000; House Joint Resolution 92, Public Law 94–311, 94th Cong. , 1976). However, the term of reference chosen for the 1980 census, "Spanish/Hispanic origin or descent," bred confusion: Which Americans counted as Hispanic and stood to benefit from affirmative action measures? In their 1987 article in the *American Journal of Public Health,* David E. Hayes-Bautista and Jorge Chapa raised a number of conceptual questions: "Is a Spaniard Hispanic?...Is a Cape Verdean Hispanic? Is a Filipino Hispanic? Is a Brazilian Hispanic? Is a Brazilian identical to a Cape Verdean? Are both identical to a Portuguese?" (Hayes-Bautista and Chapa 1987, 65). The term *Hispanic* obscures the distinctions between European Americans and groups originating from countries colonized by the Iberian empires.

Further, millions of Spanish-speaking Latin Americans with Indigenous or African lineages do not claim Spanish heritage and cannot be accurately called Hispanics (Comas-Díaz 2001).

The term *Latino* is favored in scholarly and community circles for its grassroots origins and its reaffirmation of precolonial identity (del Olmo 1981; Oquendo 1995; Comas-Díaz 2001). Although some have argued this pan-ethnic identity was foisted on the community by outsiders, the idea can be traced to the anti-imperialist writings of Simón Bolívar. It reemerged through the Brown Power political movement of the 1960s and 1970s (Alcoff 2000; Comas-Díaz 2001). By the 1980s, Puerto Rican- and Chicano-owned popular media began using the term *Latino* in marketing campaigns, aiming to foster a sense of community among the Latin American immigrant population (del Olmo 1981). The Mexican American editorialist Frank del Olmo noted in 1985 that "Latino" was already a common term of self-identity: "Walk into a Latin American barrio, from East L.A. to Miami's Calle Ocho, and ask people what they are," del Olmo instructed. "You'll get all kinds of answers, including Latino, Chicano, Boricua, Cubano, Mexicano. But unless you wander into the offices of some government-funded poverty program, you won't hear people call themselves 'Hispanic'" (del Olmo 1985).

In the 1990s, feminist scholars began proposing alternatives to *Latino*, including "Latino/a" and "Latin@." *Latinx* originated online in the queer community in the early 2000s and gained traction roughly a decade later. Unlike the binary terms *Latino/a* or *Latin@*, *Latinx* and other x-carrying signifiers (e.g. , *chicxs* for *chicos*, or "kids," *todxs* for *todos*, or "all") are intended to be gender-neutral and fluid, affirming the diversity of gender and sexual expression in the Latinx community. Although some have argued that the use of *Latinx* perverts the already gender-incongruent Spanish language and renders pronunciation difficult (Hernandez 2017), others appreciate its transgression of imperialist linguistic prescriptions and the inclusive effect of gender neutrality for trans and nonbinary Latinxs (de Onís 2017).

Latinx is not an all-encompassing term. First, it does not explicitly include Hispanos, or people living in the Southwestern United States who trace their origins to Spaniards who colonized the area beginning in the late sixteenth century. Although most writers and scholars agree that

Hispanos are also Latinos/Latinxs (Vaca, Anderson, and Hayes-Bautista 2011; Andrés-Hyman et al. 2006; Sanchez 2016), Hispanos have a vastly different history. Second, according to a 2013 survey, 77 percent of Latinxs do not use broad terms like *Hispanic* or *Latino* to identify themselves, instead preferring terms signaling national origin (e.g. , Mexican or Cuban) or calling themselves American. This tendency may be explained in part by the fact that 69 percent of those surveyed did not perceive a shared culture among Latinxs. Among those who did have a preference, *Hispanic* was favored over *Latino* by a roughly a 2: 1 ratio (Lopez 2013); However, internet search data suggest that *Latino* and *Latinx* are increasing in popularity (Google Trends 2018a, b).

The US Census uses both *Hispanic* and *Latino* and defines someone who identifies with either term as "a person of Cuban, Mexican, Puerto Rican, South or Central American, or other Spanish culture or origin regardless of race" (U.S. Census Bureau 2018). According to this definition, Spanish immigrants may be considered ethnic minorities, and the vague "other Spanish culture or origin" descriptor may be interpreted to include Filipinos. Given the homogenizing effect of racial and ethnic categories, the differences in the particular experiences of Indigenous migrants—and their relationship to long-standing Indigenous communities in the United States—may not be appreciated (Bartlett et al. 2007; Castellanos 2017).

I do not believe any of my interlocutors identified as Latinx. Most related to their national origins or used the terms *Hispana* or *Latina*. Why, then, do I use the term *Latinx?*

The use of the letter x in the Spanish language emerged long before the mid-2000s and served to indigenize the colonizer's tongue for Mexican Americans (e.g. , Xicano/Xicana). However, nowadays, the x further connotes the possibility of nonconformism, of deviance, in a culture frequently treated as monolithic. As the queer Mexican-Cuban journalist and activist Paola Ramos writes in *Finding Latinx*, many young children of Latin American immigrants experienced "an ache for change... an ache that craved more unity, acceptance, and inclusion—an ache that simply wanted us to be seen." And so, through its resistance, the x in *Latinx* soothes that ache for "queer and gender-nonconforming Latinos," "Afro-Latinos," "transgender Latinas, "Asian Latinos," young Latinos who could not speak Spanish, midwestern Latinos and Latinos in the Deep

South, "Indigenous migrants," and all those who had been left outside the "Latino" umbrella (Ramos 2020, 8).

I use *Latinx* as an umbrella term, as an act of resistance. Even *Latine*, which certainly flows more smoothly in both Spanish and English speech, conforms to conventions of a colonizer's language. Although I support the use of the *e* in gender-neutral versions of Spanish words (e.g. , *Bienvenides a todes*), I continue to favor *Latinx* precisely because of its resistance to the shapes formed by European tongues and palettes. The Kichwa *q* and *ll*, the Nahuatl *tli* or *tl*, and the *d* for *th* in African American Vernacular English contort the American oropharynx.

In this study, however, all interlocutors identified as women and all those who spoke Spanish (94 percent) used feminine descriptors for themselves. For that reason, when discussing my interlocutors, I use *Latina* to respect their gender identities.

LATIN AMERICAN MIGRATION TO NEW HAVEN

"My brother had come here first," Priscila told me, describing how he had learned about work opportunities from others in their community in Tlaxcala. Other relatives then followed. Soon, it seemed, she had a cluster of family members living in New Haven. Priscila began hearing more and more about the city through her family.

After earning her degree in mathematics, Priscila passed her licensing exam and sought employment as a teacher. But, like Almudena, she would have needed thousands of dollars more to pay for an internship that would allow her to accumulate enough hours to qualify for a job. Her mother suggested that she move to the United States to work with her brother for a few years, earn the amount she needed for her teaching job, and then return.

"It made sense at the time," Priscila told me. "There was a small group of women that my mother knew that was going to be migrating, so my mother asked me, 'Do you want to go with them?' I figured, well, if I come for five years, I will probably have enough money to come back and get this job. But the things you plan don't always work out. That's life."

Priscila followed the path worn by many in her community to get a job in New Haven. The city felt almost familiar to her given how much she had heard about it back home. "Then I met my husband and stayed," Priscila said.

Priscila's experience exemplifies chain migration, a social pattern by which immigrants from one community follow friends and family to a particular destination in the receiving country. Among my interlocutors, Célia and Juana followed their sisters, who had moved to join their husbands' families. Ascención had a brother and nephew who rented her a room while she found her feet. Raquel and her husband, who had originally come to New York City as students, moved to New Haven when they met a compatriot from Chile who offered her husband a job. Each of these women acknowledged how their connections helped them get started in the city.

The term *chain migration* took on a negative political connotation during the Trump administration, when the president inveighed against "bad hombres" and "rapists" smuggling drugs into the country and bringing along criminal family members. His language evoked images of family mafias or chain gangs, effectively dehumanizing migrants. Although United States immigration policy has prioritized family reunification, that privilege has been denied to families of the "wrong" kind, including poor, Brown migrants from Latin America. Migrants have persisted in the face of this rejection, forming networks to support one another and holding the coattails of earlier arrivals as they seek to establish themselves in welcoming destinations like New Haven.

Despite statewide declines, in the City of New Haven, the Latin American migrant population has continued to grow. With a 35 percent increase in Latin American migrants between 2000 and 2010, the group grew to constitute 27.4 percent of the population (U.S. Census Bureau 2010; *New Haven Independent* 2011). In response to a surge in violence in Central America in 2014, migrants, particularly unaccompanied minors, poured into New Haven (Orson 2014), and this pattern has persisted. Statistics likely underestimate the number of undocumented residents living in New Haven, which has designated itself a sanctuary city and is informally recognized as a safe destination for people seeking to resettle in the United States without, or prior to, legal processing (O'Leary 2016). On a grassroots level, organizations like Junta for Progressive Action, Unidad Latina en Acción, and Integrated Refugee and Immigrant Services provide resources and collective bargaining power for undocumented immigrants suffering legal and workplace exploitation. Officially, the New Haven administration also demonstrates a commitment to protecting undocumented immigrants. In January 2017, New Haven Mayor Toni Harp and US Representative Rosa DeLauro defended the community against federal deportation raids, upholding the city's priority to "safeguard the well-being of all New Haven residents," including undocumented immigrants (Stannard 2017). The city has provided sanctuary to Nelson Pinos, a forty-three-year-old Ecuadorian man and father of three placed under a deportation order despite living in the United States for twenty-six years (Villavicencio 2018). The combination of a growing Latin American migrant population and a reputation as a place of safety and opportunity for undocumented people makes New Haven an apt setting for exploring questions of trauma and survival among Latin American migrants.

CENSUS DATA AND POPULATION POLITICS

Michael Rodríguez-Muñiz divides the history of US population politics, including demographic changes in the Latinx community, into three "sedimentary" layers. At the bottom is the White supremacist "demodystopia," a term he applies to the period from settler colonialism through the eugenics movements of the early twentieth century. The second lays the foundations for the "Latino threat" narrative and the growth of "unwanted" populations through the 1970s. At the top is the third layer of "Hispanic" civil rights and advocacy efforts to statistically assess the Latinx population in the United States in order to advance civil rights (Rodríguez-Muñiz 2021).

The history of the Latinx population in New Haven is consistent with this layered narrative. In the colonial era, English Puritans displaced the Quinnipiac Native Americans to establish a planned colony around nine square blocks in 1666. In the twentieth century, the migration of Puerto Ricans and other Latin Americans raised concerns among local government officials about poverty, unemployment, welfare reliance, and overpopulation. In recent decades, advancement in politics and social organizing have resulted in huge gains for the New Haven Latinx community.

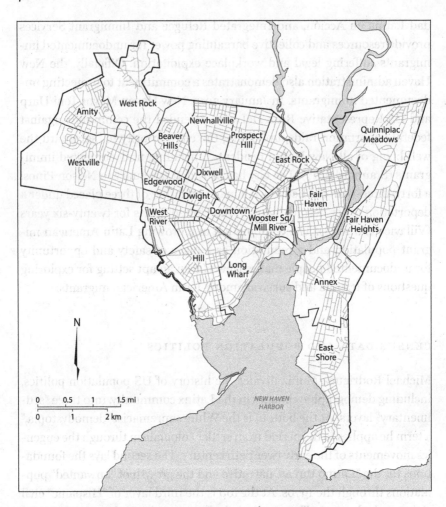

Map 1. Map of the City of New Haven, showing neighborhoods.

In my original pursuit of a Latin American history of New Haven, I sought out US census data. I thought, "Surely the US government can tell at least part of this story." I found that although I could track the growth in the Latinx population over time in the United States, in Connecticut, and in the city of New Haven, tracing the early Latin American migrants in the city was more difficult.

I dived deeper to assess the census tracts where many Latinxs live today. Fair Haven is the city's recognized Latinx neighborhood. Walking

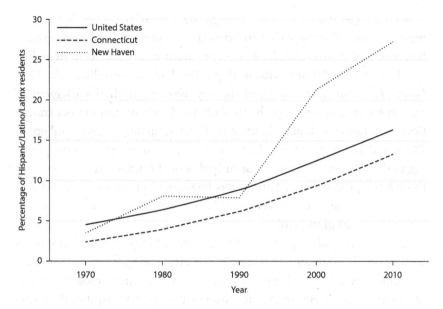

Figure 1. Growth in the Latinx populations of the United States, Connecticut, and New Haven, 1970–2010.

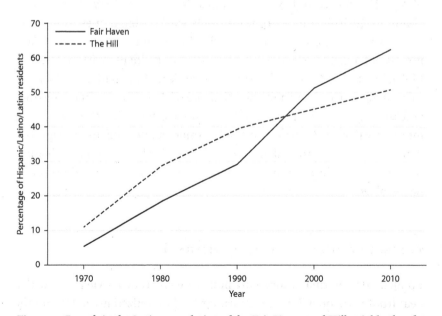

Figure 2. Growth in the Latinx population of the Fair Haven and Hill neighborhoods of New Haven, 1970–2010.

down Grand Avenue, its main thoroughfare, toward the water, it is easy to imagine yourself transported to urban Latin America, with restaurants, bodegas, and money-transfer businesses brandishing Mexican, Ecuadorian, Peruvian, and Puerto Rican flags. The Hill, surrounding Yale–New Haven Hospital in the south of the city, was the original settlement of Puerto Rican migrants, and historically the locale of immigrants transitioning to full-time homes in the city. Today it includes large numbers of Black and Latinx residents. In reviewing the census tracts corresponding to the Hill and Fair Haven neighborhoods, I found a striking pattern: though the proportion of Latinxs has increased in both the Hill and Fair Haven over time, the proportion of Latinx residents in Fair Haven was larger than that in the Hill.

Using historical city directories, I looked for patterns of residents with Spanish surnames throughout the city. For 1965, I found names like Colón, Rodriguez, Jimenez, Garcia, and Gonzalez—mostly belonging to men—clustered in the side streets around the hospital, then surrounded by vacant lots and buildings. Nearly all these names are among the most common surnames in Puerto Rico. At that time, the arteries of Fair Haven—Grand Avenue, James Street, and Ferry Street—were almost exclusively inhabited by residents with Italian names, along with a few American-sounding names, like Jones and Green, which I suspected belonged to Black residents. By 1970, residents with names like Melendez, Perez, Alvarado, Torres, Hernandez, Maldonado, and Vasquez were living in Fair Haven. Although some of these names, like Melendez and Torres, are also common in Puerto Rico, others, like Hernandez, are more prevalent in Central and South America and thus might signify a demographic shift. To flesh out these details, I asked community leaders who had spent decades in the city to tell me how their neighborhoods had evolved.

THE EARLY PUERTO RICAN COMMUNITY

I pulled up to Norma Franceschi's home, a white ranch-style house with a neat front yard, on a Saturday morning. As I organized my notes and the bag of pastries I had brought, a slim figure appeared in the front doorway.

"Pull over here, behind the house!" a woman's voice shouted from the door. "People drive like madmen on this street—they'll swipe your car." I followed her instructions and then gently tapped at the storm door. Inside, two small Yorkshire terriers announced my arrival, yapping loudly, their tails whipping back and forth. In a moment Norma appeared and ushered me inside. Her hair, once blonde and now almost entirely silver, was pulled into a neat bun. Her shoulders were hunched slightly forward.

I sat at the dining room table, which was covered with a lace cloth, and noticed a map of Italy on the wall. Next to it was a sepia-tinged photograph of a man and woman, the man resting his hands on the seated woman's shoulders. "Those are my parents," Norma told me, setting down mugs of coffee. "They moved from Italy to Argentina right after they got married. Not so dissimilar to my husband and me."

During all my prior interviews, each person had told me I *had* to speak with Norma. She knew all about the history of migration to New Haven and had supported many migrants in their transitions to the city. Her bodega on Main Street in Fair Haven had served as an informal social services hub when no others existed.

"We got married very young," Norma said. "When we first got here, it was very difficult because nothing was in Spanish. You went to the hospitals and at the hospitals, there were no interpreters. No Hispanics." Norma migrated to the United States with her husband in 1971, just a few years before a military junta took over Argentina in a coup d'état.

"Fair Haven was all Italian. There was only one single Spanish business," Norma told me. From my research in city directories, I learned that this business was a Puerto Rican grocery store owned by a man named Victor Berrios. At the time, most Latinx residents—then predominantly Puerto Rican—lived in the Hill and in the rural areas surrounding New Haven.

Norma added that no Central or South American products were available "because, at that time, the only Hispanics here were Puerto Rican. But the Puerto Ricans did not live in New Haven. The Puerto Ricans lived in Guilford, because in Guilford, they harvested tobacco.

"The gringos—the gringos were the Americans, right? —they went to Puerto Rico and looked for Puerto Rican labor and brought it here. They had these big sheds where they would bring people and then, after the

EXPLOITATION SEEN ON FARM MIGRANTS

Puerto Ricans, Employed On Area Truck Farms, Paid As Little As 51⁄ Hourly

Puerto Rican agricultural workers imported to work at New Haven area truck farms and nurseries last summer worked for as little as 51 cents an hour, according to a report released today.

Dan Donchian, former executive secretary of the New Haven Human Relations Council, released the report in connection with testimony which he makes before the Labor Committee of the General Assembly on several proposed labor measures today. In it, he outlined poor working conditions of these migratory workers.

Foundation Grant

He based his report on a survey made by the New Haven Human Relations Council under his direction, on a grant from the New Haven Foundation.

"These workers," Donchian said, "do not come under the provisions of the work agreements or contracts approved by the U.S. Employment Service and the Department of Labor of Puerto Rico. None of the group employed in the greater New Haven area has come into the States under these agreements or contracts. Many were hired through unlicensed private out-of-state 'employment' agencies or contractors who often provided unwilling, inexperienced or unhealthy workers, charged exorbitant fees and faras to both employers and workers and undercut local labor standards by providing a source of cheap labor."

11 Hour Work Day

On the farms, about 80 per cent of the workers earned 65 cents an hour; some were paid as little as 51 cents per hour. More than 80 per cent put in 11 hours a work a day or more; half of them worked 13 hours a day or more and 30 per cent worked 15 hours a day or more. Most worked at least six and a half days a week, many worked more.

More than two-thirds received no pay when bad weather interfered with outdoor work; only five per cent received full pay regardless of weather, except for 17 per cent who had to work outside, even in stormy weather. Only four per cent of the employers, provided, workers with statements of earnings and deduc-

Living Quarters

Since the primary findings of Donchian's survey were revealed, local and state health authorities have inspected housing and ordered farmers to bring living quarters up to acceptable standards, he reported.

Although housing has improved, legislation is needed to improve wage and working conditions, Donchian said. Once deductions for plane fare, food, loss of work due to poor weather and incidentals were subtracted, the average worker had some $17 a week left with which to support his family pay for his clothes and cover medical expenses.

Recommendations

In his report, Donchian made these recommendations:

1. That a minimum hourly wage standard and overtime provision be set.

2. That maximum and minimum hour limits for work day and work week be set.

3. That workmen's compensation laws be enforced to cover migratory and other agricultural workers.

4. That it be required that earning and deduction statements be given to workers, that employers maintain adequate records, which would be reviewed by a responsible agency.

5. That an appropriate agency (the subjects to the Department of Labor) be named 'to supervise and enforce standards for these workers and to establish grievance procedure.

6. That activities in the state of private out-of-state labor contractors and agencies, especially non-licensed ones, be regulated.

Insurance Programs

7. That medical and hospitalization insurance programs with small premiums to be paid by workers, be established, and that workers receive physical examinations.

8. That enforcement of uniform housing and sanitation codes for those employing live-in workers be continued.

Puerto Rican migrants are being exploited by farmers in the New Haven area, according to a report made public here yesterday by the National Advisory Committee on Farm Labor.

The report was written by Daniel Donchian for the Human Relations Council of Greater New Haven. Mr. Donchian was formerly an assistant director of the migration division of the Department of Labor of the Commonwealth of Puerto Rico.

The survey covered 186 Puerto Rican workers found living and working last summer at thirty-six truck farms and nurseries in New Haven and nine surrounding townships. "Hardly any" were recruited locally, Mr. Donchian said, because wages were so low and hours so long that not even the local unemployed could be persuaded to accept this kind of employment.

Most of the Puerto Ricans were recruited, he said, through unlicensed private out-of-state "employment" agencies or contractors.

Mr. Donchian found that "about 80% of the migrants earned 65 cents an hour or less and that some were paid as little as 51 cents an hour. Most of them worked seventy-five hours a week, he said.

Mr. Donchian plans to appear tomorrow before the labor committee of the Connecticut Legislature in Hartford.

Figure 3. News clippings from the *New Haven Register* (left) and the *New York Times* (right) from 1958, reporting on a study by Daniel Donchian of Puerto Rican farmworkers in the New Haven area.

harvest, they would send them back. At the time, many stayed, but the Puerto Rican colony was in Guilford, oddly enough."

A *New York Times* article from 1992 titled "Problems Temper Puerto Ricans' Success" describes the history and social struggles of the Puerto Rican community of New Haven. "Beginning with a small group of people who traveled to Connecticut in the 1930s to work on vegetable and tobacco farms and later settled in New Haven, the Puerto Ricans have grown into a community with deep roots in the city's political and cultural life" (Rierden 1992). Lee Cruz, a community activist who works for the Community Foundation for Greater New Haven and who is Puerto Rican himself, fleshes out this history. "A lot of people don't realize that when Puerto Ricans first came to Connecticut, they didn't come to New Haven for the factory jobs like in New York, which actually my mom did in the '50s. They came to pick apples in Guilford."

Guilford, a shoreline town known for its historic homes, hiking trails, and apple orchards, where city dwellers flock to take pictures of fall foliage, is now 92 percent White (US Census Bureau 2021). "The migrant community was moving up and down the coast [of Connecticut], following various products. And the owners of these farms and in the surrounding area really started recruiting Puerto Ricans. From Puerto Rico, it was easy because they were US citizens, you know? Just get 'em on the plane and get 'em off the plane."

These early migrations of Puerto Ricans coincided with the economic development program called Operation Bootstrap, introduced in the mid-1940s, which sought to modernize Puerto Rico's economy by disrupting the feudalistic sugar-plantation system and increasing manufacturing and exports to the mainland United States However, the resulting collapse in employment for rural sugarcane farmers led people to relocate to the mainland. In the 1930s, an estimated 1,800 Puerto Ricans left the island each year for employment in the United States; by the 1950s, that number had reached 43,000 (Ayala 1996). Unlike other regions of the United States, like the Southwest, where the earliest migrants came from Mexico, in Connecticut the original Latinx population was entirely Puerto Rican.

Over the following decades, the Puerto Rican community in the New Haven area established a vibrant social and cultural life. Lee recalls "pictures of Puerto Ricans playing congas on the green in Guilford from the 1930s and '40s because that was the only place they could congregate, because they didn't live in houses. They couldn't sit in front of their houses. They lived in these big, long shacks. And then, on the weekends, they would meet each other on the green in Guilford."

That first generation of Puerto Ricans confronted intense discrimination, workplace abuse, and language barriers that hindered their integration into the New Haven community. From the 1940s through the 1960s, many transitioned to manufacturing jobs in cities like New Haven. But these jobs—and the availability of affordable housing—began to dwindle, forcing many islanders to turn to government aid. Lydia Torres, formerly a youth development advocate for the Puerto Rican community, said, "I blame the system for damaging the people of my country. We have always come for jobs, not food stamps and drugs."

Many community leaders have argued that the US government failed Puerto Rican workers. Celestina Córdova, a long-standing leader in the Puerto Rican community, recalled that after serving in the Korean War, he went to a US work programs office in search of a job.

"Once they saw my surname," he told a journalist in 1993, "they told me, 'We have a job for you: it's working on a farm.' I thought they would give me a job as a foreman. I had never worked on a farm."

Córdova was assigned to pick vegetables like tomatoes and cabbages for a pitiful wage. "When Hispanic people go to look for a job," he explained, "there was no job for them. They made Puerto Ricans do the dirty work at lower positions."

To meet the growing need for social and cultural organizing, Córdova, along with other local Puerto Ricans, established the Spanish Cultural Association of New Haven in the Hill neighborhood in 1965. An informational pamphlet described the association as aiming to "unite, represent and strive for the interests and rights of the Spanish-American community of New Haven; to help raise the standard of living of said community, especially the cultural and socio-economic levels and to awaken underlying talents and abilities by means of beneficial program activities." To promote education and youth development, the Spanish Cultural Association launched two programs: Project Comprehension, offering educational enrichment for Spanish-speaking youth, and College Bound, which provided college and career counseling, tours of universities, and financial aid to Puerto Rican high school students. "Our Hispanic children wasn't graduating from high school," Córdova observed in a 1992 interview. "They was quitting school in the eighth grade, ninth grade. We saw the need for us to organize."

The Spanish Cultural Association preceded the current Latinx community advocacy organization, Junta for Progressive Action, which opened its doors in 1969. By that time, many Puerto Ricans had begun renting homes in the Hill neighborhood, near Yale–New Haven Hospital, or purchasing property in the Fair Haven neighborhood.

Puerto Ricans also established cultural and religious hubs. The Second Star of Jacob Church, a Pentecostal institution, opened its doors in the 1960s and became a center for organizing in the Puerto Rican community. Puerto Ricans also staged multiple festivals to preserve their culture and traditions.

As the majority group, Puerto Ricans dominated Latinx culture and politics through the 1990s. Lee Cruz described the Latinx community as roughly 85 percent Puerto Rican when he arrived in New Haven in 1983; according to Norma, the remainder were "Cubans who had fled the Bautista era" and other "upper-class" Cubans who had subsequently escaped from Fidel Castro's regime.

John DeStefano, who served as New Haven's mayor between 1994 and 2014, told me that "In the '80s... it was a largely Puerto Rican population with some Cuban feel, some Mexicans. But all the institutions of the community that were Latino were dominated by Puerto Ricans, with, in my view, distinct cultural awareness of who was Puerto Rican and who wasn't."

DEMOGRAPHIC SHIFTS IN THE LATE TWENTIETH CENTURY

In the late 1980s, the demographics of New Haven began to shift. Norma explains, "Well, after '71, Argentinians began to arrive, because in our country, the problem of the military takeover began. Those horrible years... the military killed people. If you were a student, especially of medicine, they would make you disappear." An estimated thirty thousand people vanished from the streets in illegal arrests, detentions, and killings. The students were targeted, Norma explained, because "when the guerillas were wounded, they could not obtain doctors, so they were looking for medical students to save them. All that was so horrible that we began to emigrate."

Such dangers were not limited to Argentina. "After us, the Colombians began to arrive, because of the same problem. They had the FARC [Fuerzas Armadas Revolucionarias de Colombia, or the Revolutionary Armed Forces of Colombia] and the guerrillas. After that, came the Peruvians, who also had problems in their country."

In the 1980s in Peru, the Sendero Luminoso (Shining Path), a militant Maoist organization, began an attempt to take over the country, conducting indiscriminate bombing campaigns, assassinations, and sexual assaults, channeling funds from drug production and trafficking to support their activities. The economy collapsed, and hundreds of thousands of Peruvians, including my husband's family, fled to the United States (Palmer 1994; López 2015). According to Pete Rivera, an accountant and Puerto Rican economic leader in New Haven, Peruvians established a foothold in businesses like grocery stores, meat markets, and restaurants.

In the same period, civil war, political repression, and economic devastation in Central America—particularly El Salvador, Guatemala, and Nicaragua—caused nearly a million migrants to flee to the United States. Despite the US support of brutal anti-Marxist regimes that contributed to this exodus, refugee policies under the Reagan administration denied many of these migrants consideration for asylum (Gzesh 2006). Puerto Ricans were US citizens, Cubans could claim refugee status, and many South Americans were eligible to become or permanent residents under the 1965 Hart-Celler Act, but these Central Americans were forced to enter the United States clandestinely and to live without papers.

Latinxs also migrated to New Haven from within the United States. Norma notes, "In California and Texas and Arizona, Mexican immigrants were driven out, harassed, mistreated, and abused. So [the Mexicans] saw the north as a Mecca." Similarly, many moved out of New York City in response to falling wages and increases in the cost of living, particularly in the Washington Heights neighborhood. These microeconomic shifts brought a surge of Dominicans and Ecuadorians to New Haven.

The Puerto Rican lawyer and activist Kica Matos began working for Junta in 2000. "I noticed almost immediately after I started that many of the people who came to Junta for services were not Puerto Rican," she told me. "People who seemed to be Puerto Ricans...by the cultural approach, the accent, the clothing, sometimes physical features. Culturally, what they were eating was not Puerto Rican cuisine."

She noticed that "a significant number of them appeared to be from Central and South America, especially from Mexico. As I started getting a little bit more familiar with the landscape, it seemed many of the Mexicans who were relocating to New Haven were either from Tlaxcala or Puebla. And that's when I really started realizing, wow, this is a large Spanish-speaking population that is not Puerto Rican."

The influx of migration from Central and South America presented new issues for the Latinx community of New Haven. "Now you had an undocumented population," DeStefano explained. Unlike the Puerto Rican community, which had a large organizing presence, "they did not want to play prominent, visible roles because of their immigration status."

Norma Franceschi recalled the day she realized the dramatic change in the community and its needs. "I left my home at 6:25 to open my store at 7 A.M. I had gone to Apicella's, to the bakery, to pick up fresh bread, and I go to open the store. And there, right in front of me, is one of those trucks that you rent, a U-Haul, right? The driver stops, opens the back door, and you could see, boy, how many people got out there!"

Now, standing beside her dining room table, Norma put a hand to her temple, her fingers splayed through her white-blonde hair. "And I say to myself, 'What is this?' It looks like someone had stepped on an anthill. And one of my employees, María de Jesús, tells me, 'Norma, those are Mexicans.' And they began to run everywhere. 'These are coyotes that are bringing people,' María de Jesús said. So, I say, 'And where are they going, Mari?' She says, They are renting a room.' They told me that there would be seven or eight people in one room, and that the gringos are taking advantage. They would rent these lofts without bathrooms, so they couldn't relieve themselves or bathe."

The needs of the Puerto Rican and Central and South American communities were drastically different. Whereas Puerto Ricans pursued higher education and a living wage, the new migrants focused on meeting basic needs like housing and sanitation. The difference between US citizen Puerto Ricans and undocumented Central and South Americans drove a wedge into the Latinx community. "There were divisions," DeStefano observed when he took over as mayor in 1994. "It was culture. They spoke Spanish, but they didn't speak *that* Spanish. You began to see a particular community emerge in Fair Haven, around Saint Rose of Lima's church. That's where the community began to coalesce and organize themselves."

Father Jim Manship, a former priest of the Catholic Church of Santa Rosa de Lima, says that when he first joined the parish in 1999, the community was largely Puerto Rican with "just a smattering of Mexicans." But then, "between 2000 and 2005, the parish had really transformed itself. It was no longer a predominantly Puerto Rican community: it was a very diverse community with a strong presence of Mexicans from Los Reyes, Michoacán, and from Tlaxcala." Later, he added, "you had a growing and vibrant Ecuadorian community. People from Manabí, from Quito and Cuenca, Morona Santiago, Guayaquil. So there was quite a diversity of Ecuadorians coming in, some migrating out of New York, many not having family directly here in New Haven."

Civil unrest and an economic downturn in the 1980s also drove many out of Ecuador. By the early 2000s, an estimated fifty-five thousand Ecuadorians were living in Connecticut, enough to justify the establishment of a consulate in 2008, the first consular office of a foreign government in New Haven since Italy had opened one in the Wooster Square neighborhood in 1910 (Appel 2008). Kica Matos, who worked in City Hall at the time, clarifies that "the Ecuadorian consulate set up shop in New Haven both because it was an immigrant-friendly city and also because of the significant number of Ecuadorians that were moving to New Haven."

The influx of Latin American migrants transformed the Fair Haven neighborhood, an area that had long welcomed European immigrants. Matos explains, "Fair Haven has always been, historically, the neighborhood in New Haven where migration stories begin, be it German or Russian or Italian or Polish or Jewish or Black from the Great Migration north. A lot of these immigrant folks have settled in Fair Haven first before moving on and establishing themselves, benefiting economically and then moving on. And the last waves were African Americans and then Puerto Ricans. And then all of a sudden, these Latines were showing up, and they weren't Puerto Rican. But nobody was really paying attention."

In the late 2000s and early 2010s, New Haven experienced a surge in migration from Guatemala. According to Megan Fountain, lead organizer of the immigrant rights organization Unidad Latina en Acción (ULA), "Suddenly, in 2010 or 2012, there was this influx of moms and kids from

Guatemala. Through word of mouth, they heard about us." Guatemala was then confronting its own civil unrest and economic collapse. A civil war that erupted in the 1960s over land disputes and dispossession of the Mayan Indigenous community dragged on into the 1990s. The resulting collapse of the agricultural economy, along with effects of climate change, which reduced harvests, and drug-related conflict over poppy fields along the Mexican border drove many young Guatemalans out of the country, some of whom sought asylum in the United States. "There were a bunch of moms and teens who had just crossed the border and gotten detained," Fountain explained to me.

This influx transformed the linguistic needs of the community, which up to that point, had been exclusively Spanish speaking. Fountain told me, "We had more Indigenous folks coming in. Prior to that, we had one family from Mexico who spoke the Indigenous language Totonac from Puebla, from Sierra Norte de Puebla, Mexico, but we really didn't have a lot of Indigenous folks. But then with these Guatemalan folk, a lot of them spoke Mam. Some of them speak Q'anjob'al. Some of them speak Kaqchikel. Most of them speak Mam. And yeah, it just ushered in a new dynamic at ULA."

By this time, the Latinx community in New Haven was largely Puerto Rican, Mexican, and Ecuadorian, with a growing contingent of Guatemalans—a mix that reflected a radical shift from the almost exclusively Puerto Rican community of the later twentieth century and the networks of European immigrants before them. By 2012, over half of the migrants to New Haven were from Latin America and the Caribbean, with massive increases in migrants from Mexico, Ecuador, Guatemala, and the Dominican Republic (Buchanan and Abraham 2015). John Curtis, a Spanish-speaking journalist and immigrant rights advocate, notes, "What I have observed is that there seem to be three big communities in the New Haven area: the Puerto Rican community, which is largely in the Hill, the Mexican community in Fair Haven, and the Ecuadorian community in East Haven."

Why did the women in my study move to New Haven? The answer can be as simple as Lee Cruz's refrain: "US foreign policy...the wars, the civil rights violations." Asked to elaborate, he added, "It's fear for their lives, having to do with war and a loss of economic opportunity and a loss of a sense of safety." Besides responding to the push and pull of structural forces and personal connections, migrants perceive New Haven as welcoming. "Here, you have services, you have Hispanic stores, you have the Mexican bakery, there's the Dominican hair salon that you want," Norma Franceschi said. "You can go to the Don Felix butcher shop, or the *marqueta*. You walk around and there's the record store that plays the best music. It's an inviting place. Fair Haven just invites you in."

LATINXS IN NEW HAVEN TODAY

Today, 103,000 immigrants reside in the New Haven metro area, half of whom are undocumented and at risk of deportation. Of these, 84,200 have lived in the country for more than ten years. Collectively, immigrant households in New Haven paid $339.8 million in state and local taxes and $659.2 million in federal taxes (Vera Institute of Justice 2020).

When the Department of Commerce released the 2020 census results, New Haven learned that Latinxs had become its largest ethnic group, increasing by 15 percent while the remainder of the city's population grew by just 3 percent. Now 30.6 percent of the population is Latinx, 30.4 percent identify as Black, and 27.6 percent identify as White (Kainz and Breen 2021). "In my community of Fair Haven, 19,000 people live here, 62 percent are Latino," Lee Cruz said. "Of that 62 percent, we have 18 or 19 nationalities represented. About half are either Puerto Rican, Mexican, or Ecuadorian." The city, particularly the Fair Haven neighborhood, is currently bracing for a large resettlement of Afghan refugees fleeing the resurgence of the Taliban (Vallejo 2021).

Just as the United States claims to be a country of immigrants, the City of New Haven "is and always had been a city of immigrants," according to Kica Matos (Zahn 2018). In 2016, the political analytics website FiveThirtyEight determined that the New Haven metro area was most demographically similar to the United States overall, based on age, educational attainment, and race and ethnicity (Kolko 2016). The gains of the immigrant community in New Haven, as elsewhere in the United States, have sprung from collective action and organizing, and careful coordination and competition with other racially and ethnically minoritized groups.

SOCIAL MOVEMENTS AND NEW HAVEN
AS A "WELCOMING" CITY

When I lived in New Haven, I felt part of the Latinx community. From my Wooster Square neighborhood I could walk to Fair Haven for groceries and my favorite *mangonadas* and show up to rallies and protests with ULA. While heavily pregnant with my son, I paced the fringes of Criscuolo Park, at the border of the Fair Haven and Wooster Square neighborhoods, chatting with the older Latinos who played dominoes in the shade by the bus stop. Since moving to the suburbs, I have stayed connected with Fair Haven, partly through community walks led by Lee Cruz, which promote walking as a form of regular exercise and as a way of educating outsiders— including Yalies and out-of-town visitors—about the assets and needs of the community. Although I had attended a few formal tours of local neighborhoods in medical school, I now showed up with my mother-in-law and toddler for an opportunity to speak Spanish and get some exercise. The establishment of the Fair Haven walking routes reflects a powerful dynamic of community organizing that has distinguished the local immigrant Latinx community.

Housing and Urban Safety

After witnessing the arrival of undocumented Mexican immigrants in Fair Haven and learning about their squalid living conditions, Norma Franceschi dedicated herself to improving housing in the community. "Nobody imagined that there were so many immigrants," Norma told me. She raised the issue with the Board of Alders (the legislative body for the City of New Haven) and the Livable City Initiative (LCI), a private-public partnership that aims to improve neighborhood safety and housing quality. She also turned to Rafael Ramos, then deputy director of LCI and the founder of a Spanish-speaking community theater in Fair Haven.

"I turn to him, that *coco pelado* (bald, crazy peeled coconut), and say, 'Look, Rafi, there's a problem here,'" Norma said. "And I told him what was happening. Then he says, 'Norma, I can't bring in all these people.' So, I say, 'Hey, let's go for a walk. I'm going to take you to where these people are living.' I take him to this place where the landlord has people ... who have no water. The pregnant woman living on the second floor showed him the hose and bucket she had to clean herself. And I showed him people who [were] crammed into a room, some sleeping in the closet with a mattress on the floor to have a little privacy. So, when Rafael saw all that, he picked up everyone and put them into a temporary hotel and started fining the landlords. He would scare them into action."

Issues of landlord abuse and worker exploitation persisted into the 2000s. Through the joint efforts of Fair Haven's informal immigrant-aid network and organizations like Junta for Progressive Action and ULA, temporary housing was arranged with sympathetic landlords until workers could find new apartments and jobs. Junta's emergency fund covered interim expenses. John Jairo Lugo, the founder of ULA, connected migrants with others in town and helped them navigate the local supermarket. Kica Matos invited people to barbecues at her house and to summer concerts on the Green (Bass 2007). In this way, this lattice of support both formally and informally asserted the rights of the immigrant community.

As the Ecuadorian community grew in Fair Haven, they established a collective to purchase land and dilapidated homes and construct new ones. This community project has led to increased homeownership and wealth accumulation.

In addition to workplace and housing abuse, immigrants also confronted recurrent threats of violence. Edith Ortiz, a Puerto Rican woman who arrived in New Haven in 1966, told the *New York Times* that at school, students threatened her with switchblades, shouting, "Why don't you go back to Puerto Rico?" "They wouldn't believe me when I said I was an American citizen," Ortiz recalled (Rierden 1992).

In the 1980s, gang violence erupted throughout the city. "There were crimes every day, deaths," Norma explained. "The Latin Kings and the Ñetas would fight on the street corners, for the territory. And then people started shooting." Fears of gang violence tore apart Fair Haven, prompting many businesses to shut their doors and prompting a mass exodus of earlier European immigrants, particularly Italians. As Latin American newcomers began to fill that void, they transformed the culture of Grand Avenue, Fair Haven's main thoroughfare.

Later, in the 1990s and 2000s, undocumented migrants became targets of theft and assault. "People were targeted," DeStefano told me, "because of their appearance, that they probably were Mexican, probably didn't have a bank in town, probably had cash on them at all times." Norma said, "They were killing immigrants. They were attacking immigrants to steal their wallets and stabbing them and all that."

Father Jim Manship recalled that these attacks became a major concern among his parishioners. "We had a lot of violence against immigrants," he said. "Thuggery, people assaulting immigrants and robbing them and things like that. There was one of these little hoodlums that would go and bust windows and slash tires just to make people's lives miserable. Just prior to my arrival, there was a Guatemalan immigrant who was stabbed to death just outside the convent. This was a huge thing for the community. So we went at it."

With his parishioners, Manship called on the local district manager of the police force to act. Residents shared their experiences of fear and violence and succeeded in obtaining extra police patrols in the neighborhood. Together, Latin Americans in Fair Haven improved their standard of living and, now that they had become a majority, began to claim the neighborhood as their own.

New Haven Latinxs were not the only ones organizing for a better quality of life. More famously, in the 1960s, the Young Lords—a civil rights organization led by Puerto Rican youth—mobilized to address inadequate and dilapidated housing and overcrowding, improve sanitation and removal of industrial waste, and bring an end to police brutality. Particularly in East Harlem (nicknamed El Barrio), rapid migration from the island of Puerto Rico allowed landlords of already decaying buildings to take advantage of migrants short of money and created conditions for trash and disease to fester. Inspired by Cuba, which had implemented socialized medicine and significantly improved the health metrics of its citizens, the Young Lords also advocated for preventive medicine, universal healthcare, and a patient bill of rights. Their agenda emphasized community care, access, and attention to the social determinants of health so that poor Latinxs would not be condemned to suffer from lead poisoning, asthma, and tuberculosis (Fernández 2020). Although the activity of the Young Lords declined in the 1970s, movements for improved health and environmental justice gained traction, along with campaigns for immigration rights in places like New Haven where the Latinx population included more noncitizens.

Health and Environmental Activism

"It wasn't that long ago, maybe thirty years ago or so, the Latin Kings were a huge thing in New Haven," Lee Cruz told a tour group of first-year medical students. "For those of you that don't know, go look up the Latin Kings. Really big proponents of crack cocaine. We had national gangs like the Bloods and the Crips. And New Haven was a fairly dangerous city to live in. From the mid-'80s to the mid-'90s, the police department, the DEA—Drug Enforcement [Agency]—Firearms and Tobacco, and the Department of Justice got together to address the issue of crack cocaine and the Latin Kings. So the residual effect has resulted in people feeling unsafe walking the streets."

Cruz gathered the students into a huddle in the shady northeast section of Criscuolo Park, in front of a large map of Fair Haven marked with walking routes in green and blue.

"A lot of people, about a decade ago, at the Yale School of Public Health were talking about behavioral health. Researchers say, look, you know, eat healthy and get eight hours of sleep and exercise, that [advice] has limited value when you're holding down two or three jobs, when you don't speak the primary language of the country, when you come from another culture. So, folks were interested in how we can incentivize people to do things that are good for them, like walking. So, you know, I like to say, we had the peanut butter and they had the chocolate, and by combining those things, we came up with the idea of a walking trail, or two walking trails in our neighborhood."

Lee related the efforts to establish the trails. "We got a local architect to help us with planning the routes. We got funding from the Yale School of Public Health. We raised just as much money ourselves in the neighborhood. We bought six signs and printed ten thousand cards and handed them out to students at K–8 schools."

He then got to the heart of the campaign. "What we wanted to do is to encourage students to take this map home, show it to their guardians, their parents, their grandparents, ask them, 'Can we walk around and look for these birds and look for this river?' That way, the kids can activate the adults in their house around walking."

Lee recounted that they were able to put together the entire project with just a few thousand dollars, a feat that would have been impossible without the committed efforts of residents. Although the impact of the walking trail program has not been formally studied, Lee noted that residents of the streets adjoining the walking routes constantly see folks looking for the signs and markers.

As the Fair Haven community gained strength and unity, health and environmental justice became high neighborhood priorities. Early on, with the support of local nonprofits, a community clinic began operating out of the former Columbus Family Academy on Grand Avenue, providing medical care two evenings per week. (The school has since been renamed the Family Academy of Multilingual Exploration, or FAME, a noneponymous name adopted to sidestep concerns about Latinxs displacing Italians.) In 1980, the clinic became a federally qualified health center. Over the years, it expanded its services to include prenatal care, chronic disease prevention, dental care, and school-based health programs. In 2018, Fair Haven Community Health Care (FHCHC) served eighteen thousand patients through eighty thousand office visits (Fair Haven Community Health Care 2021).

Infectious disease and prenatal care were significant early concerns. Norma Franceschi recalled, "There were pregnant women who were afraid to get care. Many had venereal diseases." Norma says that immigrant men would seek out White prostitutes for "a different flavor" and then carry home infections to their partners and spouses. "That's when we found a lot of gonorrhea, syphilis, many mothers who even tested positive for HIV. The pregnant women were also not taking their vitamins, and all that. Then the clinic began to take notice."

Advocates at FHCHC pushed for services to promote maternal health and reduce infant mortality, a serious issue at the time. This led to the expansion of care to include early childhood support services and prenatal care through coordination with the city's Head Start and Me and My Baby programs, through which many of my interlocutors were recruited. In 2003, the Progreso Latino fund, a community-based financial support organization, picked up many of the costs of Head Start outreach to New Haven Latinxs.

Local leaders also pushed to address the high burden of chronic disease in the neighborhood. "We had a lot of Hispanic people with diabetes, but it was untreated," Norma told me. The director of the FHCHC organized a fundraising walk and health fair to promote diabetes diagnosis, treatment, and education. In 2004, a group of Yale medical students partnered with the FHCHC to open a free clinic on Saturdays, which still fills healthcare gaps for many undocumented and uninsurable individuals.

Health issues in the community also stemmed from environmental contamination, including lead poisoning and air pollutants. "In Fair Haven, there is lead on the sheetrock," Norma told me, referring to the historical use of lead-based paint in the neighborhood's older buildings. "They had not removed the lead, understand? They had not scraped it, just covered it over." Paint was not the only source of lead contamination in the neighborhood. Oil tankers operated by Shell and Gulf plied the Mill River, leaking leaded gasoline into the water and the soil. Because of overcrowding, Lee Cruz told me, many residents parked their cars on the grass outside their homes, leaking oil onto the ground and tracking it inside, where crawling and toddling infants would come into contact with it and ingest it. "There was so much lead in the soil by my house that my *chickens* got lead poisoning!" Lee starts to laugh. "As far as I know, my chickens are the only ones to have undergone chelation therapy."

Standing by the bank of the Mill River in Criscuolo Park, Lee Cruz described additional sources of pollution and its impact on poor, minoritized communities like Fair Haven. "If you take a map of the United States," Lee said, the timbre of his voice darkening, "the demographics of where people of color live—whether those people are Black or Latino or Indigenous— and you overlay that on top of a map of the things in our country that cause the greatest contamination and the most health problems, we find that those maps are eerily similar. There's a part of the United States that's known as Cancer Alley, right down through Missouri and Texas, alongside all the oil refineries. So, I'm just going to point out a few examples of our own in New Haven."

Lee grasped his straw hat with one hand and extended the other upward along the Mill River, pointing out an old power plant that had been shut down "not because of pollution, but because of deregulation of electricity in the 1980s." Some entrepreneurs later bought it, promising to clean it up, but instead they wanted to reopen it as a power plant, providing backup electricity "so that when it was a hot day like today" in some of the more affluent counties in Connecticut, "when people there turned on their air conditioning and the electricity [demand] went up, this plant would come on and fuel them. So, the community organized."

"We had a meeting where we said, 'Can we just have a show of hands of how many people in the room either have asthma or someone in your family has asthma?' Every hand in the room went up. And so we told them, 'Your asthma is going to be exacerbated on a day like today when that plant goes on.'" Today, five years after the original agreement, executives and regulatory agents involved continue to debate an "allowable" level of contamination—and, by extension, allowable health hazards to residents.

Lee pointed out other sources of contamination: uncovered piles of salt and sand for winter snow management for Connecticut streets and highways, the bridge connecting a long stretch of I-95 across the rivers bounding the neighborhood, the encroachment of a gravel company along the shore. "Nothing but the hardiest reeds grow on either side of that street," Lee noted, indicating the salt piles. "The salt gets blown off the top, falls on the soil, gets absorbed in the water, and it kills the trees." Then, nodding to the highway, he added, "And that wind is blowing all of the pollution this way." Lee shook his head. "Some of these things we've tried to fight, but there's just no way to win when there are so many things that we've got to stop. We haven't lost everything, and we have a historic presence."

In her book *A Terrible Thing to Waste*, the medical ethicist Harriet A. Washington writes about the disproportionate exposures of communities of color to air pollution, industrial chemicals, and heavy metals, including lead, and how these exposures impair brain development in ways that reinforce racist notions of biological inferiority (Washington 2019). The struggles of Black and Brown communities are attributed to inherent flaws, in a victim-blaming feedback loop.

The Fair Haven community has made monumental strides toward improving the health of its residents, but many challenges remain. The neighborhood continues to exhibit rates of chronic disease and obesity above Connecticut and United States averages (Xi 2013). The

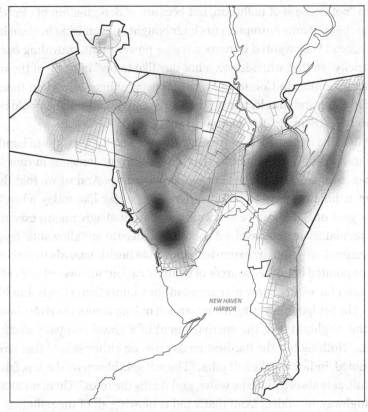

NEW HAVEN
HARBOR

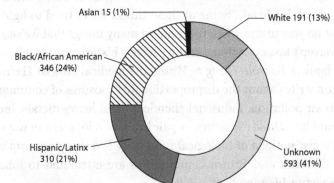

Asian 15 (1%)

White 191 (13%)

Black/African American
346 (24%)

Hispanic/Latinx
310 (21%)

Unknown
593 (41%)

Map 2. A heat map and donut plot of COVID-19 cases in New Haven by
race and ethnicity in April 2020, showing cases to be concentrated in the
predominantly Latinx neighborhood of Fair Haven.

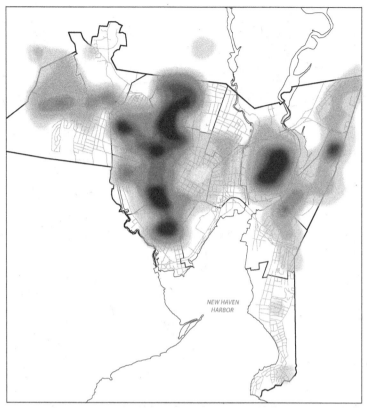

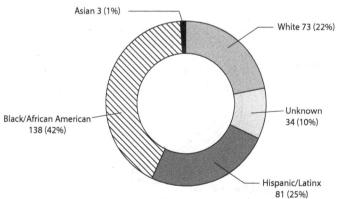

Asian 3 (1%)

White 73 (22%)

Black/African American
138 (42%)

Unknown
34 (10%)

Hispanic/Latinx
81 (25%)

Map 3. A heat map and donut plot of COVID-19 hospitalizations in New Haven by race and ethnicity in April 2020. Many patients came from the Fair Haven, Dixwell, Newhallville, and Hill neighborhoods, whose residents are predominantly Black and Latinx.

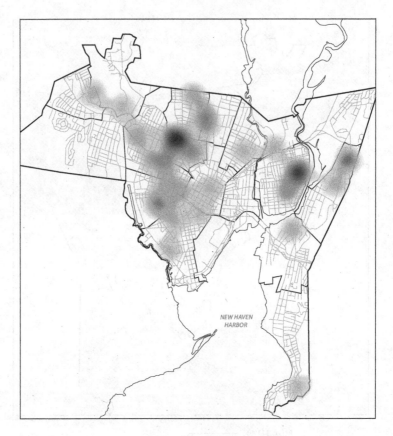

NEW HAVEN
HARBOR

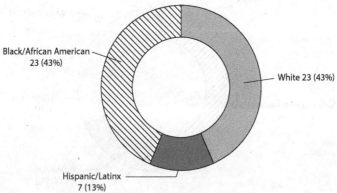

Black/African American
23 (43%)

White 23 (43%)

Hispanic/Latinx
7 (13%)

Map 4. A heat map and donut plot of COVID-19 deaths in New Haven by race and ethnicity in April 2020. Patients who died from COVID-19 early in the pandemic came from hot spots in the Dixwell, Newhallville, Fair Haven, and West River neighborhoods, whose residents are predominantly Black and Latinx.

neighborhood was also heavily affected by COVID-19, as seen in the maps from April 2020 (*New Haven Register* 2020). Fair Haven is in the northeast part of the city; if you imagine the city as a giant kangaroo, Fair Haven is the hip and rump.

In 2021, community leaders and activists again took to the streets in the pursuit of health justice, this time encouraging residents to get vaccinated against the coronavirus. The volunteers dispelled myths regarding requirements for health insurance or lawful presence in the US to receive the vaccine, and they helped residents without internet or cars to schedule and attend vaccination appointments (Leonard 2021).

Immigration

The swell of the undocumented population in New Haven shifted the attention of organizations like Junta toward the legal needs of the community. "Their solutions were not the same [as those for Puerto Ricans]," Kica Matos told me, "because many of their issues directly related to their undocumented status. If somebody came to us and said, 'Hey, I'm having a problem with my landlord, and I'm being ripped off,' and we'd offer them advocacy-oriented options, inevitably what you would hear from that person is, 'Well, I don't really want to pursue that course of action because he threatened to call immigration on me,' or 'I'm afraid that if I start advocating for myself like you're suggesting, then I'll be evicted and I'll have no recourse.' So that's when I really started getting involved in immigration law and policy."

In the early 2000s, Kica drew on her contacts at the Yale Law School to set up legal clinics at Junta. She also started raising money to focus on advocacy for the undocumented community. In 2006, millions across the United States protested proposed immigration reforms under the George W. Bush administration, particularly the Border Protection, Antiterrorism, and Illegal Immigration Control Act of 2005 (HR 4437), which proposed to harshen penalties for undocumented immigrants and to classify them, and anyone who assisted their entry into the United States, as felons. This and related policies, presented as part of the "War on Terror," constituted what the sociologists Tanya Golash-Boza and Pandierrette Hondagneu-Sotelo term a "gendered racial removal program" that disproportionately criminalized Black and Latino men (2013). Indeed, Afro-

Caribbean and Latino men are more likely to be targeted for deportation (Gomberg-Muñoz 2012; Golash-Boza 2012). On March 25, 2006, nearly 1.5 million people participated in La Gran Marcha in Los Angeles. On May 1—May Day, later dubbed "A Day without Immigrants"—thousands of migrants abandoned their low-wage jobs to demonstrate the value of their contributions to society (García Bedolla 2014).

Megan Fountain was an undergraduate student at Yale at the time. She recalled, "There was this massive mobilization. The biggest protest in the history of New Haven since 1970.... I saw this huge mobilization of immigrants, you know, people who I didn't normally see in New Haven in my day-to-day life as a student. All of a sudden, they were right there, on the New Haven Green."

That same year, New Haven established a policy of noncooperation with federal immigration authorities. Mayor DeStefano aimed to build trust between the city and its undocumented residents. He hired Kica Matos as deputy mayor for community services, and together they sought to implement policies to protect immigrant rights. The first involved formalizing the New Haven Police Department's former "Don't ask, don't tell" policy, effectively prohibiting city authorities from inquiring about a person's immigration status, and establishing New Haven as a "sanctuary city." That summer, they introduced plans to create municipal ID cards for undocumented residents (Medina 2007; Wucker 2007).

Father Jim Manship had earlier identified the need for local ID cards among his parishioners. "The discussion started around ID cards, but it wasn't progressing very quickly on a city level," Manship noted. The delay likely occurred as a result of DeStefano's reelection campaign: the proposal prompted a backlash from conservative pundits on national media streams. "Some of our leaders came forward to produce a parish ID card. So we did. We made these little laminated cards for eight hundred parishioners."

Manship says that the church leadership determined the eligibility criteria for the cards: either identification provided by a national consulate or a home country passport. Through this requirement they found that the parish community included people from eighteen countries and fifteen Mexican states. Even though the parish ID cards conferred limited political capital, they were important to the community. "Bottom line was, you're here, and you have standing," Manship asserted. "We see you; we recognize you. You are part of us, and we are part of you."

Likely as a result of these proimmigrant measures, federal immigration authorities punished New Haven. On Wednesday, June 6, 2007, thirty-six hours after the city's Board of Alders had approved plans for the municipal ID cards, Immigration and Customs Enforcement (ICE) agents swept in, starting early in the morning, and arrested thirty-four people.

"It was like five in the morning," Norma tells me, "And Mari calls me saying, 'La Migra came, and they took everyone. Then I called Kica, and she called the mayor and the police. "And then I call the church and I said, 'Father Jim, they're taking all the immigrants!'"

Thirty of the people arrested were parishioners at Santa Rosa de Lima. The Fair Haven community immediately began working on guardianship paperwork for children whose parents had been arrested. Next they began raising funds to bail the migrants out of detention centers in Boston and Rhode Island. "I don't think anyone was actually deported," Norma says. "The Yale Law School, they fought like lions."

The Yale Law School's Worker and Immigrant Rights Advocacy Clinic (WIRAC) represented eleven men who claimed that twenty immigration agents had invaded their homes without warrants or consent, illegally seizing and arresting them. In 2012, they achieved a landmark settlement. The men received a total of $350,000, and all pending immigration proceedings against them were ended (Connors 2012).

In addition, under the Freedom of Information Act, ULA identified emails between the Connecticut state police and ICE that indicated coordinated retaliation against New Haven for its proimmigrant policies. The raid in New Haven figured as part of an act of political theater on the part of the Bush administration, an attempt to appear tough on "illegal" immigration. That same year, ICE carried out dozens of raids in Colorado, Iowa, Georgia, and Massachusetts, mostly targeting communities and large businesses that were permissive of sheltering and employing undocumented migrants. Whereas powerful coordination—and the backing of Yale Law students—prevented the deportation of the New Haven migrants, elsewhere in the country the raids fractured hundreds of families, separating many children from their parents (MIT Press 2017).

Today, two major organizations lead the immigrant rights movement in

New Haven: ULA and the Semilla Collective, founded by the former ULA member Fátima Rojas, a Mexican immigrant mother who emphasizes relational organizing and *compañerismo*, or fellowship. Lee Cruz, who is godfather to Fátima's children, says, "Both of them have hundreds of people signed up who are undocumented, and they're helping them with everything from food security to health, to jobs, to housing, to legal support—the whole nine yards." During the COVID-19 pandemic, ULA and Semilla tackled the needs of the undocumented migrant community from different angles. Semilla established a mutual aid fund and food garage to support migrants. ULA provided cash assistance as well as baskets containing food, hand sanitizer, and masks for families who were out of work or had contracted the virus. Next on the agenda for these organizations is advocating for abolition of ICE, expansion of healthcare access, and a path to legalization for undocumented migrants.

Economic Development

"In 1982, I opened up my own company, Rivera and Rivera Associates, with my wife, who used to do translations at the federal courthouse, interpreting Treasury documents, and I would do the accounting, bookkeeping, and taxes." Pete Rivera pulls down his black face mask and takes a long sip of coffee across the booth from me at the Greek Olive diner. "There weren't a lot of Spanish-speaking business groups at the time, so we got a lot of experience statewide with respect to what we were doing."

Pete moved to New Haven in 1978 from the South Bronx after serving in the military during the Vietnam era. He used his GI benefits to get an accounting degree through the University of Connecticut system and held numerous accounting positions before launching his own firm. Having worked with Latinx businesses and churches, Pete quickly recognized the need for the community to organize and represent its members' interests. He established the Hispanic Merchants Association in New Haven in the 1980s.

Around the same time, the University of Connecticut (UConn) had launched a small business development program and sought business experts who could expand services to high-need communities in Connecticut. "They basically contacted me and asked if I would be interested. I became a business counselor and eventually came to be regional director for the program as a result of my interaction with the business community."

When local pastors like Father Jim Manship and other community leaders came to Pete saying that the Spanish-speaking business community in Fair Haven continued to face disadvantages, he began providing direct assistance to immigrants attempting to open small businesses and mentored Latinx business owners. "By 1988, I was probably solely responsible for about 95 percent of the new businesses of immigrants on Grand Avenue," Pete said. He also began teaching business classes, ultimately translating a statewide economics curriculum into Spanish. "I must have done hundreds of classes. I got to know Hispanics everywhere. I was like, yeah, this is the Lord's work, you know?" From his contacts with business owners, Pete concluded that immigrant entrepreneurs needed representation in city politics.

Mayor DeStefano had proposed the idea of a Latinx business program, but anytime a city official from the Economic Development Administration went to interview local merchants, they found that "no one would answer their questions before speaking to Mr. Rivera first." One of the alders asked Pete, "Is there a mafia in Fair Haven? Are you, like, the leader of the mafia?" According to Pete, Latinx business owners, many of whom were undocumented, did not trust city hall. He stepped in to facilitate the establishment of the Grand Avenue Merchants Association. Norma Franceschi remembers and appreciates Pete's role in bringing the association together.

"Pete Rivera helped me a lot with immigrants," she says. At first, the attempt to revive Grand Avenue was a project undertaken by Norma and her friend and employee, María de Jesús. They took brooms and began sweeping the street. As they recruited other locals, they began cleaning up trash and power-washing the building fronts to remove graffiti. With Pete's help, the community leaders started to meet. Overcoming their original distrust, they collaborated with a city lawyer to establish the Grand Avenue Village Association as a membership-based, nonprofit organization of local business owners in 1999. The organization began assisting merchants with issues such as increasing client capacity, financing, generating profit, and developing the Fair Haven commercial corridor. According to Norma, the organization convinced business owners to agree to a minimum wage and to resist attempts to install parking meters, which were believed to deter low-income consumers from patronizing Grand Avenue businesses.

Pete strongly encouraged Latinx business owners in his classes to expand into other racial and ethnic markets. "I'd tell people, let's look at the
Hispanic community as your saving grace. You could probably pay rent
with the Hispanic community alone. But you want to be rich, so you better
sell to the White community." To facilitate networking with other businesses and industries, Pete helped set up Hispanic chambers of commerce
in Waterbury, Stamford, and Bridgeport, as well as New Haven. Through
these organizations, Latinx business owners made inroads throughout the
state and benefited from tax credits they had been unaware of.

To Pete, the best way for an undocumented person to get ahead is to
start a business. He shared with me the story of an undocumented Argen-
tinean woman who started a cleaning business that now brings in four
million dollars a year, supporting more than one hundred employees. He
talked about a woman who had moved her home daycare business to a
commercial building in Milford, becoming one of the largest childcare
providers in the area, and about Mexican men who had expanded their
landscaping and construction company to two hundred employees, bringing in between five and six million dollars a year. "Pull yourself up by your
bootstraps," he says.

A 2014 survey of businesses in downtown New Haven found that 53 percent were owned by immigrants. Immigrant-owned businesses in greater
New Haven were more likely to be small businesses and more likely to
provide jobs than businesses with US-born owners. David Casagrande, a
longtime New Haven resident and graduate of the Yale School of Forestry
and Environmental Studies, said of the findings, "Hispanic immigrants
are 'saving' neighborhoods like Fair Haven in New Haven from economic
decay and crime" (Buchanan and Abraham 2015, 12).

Pete's other favorite quote, from the Mexican economist José Ángel
Gurria, is "It takes a collaboration across a community to develop better
skills for better lives."

The Relationships between New Haven and Yale University and Yale–New Haven Health

"You can tell when you're *at Yale*...and when you're *not at Yale*," the
campus police sergeant told my first-year medical school class during the

security orientation, her voice rising at the tail of each phrase. "And when you're *not at Yale*, we can't protect you."

I squinted. I could tell the difference between collegiate Gothic and postmodern. I knew the campus boundaries. And I also knew that crowned windows and manicured lawns would not safeguard me from crime.

The sergeant veiled her meaning, but her point was clear: any threat to our safety would come from outside the privileged elite of which the campus officers and faculty had taught us to consider ourselves a part. Yale was a group, not a place; a marker of merit, a badge of belonging built on the "accomplishments" of White imperialists (Minor 2015).

Since its inception in Old Saybrook in 1701 and relocation to New Haven seventeen years later, Yale University has had a fraught relationship with local residents. Connecticut colonists were frustrated by the university's original, inconvenient location in Old Saybrook, in the northeast of the state. To avoid long journeys from areas like Hartford and the southern coast, many students opted to seek instruction from their local pastors rather than from the university. But when the trustees accepted a bid from the City of New Haven to host the University, residents of Old Saybrook took to the streets in protest (Connecticut History 2020).

When Elihu Yale, a representative of the British East India Trading Company, donated books and funds to the newly relocated university, it took his name and cemented its ties to extraction and colonization. As waves of immigration in the nineteenth century disrupted the homogeneous Puritan ideology of the university affiliates, antagonism brewed between the college and the public over allocation of resources. Why should tax dollars support esoteric studies benefiting an aristocracy? In addition, students living in dormitories angered their neighbors with disorderly conduct and mismanagement of waste. In the twentieth century, universities like Yale received federal support and funds to clear out local areas as part of "urban renewal" programs that displaced thousands of locals (Warren 1976).

In the City of New Haven, this process is exemplified by the creation of the Oak Street Connector in the 1950s. Mayor Richard "Dick" Lee, a former director of the *Yale News,* proposed a road that would direct traffic from the Connecticut Turnpike—a section of Interstate 95—toward downtown New Haven. Ostensibly, the plan would bolster the economy of a city that many considered little more than an off-ramp between New York and Boston. In practice, however, the road dissected communities that historically were home to Black Americans and immigrants, shattering once-vibrant neighborhoods. The move reflected a shared interest on the part of the city and the university to invest in luxury economic development at the expense of affordable housing and to prioritize the interests of suburbanites over those of city dwellers. Although never stated in so many words, the plan intentionally disrupted the Oak Street neighborhood—which Mayor Lee called "a hard core of cancer, which had to be removed," implying that the racially and ethnically minoritized groups living there (Jewish, Italian, Black, Polish, Russian, Ukrainian, Irish, and Greek migrants) were responsible for crime in the city (Ansfield 2020; Gurwitt 2000). The Connector also physically insulated Yale University from the predominantly Black and Puerto Rican Hill neighborhood. A manifesto by residents of the north Hill neighborhood, which suffered the greatest blow from the construction of the Oak Street Connector, calls the redevelopment agency an "invading army" on a "rampage," questioning the mayor's respect for the community and accusing him of violence and disrespect for human life. Justifying the protests against the razing of Oak Street, the community asked, What are looted stores compared to their looted lives? (Gillette 2007).

By the 1980s, urban renewal in New Haven had screeched to a halt. In response to the uproar, the Connector was never completed. Its eight lanes of asphalt came to a halt at the sooty concrete garage where hospital employees still park their cars (Stewart 2018). Between 1960 and 2016, the area of city land dedicated to parking for suburban commuters increased by nearly 300 percent (Johnston 2016). Residents of the Hill continue to complain about the razing of homes for public projects that benefit outsiders. One resident and community activist, Dawn Gibson-Brehon, told me that she does not think Yale will stop its encroachment on the Hill until it reaches the city limits.

By the 1980s New Haven ranked as the seventh poorest major city in the nation, while the university endowment began to skyrocket: between 1980 and 1990, its market value more than doubled, and between 2003 and 2013, investment returns exceeded 10 percent each year (Yale University 2013). Its tax-exempt status frees Yale from any obligation to disburse its wealth to the city to compensate for its tremendous drain on public services, including police, fire, and sewage.

As a Yale graduate student, I sought opportunities to foster partnerships between Yale and the organizations with which I collaborated for my research, including Fair Haven Community Health Care, the Community Foundation for Greater New Haven, Junta for Progressive Action, and Unidad Latina en Acción. The responses were unequivocally negative: they agreed that Yale only cares about itself.

The economic advancement of the Latinx community in New Haven has occurred despite, rather than because of, Yale University and Yale–New Haven Hospital. Residents remain wary of Yale and the conflict between its interests and theirs. Notably, although Yale University is the largest employer of New Haven residents—and Yale–New Haven Health is the largest employer in the state of Connecticut—only one of my interlocutors reported working for either entity. Apart from occasional expressions of gratitude for student volunteers such as those at HAVEN Free Clinic, the relationship between the Latinx community of New Haven and Yale University is fraught with animosity and resentment.

CONCLUSION

In addition to trauma and loss, migration also entails homogenization and erasure of identity. *Latinidad* in the United States is a sociopolitical construction—a racial and ethnic arrangement relative to White hegemony that incorporates colorism and confounds self- and externally assigned identities. Nevertheless, the term *Latinx* can capture multiple expressions of *Latinidad*, including racial, gender, sexual, and generational diversity, as an expression of resistance against dominant social terminology. This book focuses on first-generation Latina migrant mothers, regardless of racial phenotype or social background. This population is defined by shared histories of migration, gender identity, and maternity. The cohesive treatment of the migrant mothers in my study under the "Latina" label enables the examination of the forces of xenophobia and gender discrimination in the lives of these women and their children.

The migrant communities in New Haven exhibit patterns of chain migration, a term that has been weaponized and stigmatized even though the reality is hardly sinister. The personal stories of the women I interviewed reflect historical patterns of settlement in the area, from early Puerto Rican farm and factory workers to today's clusters of Mexicans, Guatemalans, and Ecuadorians. Narratives surrounding these shifts in demographic statistics can both empower and vilify the Latinx community.

Beyond personal links to New Haven, many migrants have perceived the city as welcoming to Spanish speakers, likely thanks to the growth in businesses and culture set in motion by early Puerto Rican organizers. In addition, long histories of activism to promote health, safety, and immigration rights have built a sense of community solidarity. Despite this inviting atmosphere, the Latinx community continues to fight against powerful forces. Private industries continue to pollute the neighborhoods, like Fair Haven, where Latinxs live, and the titanic Yale University hoards its wealth and encroaches into the homes of the community. Even in a well-resourced, organized, sanctuary city, Latinx migrants still face challenges in realizing their full potential.

In my conversation with Kica Matos, I raised the issue of how much remained to do, despite what New Haven Latinxs had accomplished. "As a Black woman, as a Latina, we often minimize our own work," Kica admitted to me. "It doesn't feel significant. It feels like you're always fighting with everything you have. And when you achieve victories, you may, you know, for a day savor the moment, but then you turn to the next big battle, because there's always another big battle to be had."

I paraphrased a quote from Malcolm X: "If you stick a knife in my back nine inches and pull it out six inches, there's no progress. If you pull it all the way out that's not progress."

"Yes!" She shouted. "The knife is still there! I can still feel it!"

4 Mothering

It is 8:08 A.M., just about time for the morning "huddle" at the Women's Center of Yale–New Haven Hospital, when the providers, nurses, and medical assistants gather to review announcements and assignments for the day. Linda, a nurse and patient services manager, extends her ID badge to unlock the door. Her face is worn; her pale eyes, made up with blue eyeshadow and eyeliner, are sunken with fatigue and overwork. As she chats with the staff, her mood lightens. They discuss their children and ask if anyone has news of a staff member who had called in sick. The head nurse, Renee, reads out the day's assignments, specifying which rooms the providers, medical assistants, and patient care attendants will work in and with whom they'll be paired.

The building is drab and worn. Blue lettering on the gray facade announces its status as a primary care facility. Inside, it feels like a basement. Except in the lobby, where patients fan out toward pediatrics, adult medicine, or OB/gyn, it has no source of daylight. I often entered the clinic from the medical school, passing through breezeways and descending dim staircases until I arrived at the Women's Center.

In the time I worked there, all but two of the providers—including physicians, certified nurse midwives (CNMs), and physician assistants

(PAs)—were White; the two people of color were South Asian. All the nurses were also White. The medical assistants (also called ambulatory care associates, or ACAs) and patient care assistants (PCAs) were all women of color, except for one White student from the University of Connecticut who filled in during the winter holidays. The patients were nearly all women of color. In the several weeks I spent conducting fieldwork at the Women's Center prior to the COVID-19 pandemic, I encountered just two White women seeking care.

This racial dynamic—with White providers and nurses at the top of the medical hierarchy and Black and Brown ACAs and patients at the bottom—pairs expertise (and wealth) with racial advantage. The pattern mirrors the observations by the anthropologist Khiara Bridges at a safety net prenatal clinic in New York City. She identified ancillary staff, "composed primarily of first-generation immigrants of color," who distrust patients and their presumed dependence on welfare, alongside "well-trained, elite physicians," treating poor patients of color in a chaotic struggle to deliver high-quality healthcare in an underfunded and overburdened setting (Bridges 2011, 21). Both the clinic Bridges studied and the Women's Center where I met these migrant mothers funneled small allocations of resources from premier academic institutions to low-income, mostly Black and Brown women.

In this chapter, I discuss issues of racialization of Latina reproduction, challenging the perceptions of migrant women as hyperfertile and "obstetrically hardy" mothers who are resistant to pain. I address prejudicial attitudes toward pregnancy planning and birth control, broadening these observations beyond Latina women to examine their occurrence across different race and class strata. I also discuss gaps in the healthcare system—and attempts to fill them—alongside experiences of "bureaucratic disentitlement," or the administrative abrogation of individual rights (Castañeda 2019, 3).

THE RACIALIZATION OF LATINA BIRTH

Throughout US history, White Americans have feared and sought to control the fertility of racialized and migrant Others. In the early twentieth century, White Americans feared a "race suicide," a prediction of racial extinction based on perceptions of immigrant reproduction outpacing that of Anglo-Saxons. Restrictive immigration policies and selective marriages were promoted to "breed out" the undesirable traits of newer immigrants, including Italians and Jews (D. E. Roberts 1999, 99). As declining fertility among US-born women coincided with changes in the demographic composition of US immigrants following the Hart-Celler Act of 1965, White Americans feared that procreation by immigrant women would outstrip that of White women. These fears justified sterilization campaigns, reductions in social support for immigrants, and the vilification of Black and Brown mothers (Chavez 2013, 74).

The medical anthropologists Faye Ginsburg and Rayna Rapp advance the concept of "stratified reproduction," originally proposed by Shellee Cohen to describe overt and covert pressures by which some women are encouraged and empowered to reproduce while others are disempowered and their possible offspring stigmatized (Ginsburg and Rapp 1995, 3). According to Khiara Bridges, migrant women in the United States—whether Latin American, Middle Eastern, or African—are racialized as non-White and thereby represent a threat to the implicitly White nation (Bridges 2011, 346).

These attitudes and practices inform enduring biases against Black and Brown women. At the clinic, I overheard providers making comments along the lines of "What's the point in talking to Latinas about birth control? They're just going to be back here in a year," implying that Latin American migrant women are ignorant of their bodies, hypersexual, and irresponsible. I also heard one provider repeatedly speak of participants in the privately funded Me and My Baby program—mostly undocumented immigrants—as "ungrateful," echoing racist tropes of Black and Brown women as undeserving and exploitative "welfare queens."

In 2018, the year that the foreign-born population in the United States reached its peak, more immigrant women (7.5 percent) gave birth than US-born women (5.7 percent) (Budiman 2020). In 2019, the fertility rate for Latina women was 1.94, whereas the rate for White women was 1.61 (Statista Research Department 2021). However, most American women desire two or three children, with a growing number expressing an ideal of "as many as you want," suggesting that current fertility rates fall short of women's desires (Stone 2018). In my study of Latina women, 65 percent expressly wished for fewer than three children. Those who had more children often experienced reproductive coercion as a result of their inability to access birth control or abusive partners. Given that Latina reproduction rates align more closely with their expressed ideals than do those of White women, Chavez proposes considering White reproduction "abnormally low" rather than criticizing the supposed "hyperfertility" of Latina women (2013, 104).

When women deliberate over family size and timing, they consider familial goals and dynamics, gender balance, and finances, as well as the potential of a baby to legitimize a "strategic" relationship. Several women planned for a tubal ligation or placement of an intrauterine device (IUD) like the Mirena after birth. Just over 40 percent of my interlocutors told me that their pregnancies had not been planned, a prevalence below the national average of 45 percent (Finer and Zolna 2016). Many of those who had experienced unplanned pregnancies—and even those whose pregnancies were desired—reported problems accessing, maintaining, and tolerating birth control.

Jackelín told me, "At first, this wasn't in the plans. Because I'd had a previous C-section, I knew [my pregnancy] would be at higher risk." One of Jackelín's greatest stressors at the time of our interview had been her fear of medical complications with her pregnancy. "After having my girls, I was no longer taking care of myself [using birth control]. I had gotten the injection before, but it made me feel awful. I didn't like it. My bones would hurt, my feet, too. It felt like one bone would separate from the other.

"So I got the one you put in your arm [the contraceptive implant]. I still don't know why they gave that to me. It would move, and it felt like having a needle in my hand. It felt like it would move at night and everything, and it hurt. I made an appointment to have it removed. They told me that everything was fine, that nothing was wrong, and that they didn't have to remove it."

Jackelín lived with the pain and discomfort from the implant for another year before she decided she could no longer take it. She begged her gynecologist to remove it. After that, she became pregnant. "I tried to be careful, but in this case, we didn't take good enough care of ourselves." Jackelín blamed herself for the untimely pregnancy but still welcomes her son. "I say, he is a baby, he is a human being. He did not choose his life, to be born, and he must come to live in this world."

Women like Jackelín acknowledge pregnancy as both a biological function, one that may rebel against attempts at control, and a social one that may support companionate marriage and strengthen familial love. These reflective and intentional approaches to family building run directly counter to stereotypes of Latina women as ignorant, hyperfertile possessors of "unruly bodies" that undermine a White supremacist national collective.

The results of the 2020 US census revealed that, for the first time on record, the White population of the United States had declined. Moreover, *all* population growth—an increase of roughly twenty-three million people—occurred among racially minoritized groups. Over the past decade, Latinxs have accounted for half of the growth in the US population (Tavernise and Gebeloff 2021). Such trends are bound to lead to the revival of racist tropes regarding the threat that women of color—pose to essential "Americanness." The sociologist Michael Rodriguez-Muñiz reminds us that interpretations and projections of tabulated data induce affective responses. Latinxs might view their fast-growing cohort as a sign of empowerment, whereas White people might consider the shrinking of their population as an affront to their sense of self and belonging. These assessments "take for granted the existence of the ethnoracial populations they depict and frame the demographic future as more or less inevitable" (Rodriguez-Muñiz 2021, 92). In other words, the forging and persistence of the racial categories *Latinx* and *White* make these narratives possible, and forecasting implies certainty.

OBSTETRICAL HARDINESS AND RISK

"Last Saturday, the pains started," Célia told me. "In the morning, I went to the hospital, and they told me I was past my due date. They had already told me that if the pains did not start by Tuesday and they saw that I was not dilating, then they were going to induce labor. But then I started with pains on Saturday, and I went into the hospital, but there was no space for me yet."

Célia related the beginning of her traumatic birth story with calm resignation. Her older son, Alonso, had been born by Cesarean section, and according to her medical records, she had an "unknown" uterine scar, meaning she did not know—and her obstetricians in Ecuador had not documented—where her uterus had been cut to deliver her older son. Despite this, three months before her delivery date, Célia consented to a trial of labor after Cesarean (TOLAC). On the morning when Célia arrived at the hospital, she recalled, "I had started bleeding. That's why I went in. I was going to wait it out until the pains became stronger, but it was already too much. I went in that same day."

Bleeding late in pregnancy is a possible indicator of several complications, including placenta previa (the partial or full obstruction of the cervix by the placenta), placental abruption (premature separation of the placenta from the uterine wall), vasa previa (a condition in which fetal blood vessels protrude into the cervical opening), and most dangerous, uterine rupture (spontaneous tearing of the uterus). According to clinical guidelines, vaginal bleeding and abdominal pain in women with histories of C-sections—particularly during labor—almost always indicate an emergency (Norwitz and Shin Park 2022). Despite these warning signs, the medical team at Yale–New Haven Hospital originally turned Célia away. "They sent me back. They told me they would call me because there was still no bed at the hospital. They told me they would call that afternoon to try to check me in, but it wasn't until Saturday night that they told me to come back."

When she returned to the hospital, Célia received an infusion of Pitocin, a synthetic form of the hormone oxytocin, to accelerate her labor. "They began the induction on Saturday and from that night through the morning, the pains were very strong. In the morning, they gave me stuff for the pain. So, I had a lot of strong medicine in me, but I still could no longer bear the pain. I complained a lot, and I told them I couldn't take it anymore. The next step, they said, was to inject my back [with epidural anesthesia]—the medicine they give you when you are going to have a C-section. It was only with that medicine that I was able to endure the pain.

"Then, around four in the afternoon, he [the baby, Gabriel] was still in there, and he wasn't coming. About four or six more hours passed, and it was now ten at night. It was time, but now many hours had passed, and I was not dilating normally.

"I tried pushing but now, the baby was not coming. There was no way for him to come down. And so they realized this, but by that time it was too late. And the pains were so strong that I could no longer bear it. I was like, 'I can't take it anymore.' I don't remember very well, but they were telling my husband that my pain could be because my wound was opening—or that's what they were afraid of. I told them to please take care of it as soon as possible because the pain was very strong, and I had already pushed a lot, but the baby was not coming down.

"So, they took me away to the operating room in about ten minutes. They gave me full anesthesia. And then they realized that it was the wound that had opened, which was why my belly had grown so much. That part became very difficult. I don't know exactly what happened, but something was wrong with my uterus, I don't quite remember what it was. But the operation was no longer a normal operation, a normal C-section. They had to reconstruct something, and it became much more tedious."

Célia suffered a lateral extension of her original uterine incision, or a stretching of her previous C-section scar, that tore open her uterus. Not only this, but both her uterine arteries, the major vessels that supply blood to the uterus, had ripped open. The obstetricians noted that four centimeters of her uterus had thinned so much that her son could be seen through the tissue. "I lost a lot of blood. It was not like a normal C-section . . . it was something else. It was because it was almost as if I had had like a double birth."

Célia's red blood cell volume dropped to a dangerously low level. She received two units of transfused blood. In addition, "they injected me with a lot of things for the pain. I swelled up a lot—I was unrecognizable. The next day, after delivery, it was ugly. My entire body was swollen, from head to toe. My blood pressure went up. I got dizzy. They took a lot of blood out of me and then had to put blood back in me to be able to [recover]." Because of multiple episodes of dizziness and severe fluctuations in her blood pressure (signs of postpartum pre-eclampsia), Célia was kept under careful monitoring. The hospital eventually discharged her one week later.

Despite these harrowing events, the attending physician described Célia's C-section as "uncomplicated" in her discharge summary. This description, coupled with the possible medical blunders that occurred during Célia's birth, raise questions about how Célia was viewed as a patient and how she became a submissive subject.

First, Célia was a "Women's Center patient," a label that Dierdre, a patient care coordinator, notes is often assigned "in a derogatory tone." In
other words, Célia came from a safety-net clinic and lacked insurance.
This information, coupled with her inability to speak English fluently,
likely contributed to the delay in her admission for labor. At the Women's
Center, as at many other safety-net prenatal clinics, patients see a variety
of providers for their prenatal care, including midwives, physician assistants, and, rarely, obstetricians. They give birth attended by whoever is on
call at the time, usually a resident physician who is still in training. Célia
had no one who could advocate for her. When she called the hospital describing her early labor pains and bleeding, there was no provider familiar
with her history who could follow up and urge her admission. During the
hours Célia waited for a bed, it is likely that her uterine tear worsened.

Second, providers several times dismissed and underreacted to Célia's
complaints of pain. Célia raised concerns of severe pain Saturday night
but received no relief until the following morning, even though the American College of Obstetrics and Gynecology states that "maternal request is
a sufficient medical indication for pain relief during labor" (2019). Célia
initially received butorphan, an opioid medication generally not recommended for labor pain because it is less effective than an epidural and
because it carries risks of fetal heart rate and respiratory depression and
neurobehavioral changes in the newborn. Eventually, Célia received an
epidural, and her labor slowed.

Célia's bleeding, severe pain, uterine thinning, and history of prior
C-section should have raised red flags for possible uterine rupture. Her
experience raises concerns about racial biases in perceptions of pain and
facility of childbirth.

A study of medical students and residents found that about 50 percent endorsed false beliefs about biological differences between Black
and White patients, including the beliefs that "Blacks' nerve endings are
less sensitive than Whites'" and that "Blacks' skin is thicker than Whites."
Trainees who endorsed more false beliefs rated Black patients as feeling
less pain than White patients and offered inferior treatment recommendations to Black patients in mock medical cases (Hoffman et al. 2016).
Studies show that across care settings, patients of color consistently receive lower-quality pain care and are less likely to receive opioid prescrip-

tions for severe pain (Anderson, Green, and Payne 2009; C. R. Green et al. 2003; Pletcher et al. 2008).

These findings reflect the myth of "obstetrical hardiness," described by the historian John Hoberman as the belief that socially and politically disempowered women—including Black and Latina women—are less affected by the pains of labor and childbirth than White women (2005). This belief is based on a false, biologized idea of race in which Black people in particular are considered "a more primitive human type that is biologically and psychologically different from civilized man" (Hoberman 2005, 87). Physicians throughout the twentieth century considered "primitive" (code for "phenotypically darker") women to have "easy labors" that did not require pain relief.

In her examination of professional Black women who gave birth prematurely, the cultural anthropologist Dána-Ain Davis traces obstetric racism, and the traumatic birth experiences it produces, to patterns of exploitation, experimentation, and violation of Black bodies. Invasive examinations, diagnostic lapses, and characterizations of obstetrical hardiness derive from viewing Black bodies—particularly women's bodies—as "hardy" producers and reproducers within a slave economy (D.-A. Davis 2019a).

I often heard providers at the Women's Center speak about how "healthy" Latin American patients were and how they rarely needed epidural anesthesia. With reference to the Mexican women she studied, Khiara Bridges notes that physicians may assume women will have easy labors and deny or delay analgesia, insist upon vaginal deliveries when C-sections may be indicated, or fail to take precautions to prevent trauma or infection (Bridges 2011, 265). Such efforts are likely well-intended, intended to support empowered, "natural" births and to reduce the number of "unnecessary" surgeries and associated complications. Some facilities have goals of reducing C-sections to 15 percent or fewer births (Madden et al. 2013; Obstetric Care Consensus 2014). Still, women of color often report stressful birthing experiences and disregard for their preferences (McLemore et al. 2018).

Third, Célia was engrafted in a system of biomedicine that views women, particularly poor women, as possessors of "unruly bodies" (Bridges 2011) and pathologizes their cases. In their medical notes, Célia's providers state that she "failed TOLAC" and "did not labor," characterizing Célia's body as uncooperative and negating her experience of labor pains lasting more than twenty-four hours. The reason for her C-section was listed as "The head of the baby was big, and it never fit," ignoring her uterine abruption and the concerning signs of vaginal bleeding and prolonged labor. The medical team attributed the emergency surgery to the anatomy of Célia and her baby, rather than to a predictable complication of vaginal birth following a prior C-section.

Célia's distinctive medical history and presentation were disregarded based on her status as a poor, Spanish-speaking, Latina patient at the Women's Center. Clinicians assessed her risk based on their assumptions about "obstetrically hardy" poor women of color they imagine desire (or deserve) fewer medical interventions (Bridges 2011, 314). Calculations of risk are based on the traits of an arbitrarily defined population. This is a political act that negates individual particularities in order to produce a homogeneous group; it also serves to advance the interests of the dominant strata, in this case the time- and resource-constrained clinical teams (Rodríguez-Muñiz 2021). Such presuppositions of health, or implicit minimization of risk for Latina mothers, may contribute to harmful and even-life threatening biases in care practice (Gálvez 2011).

Finally, providers both in Ecuador and in the United States denied Célia's autonomy, violating the first principle of biomedical ethics. Célia had given birth to her first child, Alonso, by C-section for reasons that were unclear to her. Many of my interlocutors reported having C-sections in their home countries. The experience of Cintia, who was an attorney in her home country of the Dominican Republic, sheds some light on Célia's experience. Cintia described how her obstetrician attempted to schedule her for a C-section on her first prenatal visit: "I said that I wanted to have a normal delivery, but she wanted me to have a C-section. I asked why and she said, 'Oh, it's better, ta ra ra ra...' Sure, it's better for them, because then I have to pay for the hospital admission, I have to pay for the anesthesia, I have to pay for the doctor to do the procedure, and the medicines they give me for the operation and all that.

"Until the end, I said no, but she made up a story that the baby lacked [amniotic] fluid. At a routine visit, she broke [swept] my membrane, saying, 'Oh, this is going to speed up your delivery,' and since it was my first time, I didn't know any better. Then at the next visit, she does an ultrasound and says the baby has no fluid. She told my mother that the baby was going to die, that he would be born purple. I never thought to ask myself until later, 'How am I going to have fluid if you could've made a hole in me that drained it?'"

A membrane sweep is a procedure in which the provider inserts a finger into the vagina to separate the amniotic sac from the uterus to encourage the onset of labor in women who are approaching or past their due dates. Cintia did not clearly consent to a membrane sweep, as she was not fully aware of its risks in addition to its benefits. Although the risk of rupture of the amniotic sac is a small during a membrane sweep—and it is not clear whether this actually occurred in Cintia's case—it seems that Cintia would not have agreed to the procedure had she known it could increase her risk of a C-section. The fact that Cintia believes her obstetrician "made up" a reason for an emergency delivery—and her concern about clinicians' financial gains from C-sections—underscore a systemic issue surrounding the provider incentives in obstetric care (Spetz, Smith, and Ennis 2001). C-sections are especially and increasingly prevalent in Latin America, with 42.9 percent of mothers in South America giving birth via C-section in recent years (Magne et al. 2017).

Although some Latin American and Latina women may opt for C-section, often they are encouraged down this path of medicalized childbirth without fully informed consent. As a result, women like Célia may agree to this surgery not understanding whether it is truly medically indicated or how it might affect their future birth plans. Overmedicalization, like denial of necessary medical care, increases the risk of adverse reproductive health outcomes and disproportionately harms Black and Brown women (D. Davis 2019b). Such disempowerment constitutes a form of obstetric violence that follows migrant women as they journey across borders.

When Célia consented to TOLAC, she did not have the knowledge needed to make an informed decision. Her vulnerability in light of her uncertain medical history should have entitled her to even more cautious and compassionate communication about her options during her prenatal care, and timely response to her concerns at the time of her labor. Instead, Célia found herself desperately confused, her requests denied, and fighting for her own life, to say nothing of her newborn's.

THE ME AND MY BABY PROGRAM AND BUREAUCRATIC DISENTITLEMENT

"So I have a pretty unique position," Dierdre from the Women's Center told me. "People call it a hybrid job. I am trained as a family nurse practitioner. I am certified as a nurse case manager. And primarily my role is case management for the obstetrical patients in the clinic. I'm also in charge of the Me and My Baby program, which is a program that provides prenatal care for uninsured women. And initially it started in 1988. It was predominantly the working poor Americans [in Me and My Baby] before Medicaid was expanded. And then now, over time, it has evolved. It's become mostly a program for the undocumented."

According to Dierdre, the Me and My Baby program began in the 1980s amid surging infant mortality in the City of New Haven. The city's two hospitals—Yale–New Haven and St. Raphael's, which have since merged—received grants from the state to address the issue. St. Raphael's operated a "MotherCare" van, which circulated neighborhoods to find pregnant woman needing prenatal care. Yale provided the care, which extended to uninsured and high-risk patients.

"Our program was very big at the time," Dierdre explained. "It was mostly the working poor...it was women who had to string together a bunch of part-time jobs, but none of them offered benefits. So that put them over the income limit for Medicaid, but they did not have insurance. Now, at that time, we had transportation, we had outreach workers, we had a part-time patient educator, we had a transportation coordinator and we paid for transportation, we had some social work and other free services. We had a lot."

But as with all grants, the money eventually ran out. "The state said, 'Well, you're all doing a great job, now it's over,'" Dierdre told me. Fortunately, Yale made the decision to continue funding the program, which costs about $2 million per year. But each year, the hospital pared down its services. Now the program covers only prenatal care, prescriptions directly relating to pregnancy, and one postpartum visit. Women who earn up to 250 percent of the federal poverty level qualify.

Based on this description, the program seems like a godsend for uninsured women, particularly those who are undocumented. However, closer examination reveals several problematic gaps. For example, the program does not cover contraception, as the grant that previously provided this service expired and was not renewed.

JES: So, a question about contraception. If a woman wants to have an IUD placed, like if she has a C-section and wants to get her IUD while she's in the hospital for her birth, it won't be covered?

DIERDRE: It will not in this state. Maybe a year and a half ago, the state finally started paying for immediate postpartum contraception for women on Medicaid. But they were very clear to say that patients who were receiving emergency Medicaid for their hospital stays would not be covered. We did have a grant for ten years for LARCs [long-acting reversible contraception], but it ended.

In other words, women in the Me and My Baby program or those who receive emergency Medicaid for their births are not eligible for contraceptive support. These include many undocumented and "liminally legal" women like Nikki Campbell, a Jamaican immigrant and DACA recipient (see chapter 2).

"The decision was made that we can't just, you know, cover thousands of women forever," Dierdre explains. "We're giving them a significant amount of care. And there has to be a cutoff at some point. 'Cause if you gave someone an IUD or gave them Depo [Depo-Provera, a hormonal contraceptive injection] and they wanted it again, you know, it'd be a lot—I have a few hundred patients a year on the program." To Priscila, this seems fair. "Sure, so there are programs that help you when you are pregnant. To that, I say, how lovely. But there are some people who are so cushy with everything, who get everything paid for. Who is that really helping? There are people who should be working, and still they're getting support. Don't you think that changes a person's mentality? Yeah, I've asked for help—for pregnancy, for my husband's illness—but not 100 percent."

Though some participants in the program, like Priscila, view these limits on the program as reasonable, the absence of family planning and preventative healthcare struck me as shortsighted. The late South African bishop and anti-apartheid activist Desmond Tutu famously said, "There comes a point where we need to stop just pulling people out of the river. We need to go upstream and find out why they are falling in." The Me and

My Baby policy seemed committed to the Sisyphean task of constantly pulling people out of the river.

Limiting the reproductive care and family planning options offered to Me and My Baby participants has two effects. First, it centers the child, rather than the mother, as the beneficiary of free care. It casts the woman as a vessel for reproductive labor, fulfilling social and political obligations, rather than as an embodied subject herself (Mullin 2005). As the medical historian Barbara Duden puts it, the biomedical paradigm holds pregnant women hostage to their fetuses, "disembodying" the woman and subjecting her to calculations of need by healthcare professionals (Duden 1993). Second, it reinforces racialized conceptions of Latina women as "hyperfertile and ignorant baby machines" even as it deprives them of resources to control and plan their reproductive effort (Gálvez 2011).

The narrow focus of the program also restricts the care provided during pregnancy. Elyse, the project coordinator for the Me and My Baby program, who processes applications and reviews bills for potential or enrolled patients, explained, "I usually get a spreadsheet or an invoice, I guess you could say, with a list of charges for each patient. And, literally, you have to go through each charge to make sure that the ultrasound, you know, is appropriate, and that it was done in the hospital or here in the clinic."

Elyse went on to give an example. "If the patient was seen in the emergency room for something that's not pregnancy related, or they had another doctor visit or a dentist appointment or something, I will deduct those charges from the invoice. When the patients are approved for the program, we make it clear that the program only covers *some* of their medications and *some* of their doctor's visits, because if you have a chronic condition, that's something the program would not pay for. It has to be pregnancy-related."

The program separates the gravid uterus from the remainder of the woman's body, restricting care to what Elyse or Dierdre considers "pregnancy-related." To test the limits of eligible services, I proposed a hypothetical situation to Elyse.

JES: I'm just curious, because this can get a bit sticky. One could argue that if a woman has untreated dental caries [cavities], that could lead to inflammation and preterm birth. How do you make the determination of what is pregnancy-related versus what's not?

ELYSE: So, it's very strict. It's usually just your visits here in the Women's Center or your visit at maternal-fetal medicine.

JES: What about a woman who has gestational diabetes and then gets referred to the Diabetes Center [a specialized endocrinology clinic dedicated to management of complex diabetes]?

ELYSE: Well, maternal-fetal medicine has a diabetes education nurse... those are covered.

JES: But if a woman is really, really struggling to manage her gestational diabetes and dose her insulin, and she needs an endocrinologist or an APRN [advanced practicing registered nurse] who specializes in endocrinology, what then?

ELYSE: No, to my knowledge they wouldn't go. All of the patients with diabetes are managed by the high-risk group at MFM [maternal-fetal medicine].

Despite the increasing tendency of biomedicine to compartmentalize and molecularize health, pregnancy is a complex physiological process involving the endocrine, cardiovascular, neurologic, and genitourinary systems. Attempts to dissociate pregnancy from the rest of the body through restrictive care provision places women at risk for obstetric complications like preterm birth and babies born too small—or too large—for gestational age. The Me and My Baby program effectively constitutes women's reproductive labor as a requirement for obtaining care.

Although the maximum income limit for Me and My Baby program eligibility seems generous, at 250 percent of the federal poverty level, the application process nevertheless deters many women. First, women must document their income. Many, particularly undocumented women, are paid in cash and cannot provide pay stubs. The program accepts a letter from an employer; however, under the Immigration Reform and Control Act of 1986, employers are prohibited from knowingly employing undocumented workers. Verifying cash payments may place employers at risk of legal penalties. Women may forgo admission to Me and My Baby to avoid having to make such a request and risk being fired.

Second, women must apply for and receive a denial of medical insurance coverage from Medicaid (or HUSKY in Connecticut). The HUSKY application requires a woman to provide her full name, social security number, citizenship status, and home address. For undocumented women, this means disclosing their unlawful presence in the country and providing the state with a means to find them, thus putting them at risk of deportation. Although the Affordable Care Act explicitly forbids ICE from using any information from healthcare applications for immigration enforcement, individual states can retain this information, and undocumented migrants are advised by advocates not to disclose it (National Immigration Law Center 2016).

Finally, eligible women do not automatically receive referrals to the program. Although the community health centers in New Haven often refer uninsured women to the Women's Center, women who do not access routine healthcare or prenatal care may fall through the cracks. Several of my interlocutors told me they had heard about the program only through friends or family members, suggesting that an unknown number of women who lack such social capital may receive inadequate prenatal care or incur medical debt by seeking care elsewhere.

These barriers exemplify "bureaucratic disentitlement," or the subtle and harmful process by which administrative agencies deprive individuals of their entitlements and rights (Castañeda 2019, 3). Bureaucratic disentitlement may take the form of withholding information, providing misinformation, isolating or confusing applicants, or requiring extensive paperwork for simple processes. Although undocumented women are entitled to prenatal care through Me and My Baby, the lack of information regarding the program and the documentation requirements that may endanger women's employment or safety effectively strip them of their rights.

This form of disentitlement is also racialized. When Me and My Baby primarily served White women, "women who worked in Dunkin Donuts and Wal-Mart here and there," as Dierdre says, the program was more extensive—offering transportation and social services—and actively sought out eligible participants. Whether by coincidence or intent, now that the population is predominantly Latina, these services have been scaled back. The program no longer covers routine women's healthcare or contraception or provides transportation and ancillary care. Since I began collaborating with the Women's Center, the clinic has also lost its social worker,

Elaine, who previously helped with housing, food insecurity, and mental healthcare, and its coordinator for Head Start, a health and educational promotion program for low-income families. Lydia, the Head Start coordinator, used to wait outside the examination rooms of the initial prenatal visits for every patient presumed to qualify—that is, nearly everyone who came to the Women's Center. She would meet women and help them obtain services for their children. Now, women must navigate the bureaucracies of early childhood support, transportation, rental assistance, and other services on their own.

Melinda, a nurse practitioner who worked at the Women's Center two and a half days a week, also noted that even when these services existed, they rarely benefited Latin American migrant women. "Their target population is White and Black women," Melinda complained. "They have a big, wide support network. But when asked very directly, like, 'What about our patients who don't fit that category or don't speak English?'—because neither Lydia or Elaine speaks any other language—they'll say, 'We welcome anyone,' but how welcoming can it be?"

The question of who deserves prenatal care centers on the unborn child but also on the perception of the mother's ability to produce a "positive future" (Ginsburg and Rapp 1995). As a result, poor Brown women are seen as less "deserving" than poor White women, an attitude reflected in the progressive cuts and barriers to enrollment in the Me and My Baby program as the demographics of its eligible population shifted. The barriers for Latina mothers constitute bureaucratic disentitlement.

Despite being effectively deprived of their patient and citizen rights, women enact powerful strategies of coping, particularly with respect to motherhood. Here I discuss these approaches, which I collectively term *imperative resilience*, to emphasize the agency of these women and their resistance to oppression.

IMPERATIVE RESILIENCE

Though definitions vary, *resilience* generally refers to engaging resources in the face of adversity to achieve goals (Panter-Brick et al. 2015). Unlike the concepts of positive psychology and competence, resilience considers social environment as a factor influencing an individual's ability to adapt to difficult life circumstances (Rutter 2012). Resilience and its companion concept, *flourishing*, emphasize healthy functioning, or at least an absence of psychopathology. These terms often imply "well-being" and "positive" or "protective" factors, which lend themselves to measurement using pre- and postintervention assessments in behavioral health research (Willen 2022). Nearly all scholars of resilience—in clinical medicine, public health, and related social sciences—agree that resilience should be optimized and seek to pinpoint the ways that it can be cultivated.

This interpretation of resilience fixes the concept as a static characteristic, akin to "toughness" or "grit," rather than a process of rational action. A more nuanced conceptualization of resilience views it as a trajectory, or a process of adaptation or sustained, healthy adjustment over time (Bonanno 2004; 2012). Interpretations of trauma and marginalization that recognize individual identity and agency within social, political, and cultural circumstances allow consideration of mental health responses that are not uniformly negative (Wexler, DiFluvio, and Burke 2009).

When I discussed resilience, and its relevance to this project, with my research assistants, several cringed. "At La Casa [La Casa Cultural, the Latinx cultural center at Yale], we talk a lot about resilience, like it's something White people think we have for 'making it' here," one of my students commented. "But that's not it at all. I mean, we're resilient because we *have* to be." We joked that the response to "Wow, you're so resilient" should be "Thanks, it was between that and dropping out or dying."

Theories of resilience tend not to conceptualize it as a mode of resistance to oppression, but my interlocutors reveal that this is exactly the dynamic at work. Resilience is not an ability or a choice: it is a conditioned response to the multiple forms of violence they encounter through racism, sexism, immigration enforcement, and economic inequality. In recognition of this reality, I propose the term *imperative resilience* to describe the strategies women employ—cognitively, emotionally, and socially—to get by in the face of overlapping adversities.

Priscila, for example, told me that she could not afford to let her emotional responses interfere with her ability to handle stress: Instead she focuses on problem solving. "Let's say I do not have something that I should," she explained. "For example, this month I only had half the money

I needed to pay the electric bill. I couldn't make that bill this month, and so next month I'm going to have to work more hours to cover it. If I get angry about it, things will just get worse—it won't solve anything. So, I just try to calm down and look for solutions to be more economical and more organized."

Priscila seemed almost puzzled by my questions about how she bounces back from stress or other difficulties in life. "I try to keep things simple," she responded. "If I complicate things, I'm not going to solve anything at all. If I complicate things, I get home in a bad mood and take it out on my children. But they are my responsibility—I have to be the responsible one. If I get angry and yell and scream to let off steam, it solves nothing in the end, quite the opposite. It makes things worse. I just have to calm down and look for solutions. I have to accept and endure."

The themes of acceptance and endurance—and the desire to shield children from stress—echoed throughout my interviews. Women felt it was their responsibility to minimize their affective responses to difficult circumstances to preserve the emotional and physical health of their children, and their pregnancies (see table A.1).

Jenifer, a thirty-two-year-old from the San Marcos area of Guatemala, faced extreme stress when she developed thyroid cancer and doctors told her she might not survive. "When they gave me the bad news, I started to worry. But then I sat and thought, and I realized that in life, we have to fight for everything. And so I tried to focus on other things. I don't forget, I know it's there, but I try not to think about it so that I'm not thinking about this awful thing, this awful thing, all the time."

In Guatemala, we only had to worry about whether we had food to eat, how we were going to buy things," she went on. "Here, even in my condition, I knew my family would be provided for." This knowledge brought Jenifer peace. In some ways, she resigned herself to the possibility of dying. "Then again, I looked at my children and thought, oh God, my children are so young. I thought about leaving them with their father so that I could die, and they would never know. And at the same time, they smiled at me, they hugged me.... They kind of gave me strength to keep fighting and to get ahead for them."

At first glance, the coping strategies employed by both Priscila and Jenifer might be seen as maladaptive and described clinically as emotional numbing and intellectualization, repression, and cognitive avoidance. Strategies of avoidance coping have been associated with greater life stress and depressive symptoms (Holahan et al. 2005). However, these women also employ positive coping strategies, including problem solving, benefit finding, altruism, and personal or spiritual growth. Although Priscila might suppress her emotional reactions to stress, she does so out of concern for her children. She focuses on practical solutions to her challenges, like adjusting her budget and work hours. Similarly, while at first Jenifer might be viewed as avoiding the reality of her potentially terminal illness, she raises pragmatic concerns, such as economic provision for her family, and identifies the warmth and kindness of her children as a source of strength and perseverance.

I found myself in awe of these women who, despite immense economic adversity and limited social support, remained optimistic and focused on their goals. As a mother who found raising a young child challenging even with a dual-income partnership and familial support with childcare, I was humbled by the mental fortitude these women exhibited. Comparing my situation with theirs prompted me to reflect on my conventional understanding of resilience.

The social worker and resilience theorist Michael Ungar describes resilience as a quality evolving from both the individual and the individual's social ecology, with the social ecology outweighing individual characteristics. Ungar cautions against assessing "personal agency" and ignoring "the larger influence of sociopolitical, economic and cultural factors that shape developmental paths" (Unger 2011, 17, 19). Yet, if intrinsic attitudes and behaviors play a comparatively small role in determining well-being, how can we make sense of the persistence and psychological health of these structurally vulnerable women?

We can characterize their strategies for survival as imperative resilience. This is a performance that becomes actualized through practice. The necessity of suppressing negative emotions, emphasizing the positive, and strategic problem solving reflects not an inherent "grit" or "toughness," nor special access to social and material resources; rather, it arises as a form of opposition to social injustice, a way of summoning personal and social capacity to fill the voids left by society.

Monarch butterflies—with just a three- to four-inch wingspan—travel fifty to one hundred miles a day during their migration, flapping their wings five to twelve times per second. As the days shorten and the temperatures drop in their breeding areas across the United States and Canada, their primary source of food, milkweed, disappears. The butterflies overwinter in the mountains of central Mexico, shielded by oyamel fir trees whose microclimate protects them from extreme temperatures. As the days lengthen and the temperatures rise, however, this climate becomes inhospitable, prompting them to leave their roosting sites. Mated female monarchs leave first, blazing a trail that the next three to four generations will follow. These long and exhausting migrations are essential to the breeding success of the monarchs. Their resilience, like that of my interlocutors, is a necessity, a means of survival in a harsh and ever-changing world.

I understand the resilience of these Latin American migrant women as resistance to structural violence. Catherine Panter-Brick and colleagues emphasize the need to examine "how the fabric of a society impacts individual mental health trajectories" and further conceptualize resilience as a "trajectory, a sense of meaning-making that orders the world and gives coherence to the past, present, and the future" (Panter-Brick et al. 2011, 369, 385). Instead of ascribing this resilience to the social environment, I consider it as a form of psychosocial rebellion against oppressive structures. Women summon religious beliefs, self-conceptions of strength, and altruistic concerns for their families to fight against social and economic subjugation and to *seguir adelante*, or move onward.

Spirituality

When Norma Franceschi arrived in New Haven, her first priority was to find a church, "I looked for the church because I needed it." Norma, a Catholic, taught in religious education programs at her local church for nineteen years and considered it a home. At that time, she observed that many new migrants did not attend religious services, for various reasons. Early on, few churches offered services in Spanish; many migrants could not attend services because of work commitments; and others, particularly those from rural areas of Latin America, engaged in syncretic spiritual practices, like worshiping Santa Muerte (Nuestra Señora de Santa

Muerte, or Our Lady of Holy Death), that Norma and many local priests considered to be witchcraft. Over time, the parish communities of Santa Rosa de Lima and Our Lady of Guadalupe swelled to serve more than one thousand parishioners at Sunday mass. The Star of Jacob Church, a Pentecostal assembly, opened a second site in Fair Haven and provided a haven for many of the Protestant migrants, most of whom came from Puerto Rico.

However, during the COVID-19 pandemic, when I conducted my interviews, many churches canceled in-person services. Although some in the area offered services through Zoom or Facebook Live, most churches were limited in the community support they could offer, particularly to recent migrants. Even so, many women derived strength from their faith. When I asked Jackelín what gave her hope in everyday life, she responded: "That God is with us and gives us life. Another day dawns and with the life God has given us, we can breathe, we can enjoy all the gifts God has given us . . . being able to walk, see nature, to go out, to have a roof to live under, food. Most of all, to have our health, because with it we can move about as we please."

Jackelín, a forty-year-old woman from Guatemala, considers herself an evangelical, as did nine other women in the study (15 percent). A plurality of women identified as Catholics (48 percent), with varying degrees of involvement in religious activities. Two described their religion as Pentecostal, and the remainder of the women in my study either did not endorse any religion, but believed in more personal and direct means of relating with the divine, or expressed agnosticism. Whether through prayer, listening to Christian music, reading the Bible, or speaking with family members—mothers and grandmothers in particular—about their faith, religion provided many women with forms of solace and a narrative architecture with which to understand their life experiences.

New waves of Pentecostalism in Latin America—particularly in Puerto Rico—have offered the hope of subverting social hierarchies in favor of those positioned toward the bottom. Promises of direct communication with the Holy Spirit allow marginalized individuals to experience spiritual transcendence and transformation (Hansen 2018, 20, 23). Among the women I interviewed, these direct, individual spiritual practices were more common among those who identified as "Christian" (i.e., Protestant), Evangelical, and Pentecostal, and their faith empowered them to find hope despite experiencing poverty, job loss, and stress about their pregnancies and immigration status.

Additionally, for many women, believing in "God's plan" and orienting themselves to align with it helped them make sense of moments of suffering and to channel their efforts. For instance, when Jackelín endured harassment and intimidation from her coyote (see chapter 2), her faith in God helped her endure. "As I say, I trust God, and God's work always comes through. And that was what gave me consolation, that although that person [the coyote] says that I did this or that, lying about me, God knows I did nothing wrong. And my conscience, my heart was clear." Jackelín believed that if she remained steadfast in her faith in God, the words and acts of this abusive man could not affect her.

This attitude also helped her cope with a diagnosis of gestational diabetes midway through her pregnancy. Although she initially felt frightened and overwhelmed by her doctors' assessment of her risk and the intensive treatment they proposed, Jackelín trusted that God would look out for her. She said, "I believe in God, and if God exists and He can perform any miracle, He can do everything! I believed in God, nothing more."

She went on, "There were times when I felt scared. What's going to happen? How is it going to be? How's everything going to go? Most of all, I trusted that God had everything, but there are times that I felt insecure. Always, I just thought that God could help me because there was nothing else to do other than trust the doctors."

Clinicians commonly characterize this attitude of acceptance of God's plan as fatalism or *fatalismo*, ascribing it to Latinxs as a cultural trait. They tend to assume that Latin American migrants and Latinxs believe that the course of fate cannot be changed, and therefore they exhibit pessimistic beliefs toward illness and treatment. Treating fatalistic attitudes as a cultural characteristic overlooks the fact that institutional racism and social disempowerment inhibit the ability of many Spanish-speaking Latinxs to advocate for themselves or exert control over their medical treatment (Abraído-Lanza et al. 2007; Díaz 1998). Surrender to a divine plan enables acceptance and persistence in circumstances beyond a person's control. In this context, *fatalismo* is a form of imperative resilience.

Studies of Muslims in the Middle East and in the United States similarly demonstrate beliefs in "God as the great decider." Rather than rendering spiritual subjects passive and inert, this belief provides a narrative that enables individuals to understand healthcare challenges like infertility (Inhorn 2012). As such, a "fatalistic" belief in God may buffer an individual against harmful psychosocial conceptions of illness and healthcare that emphasize inherent fault or failure. Jackelín's belief that God "can do anything" increased her confidence in her obstetric care plan and reduced her anxiety.

Strategic Coupling

When I asked Priscila about her housing situation, she responded with a chronicle of her romantic relationships. "Well, . . . so my first husband and I separated. I was with him for three years. But I quickly met another person," she explained. "We were married for almost ten years. He had health problems, cancer. He passed away three years ago. Well, after he passed away, I met someone else, and now we are together. We can say it is a stable relationship, and we live in a house. And with this new partner, I try to be better for him and for my children. Thank God, both he and they accepted each other. And so, we are together—we're better off that way. When my children need something and he can do it, he does it.

"So I think we have thrived together. My children no longer have their father, but they have him [my partner]. And, with the arrival of the new baby, we will all assimilate to this new life."

Priscila framed her current partnership in economic and pragmatic terms. Her partner helps with her children, and the relationship enables her family to live in a house. Sharing caregiver responsibilities has allowed Priscila to keep her job as a restaurant worker.

Priscila also implicitly characterized her current pregnancy as a means of unifying her blended family and asserting the legitimacy of her new romantic relationship. "Although I love this man—the father of this baby— the death of my husband left a void, for my other children, for me," Priscila told me in a dispassionate tone. Although she and her current partner are not legally married, she observed: "I have always had the support of a partner. I've been fortunate to always have people on my side—I've never felt alone. Marriage is learning, it is living together, it is making and undoing, getting angry and becoming content again. This baby just gives us all new hope. So yes, yes, I have my children, I have a job, I have the main pieces in place to save and to *salir adelante*, more than anything, that, to *salir adelante*."

The blending of the family represented by the coming baby advances her goals of gaining financial security, working, and continuing onward. Priscila's assertion that she loves her partner is couched within her aims of preserving and strengthening her system of social and financial support.

Priscila fervently asserted her independence, telling me, "No, I don't depend on him. He doesn't depend on me either. We spend so much, he earns so much, I earn so much, and everything comes together." However, she admitted, "Well, now that I've stopped working [in late pregnancy], maybe yes [I depend on him]." She later added that she did not want her daughter to lean on anyone else and that she modeled this independence by never "stretching out my hand and saying, 'Give me, because I don't have it.'" She saw her relationship with her partner as enabling her own financial security and her own progress toward achieving the American dream.

Other women describe their romantic partnerships as a means of connecting to social networks or with aspects of their home communities and culture. Almudena told me, "In my culture, we children are very attached to our parents. We always depend on them, you know? Here, kids go to university and they're already independent, no longer living with their parents. Back home, I went to university and still relied on my parents. I didn't cook, I didn't know how to do anything, because I would come home from school and my mother already had food for me. She washed my clothes—I didn't do anything for myself. And so, I didn't know my husband before I came here, but I felt this emptiness from not having my family."

At that point, Almudena began sobbing. "He has his whole family here. I saw that everyone walks by his side. And so, I tried to build a friendship with him because he had so much here. While I had to eat alone and warm myself up something to eat or even cook, he had everyone who cooked for him. And so, when he was alone, I would start talking with him. Eventually we started dating and a love was born, and we decided to get together. That's how it happened."

Almudena's husband satisfied her need for community and a sense of companionship that alleviated her isolation as a solitary migrant woman. Almudena became part of her husband's robust social network. When I asked her about her forms of social support, she cheerfully cited her in-laws.

Similarly, Ascención, from Guatemala, described her marriage in terms of familiarity and the potential for logistical support. "He's from my hometown," Ascención said of her husband. "When I met him, he had a car, and he would give me rides as a favor. Sometimes he would drop me off at the hospital or clinic or take me to the Walmart. And he would pick up my child's medicine for me. That's how I got to know him. And so, the year we met, I told him that I wanted to give him . . . that I wanted to have his baby." Ascensión frames her reproductive labor as a remunerative act that sanctions strategic coupling.

Other women describe their relationships as retreats from intimate partner violence or as a means of obtaining legal residence. For Gladys, a relationship did both. "I started working in a company painting houses in Queens, and most of my clients and work colleagues spoke English, especially the owner. So I had to learn English. At the beginning, I tried, but it was so difficult," Gladys told me. "So I had this neighbor, this next-door neighbor, who was from West Virginia and didn't speak any Spanish, and we got along. I would ask him questions like, 'Wait, how do you say this?' And I would just make him repeat it. I learned a lot with him and eventually ended up marrying him."

Daniel, the man Gladys married, was a US citizen. If Gladys applied for a green card, passed an invasive interview about their marital life, and remained married for five years, he could provide her with a pathway toward citizenship. But there was an additional advantage to marrying him. "At the time, I had become pregnant with this stranger from Portugal, but I didn't want anything to do with him. I called my mom, and she told me, 'You can get married, or you can have an abortion.' I didn't want to have an abortion, so I remembered this neighbor, and I called him up—he was living in Texas at the time—and I told him I was pregnant, and I didn't know what to do. [Daniel] had fallen in love with me when we were neighbors. I told him, 'We can pretend or just marry and get divorced or whatever'—I just wanted to get my mother out of my hair. I didn't really love him, but I knew that he loved me. In the back of my mind, I also knew that he could get me a green card. So, I went down to Texas, and we got married."

Unfortunately, their marriage devolved into patterns of violence and abuse, in part because of Daniel's undertreated bipolar disorder. "He used to treat me so badly, so poorly. He used to beat me. It turned out he was a very bad guy. It was like hell—I suffered a lot in that pregnancy. He raped me and he attacked me. I was pregnant, and still he beat me. I was so miserable. So I just left him because I couldn't stand it anymore."

Gladys left for Connecticut and had her baby alone, with no husband and no green card. As she struggled to find her feet, a friend recommended she apply for a green card on the grounds of seeking protection from domestic violence as a self-petitioner under the federal Violence against Women Act. "I connected with these counselors at a place called Safe Connect. They got me a lawyer and helped me apply for my green card. After three years, I got it. And then later I applied for US citizenship."

Alone with a young child and scarred from her history of abuse, Gladys sought refuge in a relationship with a man named Elias. He provided her with financial security and allowed her a reprieve from work to care for her daughter and the child they had as a couple. Elias treated her with deep respect and kindness, a drastic change from her relationship with Daniel. With this newfound stability, Gladys invited her elderly parents to live with her in New Haven. Shortly thereafter, Elias died of a heroin overdose and her father contracted colon cancer. Gladys was left supporting a household of five on her salary as a housekeeper. Then COVID-19 hit, and her work was cut in half. "I could no longer make it. I thought I would have to move my whole family into a one-bedroom apartment."

But then she met Nicolás, who understood her situation and began to help her by picking up and dropping off her kids and supporting her father at his medical appointments. And so, although her pregnancy came as a surprise, and Gladys and Nicolás were not married or living together, they welcomed the news as an opportunity to formalize their arrangement. They agreed that Nicolás would help Gladys with the new baby while her parents cared for the older two. By merging their finances, Gladys felt she no longer had to worry about paying rent and credit card bills or about supporting a third child. "He's going to be with us," Gladys asserted about Nicolás. "He's going to be there for our child, and he's going to be responsible. I feel that I no longer have to worry."

Each of Gladys's three marriages provided her with legal, financial, or social benefit. She married Daniel to avoid stigma from her accidental pregnancy and with the hope of obtaining a green card. She married Elias for financial support and for reprieve from the abuse she endured at Daniel's hands. She partnered with Nicolás to help support her multigenerational family.

Although strategic coupling may help women fulfill their aims, it may also render them vulnerable to gendered power imbalances. Pregnancy, emotional fragility following trauma, economic dependence, and "liminal legality" contingent on marital status may place women in precarious situations that can exacerbate tendencies toward intimate partner violence. Several of my interlocutors relied on their husbands for legal residence, and more than half depended on their partners for income. These imbalances enable abusive partners to control and manipulate migrant women. Whereas Gladys benefited from an informal network that connected her with domestic violence support, most women face cultural and linguistic barriers to accessing services. Through tactics of financial control and restriction of movement and isolation, abusive partners may further prevent women from acquiring help they need (Mendenhall 2012). Finally, lack of trust in authorities may prevent undocumented women from seeking support. These factors contribute to high rates of intimate partner violence against migrant women (Holtmann and Rickards 2018; Raj and Silverman 2002; Kyriakakis 2014).

Intergenerational Fortitude

"My mother was always a hard worker," says Susana, a thirty-one-year-old woman from Ecuador. "She's been working so hard, raising my brother and sister. And she raised me. I think the way she thinks made me think the same way, you know, focusing on studying, working hard, and keeping after the things that I want. She inspires me."

Susana hopes to emulate her mother's devotion to her: "This little thing [my baby girl] will be ... my engine. My family will always be my inspiration, what pushes me forward. If I'm doing well, she will be well. If she's good, I'm good. It's a very tight connection." Likewise, Susana hopes to inspire her daughter: "I want the best for her. I want her to be better than me. I want her to grow, to learn, to learn a lot of things—good things. I want to give her every blessing."

Rather than considering the ways their mothers' adversities affected them—or the potential for their own traumas to influence their children— the women in this study more often focused on instances in which they or their mothers modeled positive behaviors for their offspring. Many women described intimate relationships with their mothers that informed their goals, decisions, and approach to parenting. "My mom is my best friend," said Elvira, a thirty-year-old woman from the Dominican Republic. "I am very attached to her. It's been difficult because I don't have the chance to visit her often, nor can she come here..." Elvira trailed off. "There are days when I wake up and I just want to cry, wishing my mother was here, but in the middle of all this [immigration challenges and the pandemic], it is so difficult.

"But my mother believes in me. She always believed in herself, and she helps me find my own strength. She knows that I, we, are strong and we endure. Like her, I have been through a lot of things, too, and I have overcome them on my own. My mother always tells me that sooner or later, I will get out of any difficult situation, that everything will get better soon. This has always shaped my mind. I always try to stay positive. And so, I don't only think about my future, I think about my mom and how I can help her. And I think about my Prince Charming." This was Elvira's nickname for her baby boy, Jacob. "The first thing I did when Jacob came out of my womb was call my mother," Elvira said. "I told her, ' Mami, if at any time I have failed you, I apologize. Because now that I am a mother, I know what we go through—the pain, the struggle.'

"At first, I asked myself, Am I really going to be a good mother to Jacob? I don't know how to explain it, but I just saw this perfect boy and said, Wow, is that really my son? I had always loved children and taken care of babies, but this felt different. I just wanted everything to be perfect."

Every day over the phone, Elvira's mother reassured her that she was the perfect mother for her son. "I love her so much more than I ever could, I value her so much more. She told me that the truth was that I was already a mother, that I already knew my baby. And gradually I saw that she was right. I got used to taking care of him, to see him, to know his needs. Little by little, I got used to it. Now I really know him, all his tricks!"

Elvira's mother instilled in her a strong sense of self-worth and modeled unconditional love, which Elvira internalized and shared with her baby. Such attitudes, coping strategies, and adaptive capacities shared across generations have been described as "intergenerational resilience" (Atallah 2017; Schofield, Conger, and Neppl 2014; Denov et al. 2019). Given the limitations I have identified in the resilience concept, I prefer to consider this process as *intergenerational fortitude*, invoking bravery and an orientation toward the future. Just as mothers in this study recognized the strength they gained from their mothers and grandmothers, they acknowledged their potential to bestow strength on their own children. Almudena said, "I believe the mother's mental health is passed on to her son or daughter. Because this way, the mother who is always happy—or courageous—well, the girl or boy will be like that."

When I asked my interlocutors whether they believed their health or mental health could affect their children, my mind was fixed on the potential for trauma to adversely affect fetal development or developmental programming. Most women surprised me by emphasizing the positive aspects. Juana explained, "I believe that everything is transmitted. If I'm weak, she [my daughter] won't have the tools, she won't have someone to give her strength. I must be strong for her to give her strength. And she will be strong. Why? Because her mother is."

Juana explained her belief in intergenerational fortitude: "My grandmother—my mother's mother—was always a very good person. She taught us to work, she was kind to other people. When my mother had to go out to work, my grandmother would watch us." Juana paused, her tone changing. "But she fell ill, and my aunts and uncles treated her very badly. And we children saw how my uncles treated their own mother, and it upset us. No, we had to be different from them, to be the best children, and to treat her better. My grandmother instilled in us that lesson: Not to be like everyone else, but to be different, kinder. And that's why I think we are like that.

"[My siblings and I] now try to take care of my mother so that she'll live longer. If she needs any medicine, whatever she needs, we children lend a hand and divide up her expenses so that she doesn't have to worry.

And so my grandmother and my mother affected me in a good way. I'm going to teach [my daughter] how much I learned from those two: to work, to study, to focus. Not to demand things from her but to give her the confidence so that, whether good or bad things happen to her, she does not dwell on them. I will listen to her, respect her—all the good things I got from my mom and grandmother."

FROM RESILIENCE TO RESISTANCE

What would happen if women could not engage imperative resilience to cope, to survive, and to press onward? According to my research assistant, they would "die" or "drop out." From a clinical or public health perspective, they might not seek prenatal care and therefore simply would not be captured by this research. They might experience such profound physical and psychological distress—or endure such punishing violence—that they could not hold down a job or care for themselves. They might have their children taken from their homes or find themselves shackled to a hospital bed or in a prison cell. Some of these women came close. Marisol told me of the time in her pregnancy when her partner left her, her house burned down, and her car broke down. She became deeply depressed.

"It was a very strong blow. It is not easy—your house burns down and the one you love leaves you like that, right when you need him the most—I fell into a depression." Marisol said she spent says without eating or sleeping, crying constantly. "When I got pregnant, I weighed 158 pounds. Four months in, I weighed just 150 pounds." Marisol added that she became overwhelmed by tasks like managing finances and caring for her children.

Had events taken a different turn, Marisol could have landed in a psychiatric hospital. Had the Department of Children and Families caught wind of her inability to care for herself and her difficulties in supporting her older two children, they could have initiated a temporary custody order and removed her children, enacting what Dorothy Roberts describes as a form of racialized violence (D. Roberts 2002). Instead, Marisol turned to spirituality to help her cope with her traumatic experiences. She began a routine of praying at dawn and listening to Christian music and motivational podcasts in moments of distress. Through their performance of imperative resilience, which enables them to envision and invest in their children's futures, the women in my study were able to resist the structural obstacles in their paths. With practices of strategic coupling, spirituality, and intergenerational fortitude, they nurture themselves, their families, and their communities. The historian Manning Marable and the anthropologist Leith Mullings note how Black descendants of the enslaved have likewise resisted and rebelled against structural oppression, "renewed" their communities by "imagining and enacting their continuity," and "created and maintained cultural forms" (2009). Pressing onward—past trauma, racism, poverty, legal violence, and healthcare discrimination—to build a future for their children transforms imperative resilience from individual coping into political defiance. To echo a slogan used in Indigenous, Palestinian, trans, and neurodiverse communities, "Existence is resistance."

In her analysis of monarch migrations, the anthropologist Columba González-Duarte pays special attention to the Methuselah butterfly, named for the Biblical figure who lived for 969 years, which can expand its lifespan from four weeks to nine months to migrate not only to Mexico but also back to Texas to lay its eggs. González-Duarte writes, "The capacity of this butterfly to survive difficulties and overcome physical barriers such as mountains, lakes, highways, predators, and a lack of healthy habitat across three countries, prompt human appreciations of this butterfly as a warrior or a heroine: a butterfly with superpowers" (2018). Rather than emphasizing its intrinsic strength, González-Duarte sees the insect as actively resisting the environmental and economic disruption of large agricultural businesses and trade agreements. The Methuselah butterfly's faded and abraded wings symbolize the continuance of the species and ongoing resistance to oppressive structures.

CONCLUSION

In their experiences of reproductive healthcare, Latin American migrant women face racialization and bureaucratic disentitlement. Célia's traumatic birth highlighted her treatment as an undeserving, poor, "obstetrically hardy" Latina woman, despite the particularities of her medical history. The scaling back of the Me and My Baby program reflects racialized attitudes about who deserves healthcare. Barriers to enrollment deprive other women of their right to care. Prioritization of the fetus over the mother's health and the "disembodiment" of the uterus treat women as obstetric vessels rather than whole people.

Women resist these adversities through the psychological and social coping strategies of imperative resilience. Using techniques of cognitive avoidance and goal setting, women focus their attention on their future and the future of their children, effectively tuning out their day-to-day struggles. Some women find strength and acceptance through spiritual practices. By selecting male partners who can provide financial, logistical, and legal support, women advance their personal and familial goals, including working outside the home and supporting their children's social and academic formation. Channeling the morals and encouragement of their own mothers and grandmothers, these migrant mothers parent their children with empathy and vision for their future. Together, the practices of imperative resilience enable women to *seguir adelante*, or press onward.

My concept of imperative resilience is intended to address the limitations of current theories of resilience. Imperative resilience is more than "grit" or "toughness," or a feature of a particular culture. Just as the medical anthropologist Nancy Scheper-Hughes understands illness as an expression of the "subversive body," we can consider tactics of avoidance, repression, and problem-solving as refusals to conform to rigidly oppositional social systems. The mind, like the body, can express suppressed feelings of oppression, frustration, and rage in settings of rampant inequality where such sentiments are disallowed (Scheper-Hughes 1994, 233). In institutions that systematically disempower poor, Brown, migrant women—such as healthcare and the justice system—imperative resilience enables women to focus on their goals and the futures of their children.

In the United States, migrant women confront sexism, racism, xenophobia, and economic disadvantage using cognitive survival techniques that psychologists might consider "negative" or "maladaptive." In its focus on the individual, however, this framing fails to consider such approaches as a form of rebellion against violent social and political systems. Imperative resilience enables migrant women to press onward against these forces and to enact political resistance by imagining the future of themselves, their children, and their community.

5 Surviving

When COVID-19 shook the United States in the spring of 2020, reports quickly emerged of its disproportionate impacts on communities of color and other marginalized groups. Headlines like the ones below filled the pages of media outlets for months.

> Growing Data Show Black and Latino Americans Bear the Brunt of COVID-19 (NPR, March 30, 2020)

> How COVID-19 Is Affecting Black and Latino Families' Employment and Financial Well-Being (Urban Institute, May 6, 2020)

> Covid-19 is Sending Black, Latino and Native American People to the Hospital at about 4 Times the Rate of Others (CNN, November 16, 2020)

Immediately, studies emerged emphasizing the potential genetic susceptibility of members of certain racial groups to infection with the SARS-CoV-2 virus, the causative agent of COVID-19. Particularly egregious reports attributed the emergence of SARS-CoV-2 in Asia to "an extremely large number" of cells expressing angiotensin-converting enzyme 2 in "Asian" lungs and higher infection and death rates in Black individuals to "racial/ethnic variation" in the expression of transmembrane serine protease 2 in nasal and bronchial epithelium (Zhao et al. 2020; Bunyavanich, Do, and Vicencio 2020).

As the medical anthropologist Clarence C. Gravlee argues in a *Scientific American* blog post, higher rates of COVID-19 among Black Americans were due to racism, not genetics (Gravlee 2020a). Gravlee dismisses claims that genetic or biological factors explain racial disparities in the incidence of COVID-19, instead noting that structural racism contributed to different risks of exposure and different presentations of the disease among racialized groups. The confluence of biological and structural factors that influence the prevalence and severity of disease brewed a "syndemic," or a synergy among epidemics (Gravlee 2020). This analysis is particularly applicable to Latin American migrant women, particularly those who are undocumented.

Women like those in my study have been particularly vulnerable to the effects of COVID-19. At the height of the pandemic, many who held low-wage "essential" jobs were unable to work from home and were at risk of exposure to the virus in the workplace (Stolberg 2020). Several lost their jobs but were barred from collecting unemployment relief or the stimulus payments offered through the Coronavirus Aid, Relief, and Economic Security (CARES) Act. As a result, they were compelled to engage in precarious work arrangements (Page et al. 2020). Many lacked the financial resources to stock up on food and household supplies, requiring more frequent trips to stores, which also increased their risk of exposure (Jay et al. 2020). For economic and cultural reasons, many undocumented families live in larger, multigenerational households. Older adults were thus at risk of contracting the disease from younger family members working and attending school outside the home (Clark et al. 2020). Immigration enforcement itself, through disease transmission by ICE agents, in crowded detention centers, and deportation of migrants infected with COVID-19, also posed enormous public health hazards (Erfani et al. 2020).

In addition, given lack of healthcare access, undocumented migrants may be less likely to receive prompt evaluation of symptoms of COVID-19 (or any other disease). Though testing for COVID-19 is free in most settings, evaluation and treatment often are not, and costs may deter low-income undocumented migrants from seeking necessary care and increase their risk of mortality (Chua and Conti 2020).

COVID-19 has also taken a high emotional toll on migrant communities. The illness and death of community members, and loved ones in
home countries, impose a burden of grief that is difficult to quantify.

COVID-19 has disproportionately constrained mobility and social interaction, exacerbated economic precarity and psychosocial stress, and
afflicted the bodies of Latin American migrant women and their loved
ones. I discuss how women make sense of racial and ethnic disparities
in COVID-19, such as by advancing racial-essentialist notions of disease
and identifying the structural factors—including legal, employment, and
housing arrangements—that these women confront daily. Examining
claims of "vaccine hesitancy" among Black and Brown communities, I
review women's attitudes and barriers to accessing COVID-19 vaccinations. Finally, I explore policy solutions to the multiple structural barriers
that constrain migrant women's life prospects both during and beyond the
pandemic.

EMBODIED EXPERIENCES OF COVID-19

"I used to work at Amazon, scanning products," says Antoinetta, a twenty-
three-year-old from the Dominican Republic. "I liked the work, but it was
so long... eleven or twelve hours at a time. But I had to quit my job when
I caught the coronavirus there. I got it there and I haven't gone back, I'm
too afraid. Especially now that I'm pregnant, I worry something will happen to me again."

Antoinetta contracted COVID-19 in May 2020 at an Amazon distribution warehouse in North Haven, Connecticut. Just one month later, alle-
gations of the company's disregard for employee safety exploded throughout the news media. Warehouse workers criticized Amazon for failure
to implement physical-distancing protocols, noting that the wearable
devices used to signal proximity of less than six feet to other employees
were useless because it was impossible for workers to keep six feet apart.
Some employees showed up to work despite COVID-19 concerns or symptoms out of fear of losing their jobs. Many workers stated that they did
not receive enough time to properly wash their hands and disinfect work-
stations, and they attested to delays—or nonpayment—of compensation

for quarantine or isolation following exposure or a confirmed infection (BBC News 2020). Particularly leading up to Prime Day in July, a large promotional sale that drastically increases the workload of warehouse workers, employees stated that relentless hassling over productivity and unforgiving performance quotas forced them to prioritize the company's profits over their own health. Under pressure from the attorneys general of thirteen states, Amazon reported in October 2020 that its COVID-19 infection rate was 42 percent below what would be expected, based on national averages. However, multiple US senators lambasted these claims, arguing that the incompleteness of data for the Amazon workforce, trends in infection rates, rates at specific facilities, and mortality undermined the company's assertions. These senators continued to raise concerns regarding worker endangerment (Brown 2020).

Antoinetta's experiences at Amazon led to her withdrawal from the workforce after she contracted COVID-19.

ANTOINETTA: It was like a week, no, two weeks, I should say. My whole body ached. I couldn't even get out of bed. I had no sense of taste, no sense of smell. I couldn't eat much. Sometimes I felt like I couldn't breathe.

JES: Did you ever go to the hospital?

ANTOINETTA: No, I never went to the hospital, I only went to get tested. I don't know. I was scared. I just went out to get tested and went home. They called me after two days to tell me I had tested positive and to stay at home. If it got really bad, they said I could go to the emergency room, or I could call and they would send an ambulance for me, but I was really scared.

Antoinetta's fears were twofold. First, she feared that if she had to be admitted to the hospital, her condition would worsen. Her cousin in the Dominican Republic, just forty years old, had died in a hospital that had exceeded its capacity. "They did what they could," she told me. "But everything had collapsed because so many people had the coronavirus, and my cousin just died." Antoinetta feared a similar fate. Second, she worried that hospitalization would incur insurmountable debt. Although she had medical coverage through HUSKY (state Medicaid) after acquiring US residency through her citizen husband, Antoinetta had been scarred by the costs of treatment when dizzy spells from dehydration and overwork at Amazon had landed her in the emergency room. "I got a big bill at Yale," she tells me. "It's still there. I have to agree to pay it little by little. It just added up."

Ten of the women in my study had been infected with COVID-19. Of those, half contracted the virus while pregnant. Cintia, a thirty-six-year-old Dominican woman, realized she had COVID-19 on Thanksgiving in 2020, when she was four months pregnant. "At first, I just felt tired and uncomfortable, and I had a headache, and that was it. I thought it was just the pregnancy," Cintia told me. "But then my little boy [my son] took the test, and he came out positive. I initially tested negative, but then as my son was getting better, I got sick. I tried to stay calm, but one day I felt awful. I was short of breath, and I worried about the baby. I figured, if I'm short of breath, she'll be short of breath. So, I called the doctor, and they just told me to wait it out. Eventually everything was okay."

Still, Cintia worried about her daughter's future. "I'm scared because she will be such a defenseless creature, and she could get infected with [COVID-19]. It worries me a lot. Also, the fact that we cannot have our freedom, that we must be so worried about our health."

In response to pandemic conditions—and their own infections and pregnancies—both Antoinetta and Cintia avoided going out. "I just stay here in the house, making sure that nothing happens to the baby or my son or me again," Antoinetta said. "It hit me hard, because when that happened to me—the coronavirus—I didn't know whether or not things would get better. So we rarely go out. My husband is the one working, but he comes into the house and immediately bathes, disinfects himself. I don't let many visitors come."

"I avoid going out unnecessarily," Cintia told me. "I don't go to crowded places. I always wear a mask, although now it's getting a bit difficult for me [with the pregnancy]. . . . I feel that I get a little more short of breath the more I walk with the mask. I try not to be afraid of the virus, but I respect it. I respect it and I give it its space, and I do what I have to do so as not to contract it again."

Staying at home and avoiding contact with others was the most common precaution undertaken by women in this study, with more than ⅔ of interlocutors doing so even in the absence of local stay-at-home orders. However, staying home often exacerbated the social isolation and economic concerns many women already endured as undocumented migrants and Spanish speakers. Thirty-eight percent of women in my study either left the workforce or chose not to return for fear of contracting COVID-19 while pregnant. This left many at home alone during the day, compounding their dependence on partners and their financial strain.

I was surprised how seriously Jackelín took infection precautions. She told me, "At first, before we were in the thick of it, just hearing about COVID-19 hit me, scared me. It was like a trauma. I didn't ever want to leave the house. Suddenly, I was afraid of what would happen if I got sick—my children so young, me pregnant. That's why for three months, I didn't go out at all. Being at home, I felt safer. We kept hearing from our neighbors about people losing someone close or about pregnant women dying. Now we don't see anyone. It feels normal. Even if we don't like it, it is necessary."

ILLNESS AND DEATH OF LOVED ONES

"We lost a bunch of residents," Nikki, a hospice and home health aide said, her tone somber. "In the assisted living part of the facility, they lost thirty-six residents. I lost seven of my home-care patients. I think that's been the hardest one for me. I'd been going to one client for almost two years, she was ninety-three. And, I mean, the moment I walked through the door, you know, you could just tell right up when they see you coming that they can't wait to talk to you. . . . They look forward to you coming. But then she got sick. And I was so scared. And even though she was dying, she was still able to talk, and she told me, 'It's okay. When I'm dead, I won't know what it's like to be alive.'"

"I was used to seeing people dying," Nikki went on. "There was this one client I went to where we would just talk and watch the news. Hospice. And, you know, very gradually he just died. But now there's too much death that's happening so rapidly. It was a lot of deaths. And so even though I was happy about the money I was making, I couldn't handle the guilt of the loss of life. It wasn't worth it."

Nikki had cut her hours dramatically in the first few months of the pandemic to protect her mental health, reduce her exposure to the virus, and assist her son with remote schooling. Even though she continues to work in hospice and elderly care, Nikki has been scarred from the loss of life she witnessed.

For other women, the loss was more personal. Several related the passing of uncles, cousins, brothers, friends, in-laws, and grandparents who succumbed to the virus. Living in a high-risk area—the metropolitan region surrounding New York City, the original epicenter of the virus in the United States—and worries about hard-hit relatives and friends in medically underresourced home countries took a profound toll on these women. Cintia and Célia both described it as "traumatic."

Experiences of loss and grief or fear as a result of the close proximity of COVID-19 infection were nearly universal among the women in my study. Just two did not know anyone who had contracted the virus. Scholars at Harvard University found that years of potential life lost to the pandemic were 6.7 times higher among Black people and 5.4 times higher among Latinx Americans than among White people (Bassett, Chen, and Krieger 2020). A calculation of the "bereavement multiplier" suggests that for every COVID-19 death, approximately nine surviving Americans lose a grandparent, parent, sibling, spouse, or child (Verdery et al. 2020). This signals a dramatic psychological and emotional impact, particularly among communities of color.

Fears of contracting COVID-19 deterred women from seeking medical care, including prenatal care. Jackelín told me that she did not attend her first prenatal appointment until she was almost eight months pregnant. "I was afraid to go to the appointments," she said. "I thought if I go, I could get [the coronavirus], or they would keep giving me more appointments and I could get it then. I think I waited almost until I was eight months."

Other women expressed similar fears. Juana worried about going to the hospital for prenatal visits and to give birth because "no one knows how many people enter the hospital, many people come in, and maybe they leave behind some of the virus." Adelina, a twenty-one-year-old from Puerto Rico, believed that the disease was a government plot. "When it first started, I believed the coronavirus was like, that they [the government was] trying to make the population smaller. I have a feeling like they was just killing people. Like with a vaccine or something." I spoke with Adelina over Zoom. She issued these comments matter-of-factly while chopping an onion for dinner. When she finished, Adelina moved her phone to her bedroom, where she lay on her bed, clutching a pillow. "We have all these debts, and people in the population just keep growing and growing, and they just . . . they have no control over the world. So, I feel like this is a way of them trying to control the world, taking people away because they know more people is coming into the world."

Adelina wiped her nose with the back of her hand. She had told me she was getting over a cold. "I've seen a lot of videos of things where they was saying on Facebook, like, they work for the hospitals and they were like, 'No, let people die,' and then say that it's just 'cause of the coronavirus and when somebody need help, they would do a procedure wrong or something, and they just blame it on the COVID. . . . Maybe like whenever they get their blood drawn or get like a vaccine. But like, you know, how they put things in your IV, some type of liquids or something, 'cause there's a lot of cases that people went into the hospital and then some of them was being positive [afterward]. And there was just a lot of like, nurses and stuff, that was saying that, like, they killing people."

Adelina told me that she planned not to accept any intravenous medications or an epidural for pain relief during her labor out of fear they could infect her with COVID-19. Her belief in COVID-19 as a government conspiracy echoed common myths that circulated about the virus early in the pandemic: that COVID-19 was a biological weapon or part of a plot to control the population, that a "deep state" manipulated the pandemic, and that COVID-19 death rates are inflated (Lynas 2020). Adelina's understanding of the pandemic echoes long-held attitudes of distrust toward government and healthcare systems, particularly among Black people. Its effects on her were, however, similar to the experiences of her peers who fully believed in the virus. Adelina lost work, isolated herself at home, and minimized interaction with the healthcare system because of the virus.

SOCIAL IMPACTS

In February 2020, shortly before the COVID-19 pandemic hit the United States, the US economy and labor market were enjoying a boom. Unemployment stood at 3.5 percent, the lowest rate since December 1969. By April 2020, however, unemployment had spiked to 14.7 percent (though it had dropped to 6.7 percent by November). COVID-19 affected the labor market in multiple ways. First, consumer and business activities voluntarily decreased—particularly those that involved high levels of contact with other individuals, such as restaurant work and retail shopping—because of fear of infection. Second, government-imposed public health measures, including lockdowns, stay-at-home orders, and requirements for physical distancing, shut down broad sectors of the economy deemed "nonessential," like hair salons. Given existing disparities in employment and wealth, scholars warned that women and racialized minorities were likely to be harder hit by the economic effects of the pandemic, because their typically lower wages, unpredictable and unstable work arrangements, and greater representation in high-contact fields would reduce their potential to absorb and recover from the large-scale economic shock (B. Hardy and Logan 2020; S. Y. Lee, Park, and Shin 2021).

Latinxs experienced the most severe losses of employment: among Latinxs who were previously working, unemployment rose by 15.1 percentage points, a greater spike than for any other racial or ethnic group (S. Y. Lee, Park, and Shin 2021). Latina women were the most likely to be unemployed during COVID-19, followed by Black women, who were also more likely to be unemployed than White women (Gezici and Ozay 2020). Controlling for all other factors, downturns in employment most severely affected women, Latinxs and Asians, those with lower educational attainment, and younger workers.

My interlocutors mostly worked in housekeeping, caregiving (e.g., childcare and eldercare), and food service, all high-contact industries with elevated risk of exposure to the virus. Their partners often worked in construction, landscaping, agriculture, manufacturing, and custodial or janitorial jobs, work often designated as essential during lockdowns and characterized by instability, unpredictability, low wages (see table A.3).

The economic toll of COVID-19 also has psychological and emotional effects. More than half of the women I interviewed cited financial concerns related to the pandemic as a major source of stress. Comments along the lines of "I'm worried about losing my job," "I'm worried that my husband won't be able to bring enough money home," and "I'm so stressed about not being able to work and being stuck at home all day" were repeated throughout the interviews. The patterns of anxiety changed over the duration of my study, with women shifting from expressing no pandemic concerns in the era before March 2020 to voicing extreme anxiety in the fall and winter of 2020 and optimism in the spring of 2021.

Racial Inequities in COVID-19 Attribution

In August of 2020, the *Washington Post* reported that Latina mothers accounted for nearly half of the cases of COVID-19 among pregnant women in the United States (Schmidt and Tan 2020). That statistic shocked me, but when a colleague shared the article, I thought that it might catalyze conversation regarding the disproportionate impact of COVID-19 on Latina women. Asking about my interlocutors' reaction to this statistic became a standard question in my semistructured interview schedule and prompted a bimodal pattern of response. Though many women understood the disparity to result from structural factors like racism, lack of health insurance, and disproportionate involvement in high-risk, essential work, even more considered it to be due to genetics, nutritional deficiencies, and individual irresponsibility.

Jackelín told me, "Yes, I've heard in the news that more Latinas get the disease. In the beginning, I would hear from people that So-and-so had gotten it. But the people around me were all fine. And so, we thought it was a conspiracy or something they had invented, because everyone around me, the people I knew in the town, everyone was fine. We only ever heard of random people who had gotten it, not neighbors or acquaintances. And so, we did not believe.

"Later, we started hearing of more people who had it, and so we began to take more serious measures, to avoid going out a lot. But I have neighbors, acquaintances, friends who continue to have their parties. My neighbors next door, they just party, they don't wear masks, they just play their . . . I don't know what it's called, some kind of board game, every weekend and they're not scared, they think they won't get sick. My husband says they think the beer protects them."

Jackelín, like Adelina, believed that the pandemic had been "invented" as a form of population control. Popular media reports of adherence to conspiracy beliefs emphasized education, individual judgment, and choice of news media as factors contributing to the uptake of misinformation. However, anthropological interpretations of health beliefs can provide more insights into their underpinnings and situate them in paradigms of rationality and empiricism. Interpretations of health beliefs as irrational reflect hierarchies of knowledge imposed by European thinkers. As Byron Good has noted, when an idea put forth by a White person (often a man) is thought to characterize objective reality, it is termed "knowledge"; when an idea describes something false or "cultural," it is considered a "belief" (Good 2010, 67, 71, 73). Categories of knowledge emerge through social and political organizations (Good 2010; Haraway 1988).

Closer examination of Adelina and Jackelín's narratives reveals a rationale for their beliefs. Adelina heard about nurses who intentionally killed hospital patients, or left them to die, blaming COVID-19. Jackelín initially did not know of any personal contacts who had been infected with the virus, so she had no direct evidence for its existence. These observations supported their hypotheses of conspiracy. Furthermore, long-standing trends of racial capitalism have dynamically transformed how racialized individuals express, understand, and remember their everyday experiences (St. Jean and Feagin 2015). Processes of medicalization and biopolitical governance of the body shape interpretations of public health crises as tools of population control (Biehl, Good, and Kleinman 2007).

Jackelín's emphasis on individual behavior as a driver of disease also reflects ideas expressed in neoliberal discourses of health. Claims that Latinas suffered high rates of COVID-19 morbidity and mortality were attributed to various behavioral failings: my interlocutors made statements such as "We don't take care of ourselves," "We go out too much," "We have lots of parties," "We don't take things seriously," "We ignore what we are told to do," "We have little discipline and don't like rules," "We're stubborn," "We think everything is a matter of politics," or "We don't measure the consequences." Such assertions reflect intersubjective knowledge and also uphold structural oppression, exculpating policymakers from addressing social stratifications that sustain health inequity.

Many women understood the high COVID-19 rate among Latinas to be a consequence of inadequate nutrition. For instance, Maribel, a thirty-three-year-old from Ecuador. told me, "I think it's because of nutrition.

Maybe we're low on vitamins. It's very necessary for the body so that we don't have low defenses. I always know how to take vitamins. Whether it's for the cold or for allergies in the summer, I always take vitamins." Alejandra, a thirty-four-year-old from Tlaxcala, Mexico, commented: "I think it's because of our bodies. We don't have enough of...how do you say it? We're kind of weak. We maybe lack healthy food. We don't take care of ourselves."

Many of my interlocutors emphasized the importance of proper nutrition and a balanced diet. They described preparing nutrient-dense, plant-based meals rich in fruits, vegetables, pulses and legumes, whole grains and starches, with lower amounts of meats and dairy products. The medical anthropologist Anna Waldstein, in her study of Mexican migrants living in Athens, Georgia, found that they stressed the importance of nutritional balance, supporting diets abundant in "vegetables, fruits, plenty of water and perhaps some vitamin supplements "(Waldstein 2017, 112). Similarly, Alyshia Gálvez noted that pregnant Mexican women living in New York City were attentive to eating well and exercising (Gálvez 2011, 58). The women in these studies, like my interlocutors, held themselves accountable for their health, avoiding highly processed foods and excessive quantities of fats or meats and supplementing their diets with vitamins, herbs, and spices. In addition to their prenatal vitamins, women also took multivitamins, iron supplements, vitamin C, proteins, and herbal teas like *hierbabuena* (mint). Understandably, these women believe that nutritional imbalance renders people susceptible to infection.

Another explanation attributed a "predisposition" to developing COVID-19 to genetics or intrinsic features of Latina biology. Meliza, a forty-year-old from Mexico, said, "I think it depends on our race...maybe our food, or sometimes because people don't take the situation very seriously. I think, unfortunately, sometimes we Latinos don't believe. Some only began to believe when they saw many deaths of people they knew, sometimes their parents, their own families. But to this day, many people go out and walk out without a mask. I think it also depends on your immune system or your blood type, I don't know. There are many, many question marks as well, but they say that they also see that, scientifically, it depends on your DNA."

This framing echoes biologized notions of race that are widespread in biomedicine. Authoritative regimes of biomedicine combine both "rational" and "irrational" elements. Racial essentialism, or the assumption that racial groups are delineated by innate, genetic differences, stands among the "irrational" elements, exposing the ideas and prejudices of European colonization and Enlightenment ideals at the root of modern medicine (Tsai et al. 2020). Race-based medical practices, including racialized screening tools, treatment algorithms, and framings of pathology, promote ideas that Latinas are biologically different from women of other races, and these beliefs may then be internalized by patients. For instance, many of my interlocutors with histories of births by C-section—a common experience, as Latin American and Caribbean countries have the highest C-section rates in the world (Magne et al. 2017)—were told by their providers that they could not plan a vaginal birth for their current pregnancy. This warning likely emerges from the race-based clinical calculator for risk of vaginal birth after C-section (VBAC). The VBAC calculator takes into account health data like age, body mass index, and prior obstetric history. It also initially included two correction factors for "African American" and "Hispanic" race that reduced estimates for successful VBAC by 67 to 68 percent (Vyas et al. 2019). These factors were only removed from the calculator, under intense pressure from scholars and activists, in May 2021.

Unsurprisingly, given personal experience and media narratives, some women attributed COVID-19 disparities to racism. Meri, a twenty-six-year-old from Ecuador, reasoned, "It might be because of the fact that most Latina women are working in things like cleaning, in jobs that expose them to more people. But apart from that, it could be because of racism. You can get infected or even poisoned with all the fluids that are used for cleaning. Most of the time, when you want to look at it through the lens of racism, you see that most of us are more exposed to infection because we live in large groups, and we have to get out to work." Meri's observations identify inequities in employment and wealth accumulation.

Several women expressed keen awareness of the structural factors that rendered them more vulnerable to COVID-19 infection and death. Nikki said, "I think women like us, you know, we put on our makeup, we're very hardworking. For example, I'm pregnant, and I'm still working in that [healthcare] field. So sometimes, you know, we don't have the ability to say, 'Oh, I don't want to work, or 'I can just work from home.'" She sighed.

"Some of us don't have that choice. And we're definitely on the front lines." Célia also pointed out the exposure risk from the work many Latino men undertake. She said, "I think it is because . . . that their husbands work in essential jobs. Farms. Cleaning. Construction. All those things. There's more risk." Elvira, from the Dominican Republic, added that "especially for those of us who do not have residence, we do not receive help from the government," and so "we must go out and expose ourselves, be at risk."

All these interpretations—behavioral, nutritional, genetic, and structural—reflect women's lived realities and experiences, their subjective knowledge. In addition to facing greater disease exposure risk from being low-wage essential workers, or having partners who were, many of undocumented or liminally legal women derived no benefit from government measures designed to mitigate the financial effects of the pandemic, like economic stimulus checks or unemployment assistance.

How these inequities exacerbated the effects of the pandemic for Latina migrant women is evident from comparing my personal experience with that of one of my interlocutors. In November 2020, my husband, in-laws, year-old toddler, and I contracted COVID-19 after my father-in-law attended an in-person business meeting (on census outreach to undercounted Latinx neighborhoods) and brought the virus home. My husband required emergency room attention when his fever spiked and pockets of fluid accumulated in his lungs, and I needed antibiotics after developing a secondary bacterial infection that caused pneumonia. We were out of commission for two weeks. Fortunately, my husband, my father-in-law, and I could use sick leave and then transition to working from home, and my mother-in-law was not working. We suffered no loss of income. Our family and friends organized a meal train so that when we were all feverish, coughing, and buried under blankets, we did not have to worry about making dinner. Our healthcare access afforded quick testing and contact tracing and frequent follow-up on our health status. Our healthcare provider called both my husband and me regularly to check on our symptoms and remind us about remaining in isolation. We were insulated against the disruptions of the illness by multiple layers of social and institutional support.

Contrast this with the experience of Elvira, who moved to the United States from the Dominican Republic on the advice of a friend who had opened a hair salon. Aside from this friend, Elvira had no close contacts in

Connecticut. When she contracted the virus at the start of the pandemic, she immediately had to stop work at the hair salon; shortly thereafter, the state forced the closure of hair salons and other nonessential, high-contact businesses. Elvira's friend's business did not survive the shutdown, and Elvira lost her job. Living alone, Elvira had no one to care for her during her illness. She was also pregnant at the time, fearful of how her infection might harm her developing baby, and unable to access healthcare because of her undocumented status. Then Elvira's mother in the Dominican Republic lost her job and was struggling to support herself and Elvira's brother, thirteen years old. Elvira not only lacked money to attend to her own needs but also worried about how to provide for her mother and brother. Despite the risks, she began going to clients' homes to give manicures and pedicures.

"You have to go out, even if you don't want to," she told me. "You have to push your fear aside and go out to work, even if you expose yourself."

In this country, both Elvira and I can be racialized as Latina (even though she considers herself White). Yet our risk environments are shaped by differential access to social, financial, and cultural capital. Whereas my family and I could safely isolate without concern about lost income, healthcare access, or meal preparation, Elvira felt there was no one—not friends, family, or the state—who was concerned with her welfare. She suffered economically and emotionally, struggling to meet her expenses, worrying about her pregnancy, and ultimately putting herself and others at risk by returning to work in close contact with others.

These divergent experiences suggest that it was not "race"—or DNA, or biology—that determined our experience of the pandemic; rather, it was our respective positions within societal structures, or structural vulnerability. Although assigning risk based on race aligns with human impulses to categorize our surroundings quickly and concretely, public health realities arise from more complex interactions.

ATTITUDES TOWARD VACCINATION

In the late fall of 2020 and spring of 2021, conversations regarding the COVID-19 pandemic began to center on the supply and uptake of vaccines. In January 2021, President Joseph R. Biden announced the goal of administering one hundred million shots in his first hundred days of office, a goal that was met in just fifty-eight days (Soucheray 2021; White House 2021).

Attention soon turned to individuals who intended to refuse the vaccine. A January 2021 report by the Kaiser Family Foundation (KFF) found that 43 percent of Black people and 37 percent of Latinx people were likely to "wait and see" how the vaccine was working before pursuing it for themselves, compared with 26 percent of White people (Hamel et al. 2021). A follow-up report in August 2021 found that Black and Latinx American populations had received fewer COVID-19 vaccinations relative to their shares of the total population in most states. For instance, in California, 30 percent of vaccinations reached Latinx people, even though they accounted for 63 percent of cases, 48 percent of deaths, and 40 percent of the population of the state (Ndugga, Hill, and Artiga 2021).

Many scholars and pundits attributed this racial variation in vaccine uptake to "vaccine hesitancy"—delay in acceptance or refusal of vaccination despite availability. However, this framing ignores important dimensions of the power dynamics between government and healthcare institutions and people of color. Black and Latinx people may be considered "hard-to-reach" populations because of mistrust of government, language barriers, and limited healthcare access (Vlahov et al. 2007). Efforts to achieve herd-immunity levels of vaccination in these communities require careful targeting and a commitment to addressing community concerns (Artiga and Kates 2020). As Tiffany Donelson, president of the Connecticut Health Foundation points out, "It's not hesitancy. It's access" (Brindley 2021).

In my study, women were fairly evenly split between wanting the vaccine as soon as it was offered and preferring to hold out to observe other people's experiences of vaccination. At the time I completed my fieldwork in May 2021, none of my interlocutors had been vaccinated. Many of the women who eagerly awaited their chance at the shot told me that it simply had not been offered, or they did not know how to get it.

Newborns and children were strong motivators for seeking vaccination. Although the various COVID-19 vaccines were not available for children five through twelve years of age until October 2021—and not for children under five until June 2022—women believed that they and their partners should be vaccinated to protect their young children. Marta made a careful calculation regarding the vaccine, ultimately prioritizing the health and safety of her newborn daughter.

MARTA: There are many myths about the vaccine. I have heard ugly things. They say the vaccine is dangerous, that they're going to chip us. But no, I don't think so. I have to think about the sake of my baby.

JES: So, for you, it would be more to protect your daughter, even though you would be the one to get the vaccine?

MARTA: Well, of course, it is for my health, too. But when I think about the vaccine, when it comes to getting vaccinated, I think about her first.

Similarly, when I asked Ivette whether she would get the vaccine, she told me, "Yes. To take care of them [my two children]. It would be more of vaccine for them. They say that the first one [shot], those who have gotten it—residents and citizens—is rough, but it would be better to prevent the virus because even if it hits you, it would be much less severe. As a precaution, [the vaccine] would be everything."

Other women were less concerned about potential adverse effects of the vaccine. They had received many vaccinations throughout their lives, including flu shots, and trusted the science. This view may reflect differences in vaccination policies between Latin American countries and the United States. An analysis of vaccination legislation for forty-four countries in Latin America and the Caribbean found that 96 percent of the laws mandated immunization (Trumbo et al. 2013). By contrast, vaccination mandates in the United States have steadily declined since the 1990s (Salmon et al. 2006). States with more permissive exemption laws experience higher rates of infectious diseases like pertussis (whooping cough) and measles (Bradford and Mandich 2015).

Célia and Ysabel believed that concerns about vaccination had been overblown. "Many people are already doing it," Célia said. "The time will come when I will be vaccinated, especially for the children. At school, they will require it. For now, they do not, but they will. I don't think there are concerns. I mean, it's really something that they did that [developed the vaccine] so fast, but I have hope and faith in God that everything is fine."

Ysabel echoed this sentiment. "You have to believe in science. I imagine when the flu thing [the 1918 flu pandemic] happened, many people were in the same situation, but they proved that it worked. I mean, it can help us. It's the way to get out of this situation, because we've been in it for a year already. So, there may be some not-so-good side effects, but it might make the difference to change the situation."

Other women expressed doubts. When I asked Jackelín if she would get the vaccine, she told me, "Well, I don't know anymore. Because, sometimes I think that, how can I really know if it's truly for coronavirus. Because... sometimes in the news, they say that there are so many negative [side effects]. Who can guarantee, or how can I tell if it's true, that that's what it's for? Now that older people are getting it, some have gotten terrible fevers for three or four days, and it makes me think, if the vaccine is supposed to take care of them, then why does it have to give you a fever?"

Some skepticism about the vaccine among Latin American communities may have been based in part on experiences reported in Latin America—including Mexico, Colombia, Peru, Brazil, and Panama—where some citizens received counterfeit vaccines that, though likely harmless, offered no immunity against the virus (Sullivan 2021; BBC News 2021). Delia, a twenty-nine-year-old from the Dominican Republic, expressed fears of the vaccine that stemmed from the experiences of peers in her home country. "They're all very scared," she said of her family. "There, they don't know if the vaccine you receive is the original. So they're scared not to get the vaccine and they're scared to get it, as well."

Women's opinions on vaccination, informed by personal experiences and varying by home country or territory, time in the United States, and media consumption, reveal informed calculations of risk, uncertainty, and benefit. These varying attitudes reflect their distinctive situations and intersubjective realities.

POLICIES FOR MOVING ONWARD

With permission and input from Nikki, I shared the following testimony at the New Haven Board of Alders public hearing on racism as a public health issue in October 2020. I described the experiences in Nikki's life that related to interpersonal and structural racism, including the untimely death of her younger brother. In that hearing, I listened to other residents protest the food apartheid affecting the West River and West Rock neighborhoods and the high prices at Stop & Shop, mourn the loved ones who had died of COVID-19 after contracting the virus at their warehousing or food service jobs, and decry the alders for only now acknowledging the health harms of racism.

"You're pretty for a Black girl."

"You're so articulate."

"I thought you people like watermelon."

"I've been so nice to your kind."

"You Black [N-word] bitch."

These comments punctuate the memories of Nikki Campbell, a thirty-three-year-old Jamaican immigrant living here in New Haven County. Words carry weight, but the textbooks from which they're taught—of White supremacy as mass incarceration, redlining, and restrictive immigration policies—take lives.

Nikki's brother Dante struggled growing up. Their father was always working, and their mother was back in Jamaica, so it was easy to get in trouble. He was handcuffed for the first time when he was nine. Then again at eleven. Then again and again until he dropped dead of a heart attack at age twenty-eight.

I cannot say for sure that racism killed Dante Campbell. But racism does kill. Racism is linked to increased death rates due to cardiovascular disease, cancer, and more. It contributes to chronic stress that affects not only physical health but also mental health. Racism may also cause premature aging.

These adverse health effects also show up when racist immigration policies meet the healthcare system. Nikki has DACA [immigration status] and thereby cannot receive HUSKY. Currently pregnant, she relies on free care through Yale–New Haven Hospital for her prenatal health. Despite financial challenges, she worries that accepting WIC will affect her ability to obtain a green card.

So, what can the City of New Haven do to protect people like Nikki and Dante Campbell, may he rest in peace?

First, we need to decriminalize petty crimes like drug use, sex work, loitering, sleeping in public, and minor traffic violations. We can look to our neighbor Massachusetts for their example of the Decriminalization of Misdemeanors Law.

Second, we need to increase investment in building healthy communities by supporting equity in education, affordable housing, and equal opportunity in employment. New Haven has a rich history of this, but there is more to be done.

Third, we need to expand healthcare to all, including members of our undocumented community who have been systematically excluded from protections due to racist immigration policies. We can follow the example of New York City, which offers free care to all undocumented individuals at public hospitals.

I am glad that we all agree that racism is a public health issue. With this knowledge, we must move forward together to build a healthier and safer city.

Following the public hearing and further deliberation from the working group, the alders presented ten recommendations to the city's Health and Human Services Committee, including revamping the city's affirmative action program; expanding COVID-19 testing and vaccination outreach to communities of color; supporting state legislation for healthcare access for Black and Brown communities; expanding mental health outreach and trauma-informed care services; increasing economic development in Black and Brown neighborhoods and advocating for expansion of cash assistance; increasing affordable housing; strengthening accountability for racist policing; guaranteeing healthy food for all children and advocating for more robust food assistance programs; and supporting free public transportation for all residents (Brackeen et al. 2021). Many of these issues directly parallel the concerns and hopes raised by my interlocutors.

I knew that by studying trauma and structural vulnerability among migrant mothers, I would inevitably run up against policy issues, particularly during the COVID pandemic. Here I discuss the policy needs of the Latin American migrant community—particularly migrant mothers—and advocacy work emerging from this project, focusing on healthcare access, protection against intimate partner violence, support with necessities like food and housing, and immigration reform.

Migrants and Erosion of the Social Safety Net

More than one in seven Connecticut residents, or approximately 520,000 people, are migrants, a number that has increased by 30 percent over the past two decades (American Immigration Council 2020; Buchanan and Abraham 2015). Migrants constitute 17.6 percent of the Connecticut labor force and are numerous in the state's healthcare, manufacturing, retail, and construction industries. In addition, one in four self-employed business owners in Connecticut is a migrant. These entrepreneurs are responsible for over $1.8 billion in business revenue. Collectively, immigrant households generate another $6.2 billion in state and local tax revenue (American Immigration Council 2020; New American Economy 2016). Despite these contributions, migrants are excluded from several social programs, including food stamps (Supplemental Nutrition Assistance Program, SNAP) and cash assistance (Temporary Assistance for Needy Families, TANF).

Despite the nation's long-standing recognition of the value of migrants, the Illegal Immigration Reform and Immigrant Responsibility Act of 1996 increased border enforcement and restrictions on public assistance for new permanent residents and unauthorized immigrants (Cohn 2015). The 1996 Personal Responsibility and Work Opportunity Reconciliation Act (PRWORA) restricted immigrants' access to health insurance, nutritional support, and cash assistance. PRWORA increased the proportion of uninsured migrants (see table 1). The act laid out a vision for a "successful society" that included promoting sexual abstinence outside marriage, supporting two-parent households, and discouraging welfare dependence. Specifically, the act established "self-sufficiency" as a standard of immigration policy, calling for "aliens within the Nation's borders not [to] depend on public resources to meet their needs, but rather rely on their own capabilities and the resources of their families, their sponsors, and private organizations." By doing so, these "aliens" would become "self-reliant" and no longer "burden the public benefits system" (Personal Responsibility and Work Opportunity Reconciliation Act of 1996, www.congress.gov/bill/104th-congress/house-bill/3734/text). One study found that the proportion of single migrant women with limited education receiving Medicaid—a group most vulnerable to change—fell by 12 percentage points following the passage of the act (Kaushal and Kaestner 2005). Participation in state insurance programs decreased among permanent residents and refugees at rates three and seven times greater, respectively, than among US citizens (Fix and Passel 2002).

The Trump administration further restricted social protections for migrants. Examples included "zero tolerance" policies justifying family separation at the border, an expanded "public charge" rule to further penalize migrants receiving public benefits, and xenophobic rhetoric. Additionally there were efforts to require collection of social security numbers for COVID-19 vaccine recipients and actions to prevent migrants from receiving asylum, necessary benefits like Medicaid, food stamps, housing support, and even life-saving immunization (Dickerson 2018; Parmet 2019; Ellis 2020; Stolberg 2020). As the need for these services increased during the COVID-19 pandemic, the administration slashed the social welfare assistance available to immigrants.

Together, these policies demonstrate that the United States values migrants primarily as instruments in a capitalist regime. The anthropologist Jason de León describes migrants as "excluded subjects," on which sovereign powers inflict violence "while simultaneously neutralizing their ability to resist or protest" (de León 2015).

Healthcare Access

The COVID-19 pandemic exposed deeply racist fault lines in the US healthcare system that rendered undocumented and documented migrants particularly vulnerable. The Affordable Care Act that made health insurance more widely available in the United States expressly excluded undocumented migrants. In a joint congressional session on September 9, 2009, President Barack Obama felt compelled to state: "There are also those who claim that our reform effort will insure illegal immigrants. This, too, is false—the reforms I'm proposing would not apply to those who are here illegally." This promise prompted Republican Rep. Joe Wilson to shout, "You lie!" (Jackson 2009). The implicitly discriminatory attitude of both the president's reassurance and the representative's skepticism conveyed the view that undocumented migrants who could not pay for healthcare did not deserve it (Fassin 2012).

Healthcare providers, and the broader public, persistently view migrants as undeserving of free care, considering healthcare a privilege rather than a right (Vanthuyne et al. 2013). Some particularly fear provision of pregnancy care to undocumented women because of racist and xe-

Table 1 Noncitizens' Eligibility for Benefits under the Personal Responsibility and Work Opportunity Reconciliation Act of 1996

Group status	Exemption criteria	SSI[1]	Food stamps	Medicaid	TANF[2]	State/local public benefits
		Immigrants arriving on or before August 22, 1996				
Qualified immigrants		Eligible	Eligible	Eligible at state's discretion	Eligible at state's discretion	Eligible at state's discretion
Groups exempted from bar on federal assistance ("exempted groups")	Individuals with 40 quarters of work history	Eligible	Eligible	Eligible	Eligible	Eligible
	Military personnel and their families	Eligible	Eligible	Eligible	Eligible	Eligible
	Refugees/asylees	Eligible for first 7 years	Eligible	Eligible for first 7 years; thereafter at state's discretion	Eligible for first 5 years; thereafter at state's discretion	Eligible for first 5 years; thereafter at state's discretion

Immigrants arriving after August 22, 1996

Qualified immigrants	Ineligible	Barred for first 5 years (except children and persons receiving disability benefits)	Barred for first 5 years; thereafter eligible at state's discretion	Barred for first 5 years; thereafter eligible at state's discretion	Eligible at state's discretion
Exempted groups — Individuals with 40 quarters of work history	Barred for first 5 years	Barred for first 5 years	Barred for first 5 years	Barred for first 5 years	Eligible
Military personnel and their families	Eligible	Eligible	Eligible	Eligible	Eligible
Refugees/asylees	Eligible for first 7 years	Eligible for first 7 years	Barred for first 7 years; thereafter eligible at state's discretion	Barred for first 5 years; thereafter eligible at state's discretion	Barred for first 5 years; thereafter eligible at state's discretion
Unqualified immigrants	Ineligible	Ineligible	Eligible for emergency services only	Ineligible	Ineligible

[1] SSI: Supplemental Security Income
[2] TANF: Temporary Assistance for Needy Families

nophobic concerns about "anchor babies" whose birth in the United States would make them eligible for citizenship (Vanthuyne et al. 2013; Chavez 2013). The stratified US healthcare system effectively classifies those who are uninsurable—particularly those who are undocumented or "liminally legal"—as expensive drains on the system. The medical anthropologist Khiara Bridges notes that the absence of universal healthcare pathologizes poor people, as the lack of financial means to maintain health perpetuates a vicious cycle of sickness, medical expense, debt, and deteriorating health. Equalizing healthcare access would ensure that poor people have as much opportunity for good health as wealthy people (Bridges 2011, 36).

When I asked my interlocutors about policy needs—or the gaps in the social welfare system—affordable healthcare surfaced as the most common concern. Almudena told me, "The support I need is insurance, healthcare. I applied [for free care] because I had received bills to pay. The worker told me that they had accepted me into the program but that I did not technically have insurance."

Even though Almudena qualified for a private, unadvertised program of financial assistance for healthcare for uninsured individuals—Yale–New Haven Health's "free care" program—she constantly received high bills for medical care, which caused her considerable stress. To get these bills covered, Almudena had to present them in person to a Yale–New Haven Health administrator. "She said that every time I receive a bill, I have to take it to her so that she can take care of it. It's very stressful. For example, I got a bill for $750. Imagine! That's the amount we earn in a week. Can you imagine paying each time you arrive or each time you have a visit with the doctor? The support I would like would be to not have to worry about that."

Seventeen of my interlocutors reported outstanding medical debt. Most of these debts resulted from emergency care they sought when no free or sliding-scale clinic was open. Other debts reflected accumulated costs from routine healthcare. Ascención, from Guatemala, told me, "Sometimes, when I go to the clinic, I cannot pay. The last time I took my child in, they told me I owed $40. I told them, 'I don't have it.' I asked them, 'Don't you understand? It's expensive for me to take off [from work] and to come and bring in my child. I have to pay for a taxi to get here.' I don't have money to pay these clinics anymore."

Ascención worked in a food cart, likely earning ten dollars an hour or less. In addition to the cost of the medical visit, the $10 to $12 for a taxi ride, minus the lost earnings from the work time she missed, would leave her with costs amounting to a full day's pay. Although undocumented migrants can apply for emergency Medicaid for situations that require immediate medical attention or severely jeopardize health (such as pregnancy, dialysis for kidney failure, or a severe injury requiring urgent surgery), this provision does not cover necessary preventive and primary care (Edward 2014).

High costs prompt many migrants to avoid routine healthcare. Particularly in areas with more restrictive healthcare and immigration enforcement policies, migrants and their children have been shown to be less likely to seek and obtain routine services, an effect the sociologist Meredith van Natta refers to as "medical-legal violence" (2019). This pattern is particularly concerning for pregnant women, because the lack of prenatal care may increase the risk of newborn death by 40 percent (Rosenberg 2002).

Raquel, from Chile, said, "Recently, we had a very large debt. We were already in for five thousand dollars. My husband was very stressed about it. But he filled out some papers [for the free care program], and it took a long, long, long time. It actually delayed me from going to the clinic in my first four months of pregnancy." Raquel told me she worried that she would continue to accumulate bills by going to the clinic, and if her application for free care was not approved, she and her husband would never be able to pay off their outstanding balance. As a result, she went without care for almost half of her pregnancy, a calculated decision that endangered her and her unborn child.

As I completed my fieldwork, the HUSKY 4 Immigrants movement was strongly advocating for the expansion of Medicaid to undocumented immigrants. In July 2020, I collaborated with directors of the student-run HAVEN Free Clinic to write letters and policy memos to key legislators—and the Connecticut governor—in support of this cause. We worked alongside the mayor of New Haven, the city's Health and Human Services director, and the Center for Children's Advocacy to demonstrate the need for and interest in Medicaid expansion. In June 2021, State Senator Martin M. Looney, who represents New Haven, cosponsored H.B. No. 6687, which proposed medical assistance to children and adults without health insurance. The amended version of the bill was signed into law on July 13, 2021, by Governor Ned Lamont, providing Medicaid coverage to children eight years old and younger and to pregnant women. The measure also called for the future expansion of coverage to all children eighteen and under (Carlesso 2021). Currently HUSKY 4 Immigrants is working to expand emergency Medicaid coverage to cover outpatient dialysis treatment. At present, the need for dialysis traps dozens of uninsured individuals in hospitals throughout the state, as these are the only sites where their dialysis treatment is covered by Medicaid (Rabe Thomas and Smith-Randolph 2021).

Most undocumented migrants in Connecticut currently have no healthcare coverage. This situation leaves them at risk of accumulating overwhelming medical debt or having to overcome the bureaucratic disentitlement surrounding private charities like the Yale–New Haven free care and Me and My Baby programs. By contrast, the State of California and New York City offer programs that fund healthcare for the undocumented community. In July 2019, Governor Gavin Newsom of California extended state Medicaid coverage to low-income, undocumented adults aged fifty and under (Gutierrez 2021). Similarly, local policy in New York City expands the MetroPlus Healthcare program, provided by the New York City hospital system, and has allocated $100 million to ensure that undocumented residents can access and receive necessary healthcare (Goodman 2019). Other states and jurisdictions can follow these leads.

ESSENTIAL SERVICES

"I need both economic and emotional support," Raquel told me. "If we could receive financial aid, it would be so welcome. It is very difficult when an immigrant arrives, and the situation is not the best [like during COVID-19]. I wouldn't turn away that help. Emotionally, it would be so nice to be able to talk through things with someone.... to not feel so invisible to society."

Raquel and I spoke for over four hours. Other than her husband, I was the first person she had spoken to in weeks. Isolation due to the pandemic, her immigration status, and her financial precarity prevented her from seeking out support or companionship. Nearly one-third of the women in my study shared Raquel's experience of social isolation, describing themselves as "alone" with limited social lives as a result of pandemic precautions and fear of exposure of their undocumented status. In addition to the psychological toll, this self-sequestration separates women from sources of social and financial capital. Women with more robust social networks expressed greater awareness of resources like Me and My Baby, food banks, diaper banks, and mutual-aid funds that helped soften the blow of the COVID-19 pandemic. Those without such networks felt they needed to handle things on their own, particularly mothering their newborns. Juana told me, "Everything is harder in this pandemic. Being a mother can be isolating enough when you don't have the help of your family. But on top of that, when you're not able to have visitors over, it's harder. There is no one. I have to just learn to cope."

Juana sounded desperately frustrated. "Once my husband went back to work, I had to do everything on my own, with my baby. I could no longer ask anyone for help, like, 'Oh, just put a blanket over her,' or 'Check her diaper.' I have to do everything myself: feed her, bathe her, change her diaper. I don't have anyone to help me." Juana and Raquel's narratives illustrate the importance of two policy interventions: behavioral health services and critical human services for migrants.

Behavioral Health Services

Social isolation and loneliness are associated with higher levels of depression, suicidality, psychoses, and personality disorders (Wang et al. 2017). Migrant women, many of whom carry histories of trauma and confront social and economic disenfranchisement, are at increased risk of mental distress. Mental healthcare remains inaccessible to migrant communities, particularly undocumented communities, because of cost, availability, and language and educational barriers. Community health worker (CHW) or *promotores de salud* (PdS) programs, which have grown extensively over the past few decades, seek to dismantle these barriers by collaborating with individuals with lived experience and cultural knowledge who undergo specialized training to promote health and wellness among their peers (WestRasmus et al. 2012). CHW and PdS programs have demonstrated promise in improving health outcomes by increasing access to care, facilitating appropriate use of health resources, and providing health education and screening (Witmer et al. 1995). Massachusetts and Minnesota have implemented successful CHW programs to overcome the challenges of providing healthcare to diversifying populations (Rosenthal et al. 2010). These programs can serve as models for wider implementation. Such programs require sustainable financing (through services like Medicaid and the Children's Health Insurance Program [CHIP]), investment in workforce development, standards for training and certification, and guidelines for assessing effectiveness.

A free clinic run by Yale students adapted a behavioral health *promotor* program to assist Spanish-speaking migrants. A study of the program found a significant decrease in depression symptoms among participants and increased interest among student facilitators in working with underserved populations (Rodriguez Guzman et al. 2018). *Promotor* programs throughout Connecticut and beyond could support migrants coping with social isolation and prior migration-related trauma.

Food, Housing, and Financial Support

"With the pandemic, there is no work. You cannot pay your rent, buy food," Noelia, a forty-year-old woman from Mexico, lamented. "There are many places that provide help, like food pantries, but it's not enough to survive." In Connecticut, residents can call 211 or visit 211ct.org to access critical human services. "Just call 211" is a common refrain among the state's healthcare providers and nonprofit workers. However, many services and programs are not accessible to undocumented migrants. The main needs my interlocutors expressed were for food, housing security, and financial support. The corresponding federal programs—SNAP, Section 8, and TANF—do not cover undocumented migrants.

At the start of COVID-19, when I was barred from conducting research at the clinic because of infection precautions, I joined ContraCOVID, a healthcare navigation resource that facilitates access to educational and social services in multiple languages for migrant communities. As the Connecticut liaison, I pooled information on food, cash assistance, employment support, and COVID-19 testing services from a hodgepodge of sources, including the state government, local Facebook groups, immigrant rights organizations, and mutual-aid networks. I learned that the resources available to migrants were sparse, fragmented, grassroots-developed, and ephemeral. No stable infrastructure of aid existed for Spanish-speaking migrants.

The devastation of COVID-19 has increased the need to reform policies that cast migrants as excluded subjects. In the absence of comprehensive immigration reform that provides pathways to legal residence and citizenship for undocumented individuals, responses include improving wages and workplace conditions for undocumented workers, providing higher-education tuition support for undocumented youth, compensating communities that provide social services to migrants, and expanding rental assistance to migrant communities (Vazquez 2019; U.S. Department of Education 2015; Yoshikawa and Kholoptseva 2013).

Intimate Partner Violence

Latina mothers are particularly vulnerable to intimate partner violence because of the barriers they face to escaping from abusive relationships. These include limited financial resources, language difficulties, social isolation, and, if they are undocumented, the risk of deportation (Hass, Dutton, and Orloff 2000). Although intimate partner violence may not occur more commonly among Latinx migrants, research suggests that Latina women are significantly more likely to be killed by their partners than women of other racial or ethnic groups (Runner, Yoshihama, and Novick 2009). A study of intimate partner violence in New York City found that 51 percent of intimate-partner homicide victims were foreign born (Futures without Violence 2021). Many of my interlocutors, including Teresa and Gladys, reported intimate partner violence and other forms of gender-based violence.

PRWORA and the Illegal Immigration Reform and Immigration Responsibility Act of 1996 (IIRIRA) exacerbated the risk of intimate partner violence for migrant women by restricting access to benefits and imposing harsh penalties for undocumented residents. To be exempted from these restrictions, women must demonstrate experiences of battering or "extreme cruelty." Similarly, provisions for migrant women in the 1994 Violence against Women Act require evidence of physical or mental injuries, or threats to that effect. Psychological abuse equating to dominance and isolation may not meet these criteria and is difficult to prove before judges (Hass, Dutton, and Orloff 2000). To address these problems, healthcare providers, community workers, lawyers, and judges should be trained to recognize abusive behavior that can lead to battering or homicide, to advocate for women trapped in controlling relationships, and to support their need for legal restitution, independence, and lawful residence. Intimate partner violence screening should be universal at all sites of service provision, including healthcare and private charities (e.g. , food and diaper banks), and effective tools should be deployed to probe for more insidious forms of abuse, like intimidation, financial abuse, social isolation, and other tactics of coercive control (Rabin et al. 2009).

Immigration Policy

Adequate remedies to the intense structural vulnerability encountered by migrant women require reform of US immigration policy. At present, pathways to legal residence are extremely limited and require the accumulation of social and financial capital, along with some luck and patience.

Comprehensive immigration reform, a phrase that has circulated in US political circles since the early 2000s, became a point of debate during the 2020 elections. The former secretary of housing and urban development, Julián Castro, made headlines in 2019 when he proposed a repeal of Section 1325 of Title 8 of the US Code, which criminalizes unlawful entry into the United States (Lind 2019). This spurred debate among Democratic candidates, who also argued over whether to expand public healthcare to undocumented migrants, abolish or disband ICE, and provide expanded services to migrant communities. They also discussed the timelines and requirements for extending legal residence to undocumented migrants already in the country (Mehta and Gomez 2019).

The Migration Policy Institute (MPI) highlights groups of undocumented migrants with "strong equities" for expedited citizenship review, particularly amid the COVID-19 pandemic. These groups include DACA recipients and "Dreamers," TPS recipients, essential workers, farm workers, migrants sponsored by families or employers, and parents of US citizens and permanent residents. The MPI encourages a broad legalization program for migrants present for three years or longer, paralleling the allowances of the 1986 Immigration Reform and Control Act. An alternative option would be updating the provisions of the 1929 Registry Act, which allowed migrants to apply for permanent residence if they had abided by US laws and resided in the United States for a significant number of years. The MPI estimates that replacing the eligibility date for registry-based migration would render between 2.8 and 8 million people eligible for green cards (Bolter, Chishti, and Meissner 2021). In July 2022, companion bills were introduced in the House and in the Senate that would enable about 8 million undocumented individuals to adjust their status (Moriarty 2022).

In addition, legislative solutions could expand mechanisms for establishing lawful presence short of permanent residence, including expanding the current DACA, TPS, and work visa programs. The Trump administration's suspension of the DACA program left an estimated 1.3 million eligible young people unable to access it (Beitsch 2021). The Migration Policy Institute also proposes eliminating the three- and ten-year bars to reentry from abroad for migrants sponsored by family members or employers who initially entered unlawfully, a policy that would benefit nearly 2 million people (Bolter, Chishti, and Meissner 2021).

My interlocutors specifically articulated interests in expanded work visas, legal and social services to support acquisition of citizen rights, and investing in the economic development of their home countries. As Almudena suggested, "Maybe with a permit you can travel to where you want to go and then return, right? Why not give us permits for a while so we can make the decision to stay or go back? Why don't our presidents work on the economy, on employment, on creating more jobs? Maybe by giving us more jobs, people wouldn't need to migrate to other places to look for something better, right?"

On his inauguration in 2021, President Biden proposed a legalization framework to Congress that would make anyone unlawfully present in the country as of January 1, 2021, eligible to apply for adjustment of status (Bolter, Chishti, and Meissner 2021). The $3.5 trillion budget package includes $107 billion for the Senate Judiciary Committee to spend on charting pathways to citizenship and investing in border security (Beitsch

2021). The wheels are in motion to significantly improve the legal condition of many undocumented migrants; however, we remain far from full realization of this ideal.

CONCLUSION

On one of his community tours for medical students, the New Haven community leader Lee Cruz uses the metaphor of seagulls to impart a lesson on deconstructing hierarchies of knowledge. Walking on the riverside of Criscuolo Park, at the confluence of the Quinnipiac and Mill Rivers, Lee calls attention to the "white stuff" along the path. On a closer look, the "white stuff" takes the shape of shell fragments.

"Now, how did they get there?" Lee asked, tilting his straw hat up.

"Seagulls," a student answered tentatively.

"That's right, seagulls. The seagulls have learned that if they drop their clams on this black stuff—the pavement—the shells will break. Now, people consider seagulls to be dumb animals, but they figured this out on their own, and it helps them survive. The point is, just like we have our prejudices about what we believe intelligence is, . . . we also have prejudices against each other, in terms of other people's culture. 'We know better than those people.'"

Lee tells a story from when he worked in Nicaragua for twelve years. The assumptions of public health interventionists and researchers caused them to miss their targets by failing to pay attention and listen to the members of the community. In one example, attempts to prevent infant deaths from diarrheal diseases did not take account of the local approaches to caregiving and access to supplies. The teams taught women to mix oral rehydration packets with water, overlooking the fact that it was young girls who cared for the babies while their mothers worked, and that water was not reliably clean. When they paid closer attention, and listened to community members, they focused their efforts on these daughters and local bodega owners, who sold sanitary, bottled, carbonated beverages that could be used to mix the rehydration packets.

"So again, this all started with the seagulls and dropping the shells, but all of this is part of a spectrum of intelligence, a spectrum of viewing the world, a spectrum of looking at the people that you're going to be serving as not only people to be served, but as people with understanding of their own reality, of their own history, of their own culture," Lee said. "And when you do that, there *will* be times when what you know is better. That will actually be true most of the time. But if you make the assumption that because you know better, you will make things *be* better, then you are always going to lose. If you make the assumption that there's someone here that has value to be respected, and you listen to them and try to understand them where they're at, then when the right time comes and you have to say, 'You should take this into account,' or 'There's a different way to do that,' there'll be more of an openness to that. And that is a lesson that you'll either trust me [on], or you're going to learn it the hard way. And that can be here, it can be in a developing country, or it could be in Beverly Hills."

Ethnographers, just as much as clinical scientists and outreach workers, bear responsibility for thinking we know better than our interlocutors. This assumption stems from the imperialist origins of anthropology. However, as Lee points out, an attitude of superiority, whether conscious or unconscious, impedes our ability to effect change.

On the issues of COVID-19 disparities and vaccine hesitancy, many scholars and public health officials blamed genetics and unwillingness to participate to explain the high rates of morbidity and mortality from the virus and low rates of vaccination among certain populations. Listening to the people most affected reveals a different story: Although a few women in my study believed that Latinas were more susceptible to COVID-19 because of genetics or behavior, many others noted increased risks of exposure from having to work in high-contact settings outside the home and the lack of financial support that would have given them other options. When I probed about their willingness to receive the COVID-19 vaccine, women conveyed valid concerns based on the knowledge and information to which they had access. Those who wanted the vaccine simply did not know how to get it. This conflict between authoritative characterizations of two public health challenges and local, embodied renderings emphasizes the need, as Lee would say, to abandon our assumptions and attitudes of superiority, to humble ourselves and to listen.

In his original conception of structural violence, the Norwegian sociologist Johan Galtung notes that personal and structural violence are often massively evil and coupled, but he retains the hope that research and practice will yield social action to combat injustice (Galtung 1969). Medical anthropologists have written in considerable volume and detail about the human toll of structural violence. These narratives have the power to shape policy, to leverage our cultural capital and amplify the voices of vulnerable communities to reform the policies that disproportionately harm and dehumanize them.

Models of applied or engaged anthropology encourage scholars to collaborate with communities to generate data that informs and propels systems change (L. Hardy and Hulen 2016). Decolonial methods require community engagement prior to and during data collection, as well as in processes of dissemination (Smith 2012). To this end, anthropologists should receive training in decolonizing methodologies and policy advocacy. The urban anthropologist Eleanor Leacock argues that anthropological perspectives, combined with historical and advocacy approaches, "offer the possibility for defining the potentials for action and the ambiguities that hinder it, as individuals and groups in part accept and in part resist the existing power relations that oppress them" (Leacock 1987, 314). Strengthening community assets with university resources and critical analyses can help to overpower structural inequities. As the scholar and activist Angela Davis says, "You have to act as if it were possible to radically transform the world. And you have to do it all the time" (A. Davis 2014).

Conclusion

ONWARD

In front of Lee Cruz's home on Clinton Street, a beautiful Victorian-style home with a green-painted wood exterior, a sign calls attention to the surrounding milkweed. It reads: "MONARCH WAYSTATION. This site provides milkweeds, nectar sources, and shelter needed to sustain monarch butterflies as they migrate through North America."

Lee and his sons, along with other organizers and managers of local community gardens, have taken an interest in supporting the endangered population of monarch butterflies that pass through Connecticut each year. Lee calls the milkweed planted throughout the neighborhood a "picnic" for the butterflies. Connecticut lies in the butterflies' northern roosting territories. Each fall, the monarchs leave for their overwintering grounds in southwestern Mexico, and their descendants return to Connecticut.

"First they'll go to Texas," says Diane St. John, the manager of a New Haven County garden center. "The milkweed is already coming out there. They'll stop and lay eggs; those butterflies will die, but their babies will be born and fly farther north. The great-great-grandchildren, the fourth generation, will come [back] to Connecticut" (Beach 2020).

"The butterflies have been migrating for ten thousand years," Lee says, his voice raised in wonder. It was not until the 1970s that scientists began to ask where the monarchs go. Information from monarch watchers throughout North America enabled the mapping of the butterflies' migration paths, which had previously been a mystery. We had to listen, observe, and learn to understand their truth.

Humans, too, have migrated across the Americas for tens of thousands of years in search of resources. The process has become increasingly dangerous with the establishment of nation-states, borders, and policies that criminalize those seeking new terrain. The women whose stories I have attempted to narrate here are like the female monarchs: intrepid travelers, gatherers, and bearers of life. Their journeys and triumphs shape the worlds of the generations that follow them. Like the monarchs, these women rely on their children to preserve their histories, transmit their legacies, and continue to *seguir adelante.* As Ocean Vuong says, "Only the future revisits the past" (2019).

The ability of these women to press onward is often attributed to their "resilience." Scholars tend to imagine resilience like a savings account: something you are born with (thanks to your parents) or something you can increase through skilled investment. In reality, resilience is more like a line of credit that you do not know when or if you will ever pay back. You hold on to your family's belief in you, your faith in God, your confidence in your partner, and your dreams for the future, and pretend not to notice that number turning bigger and redder. Resilience is not an asset acquired by anyone with resources; it is a cost selectively paid by those without.

For many women, pressing onward—past the insecurity they face in their home countries, the traumas of migration, and the dual oppressions of racism and migration enforcement—centers on improving the lives of their children. They aspire to financial stability, owning a home, obtaining legal residence, and investing in their children's education. As Ysabel puts it, "My baby has given me the strength to carry on. There are so many opportunities here. I want her to study well, and—as all mothers do—I want her to build a life for herself." By advancing the futures of their children, often at the expense of their own dreams, these migrant mothers enact resistance against political oppression. They press onward for their descendants and for their communities.

We can envision a more nurturing future, one in which monarch butterflies can pick waystations the way we choose between fast food stations along the interstate, and in which Latina migrant mothers can invest their cognitive, social, and emotional energies in art, community connections, entrepreneurship, and the blessings of kinship, rather than in coping with trauma, racism, and poverty. A robust social and economic safety net and an attainable pathway to citizenship would enable them to enjoy their lives instead of pushing toward the next moment. We can work to realize this vision of a "livable life" (Willen 2019). Organizations that support this effort are listed in appendix 3.

Through person-centered ethnography and oral history, I listened, observed, and learned from these women. They are the ultimate, authoritative narrators of their lives. I merely share what they have taught me and what I have come to understand.

In Fair Haven, an ongoing youth project tracks the monarchs. Children like Lee's son, Mateo, wait until the monarchs settle on a milkweed plant and then tag their left wings with tiny numbered adhesive tags. The Monarch Watch Tagging Program is a community science initiative that allows residents along the monarch migration route to obtain tagging kits, submit tagging data online, and search for records of tagged monarchs recovered in the United States, Canada, and central Mexico (Monarch Watch 2022).

"We're waiting one day for our numbers to show up," Lee says. "That will show me that a butterfly born in our backyard actually made it to Mexico."

APPENDIX A Methods

The study on which this book is based was originally designed to explore intergenerational trauma. To that end, I intended to examine biomarkers for epigenetic change (i.e., DNA methylation) at stress-related genes, maternal hair cortisol, and newborn cortisol reactivity from saliva samples in response to vaccinations administered during the two-month well-baby checkup. My original biomarker study required a sample size of 98 to detect a significant difference in methylation levels at my primary gene of interest. To account for attrition, the study originally planned to enroll 112 maternal-infant dyads. As I began to approach code saturation, or when no new analytical codes emerged from my transcripts, I determined my final target number of interviews; I achieved thematic saturation, or a point at which no new issues arose from my conversations, with considerably fewer interviews and determined to conclude at a final sample of 65 women (see Lowe et al. 2018; Guest, Namey, and Chen 2020; Hennink, Kaiser, and Marconi 2017). The Yale Human Investigation Committee (HIC) for biomedical research approved my study.

I obtained oral rather than written consent from interlocutors in order to facilitate phone and Zoom interviews. I used a Zoom H6 audio recorder and my personal cell phone with a Google voice number to contact interlocutors and conduct and record interviews. Prior research demonstrates that phone interviews can be as reliable and valid as in-person interviews (Cook et al. 2003; Pattnaik et al. 2020). Because historical methods do not meet the criteria for human subjects research (because they are not intended to draw conclusions or generalize findings and are not subject to IRB regulations), I conducted many oral history interviews in person, following guidelines for masking and physical distancing. I conducted interviews in Spanish and English and initially transcribed and translated the audio recordings using the multilingual automated transcription software Trint. My bilingual research assistants reviewed the transcripts for accuracy and fidelity to the meanings of my interlocutors and added their own field notes of the process with analytical memos when relevant. I personally reviewed any discrepancies in translation or audio files that rendered transcription more challenging.

Given the sensitive topics addressed in my interviews, including histories of trauma exposure, I worked closely with the social worker at the Women's Center of Yale–New Haven Hospital and a team at the Hispanic Clinic of the Connecticut Mental Health Center to safeguard the mental health and well-being of any women who became distressed during our conversations. I also trained in mental health first aid, motivational interviewing, substance use intervention, and psychoeducation at the Hispanic Clinic. I partnered with on-call mental health clinicians who could intervene if the need arose. Fortunately, no woman became acutely upset during any of the interviews.

APPENDIX B　Ethnographic Tables

Table B.1　Comments Describing Imperative Resilience

Name	Home country/ territory	Age	Comment
Susana	Ecuador	31	I just try not to think of the thing that is stressing me. I just treat it as a learning process.
Ysabel	Ecuador	19	I just have to face things and get ahead. I don't feel those emotions. I just try to focus on getting ahead.
Adelina	Puerto Rico	21	I don't stress. Whenever something seems stressful, I just don't think about it. I'm just like, it's whatever, there's going to be another day where you can make it better. I try to brush it off or look for advice. There's things that people probably went through that you're going through, you know? Who understand the situation and can help you through it.
Célia	Ecuador	35	I try to talk to my husband, and we figure out how to get things under control. If it's because of finances, then we talk about it and economize. If you have children, you have to be calm for them— they should not feel tense or see a fight. Everything can be overcome.

Table B.1   (continued)

Name	Home country/ territory	Age	Comment
Elvira	Dominican Republic	30	You have to just accept it and adapt, create something nice out of it so you don't focus on the bad. I try to think positive, stick to my plans, and always have a steady mind. I don't throw in the towel easily. I am strong. I endure. I have been through things, and I have overcome them. I try not to think about things because if you dwell on them, you feel sadder.
Nikki	Jamaica	33	I just deal with things because I feel like I don't have a choice.
Jackelín	Guatemala	40	I try not to focus on the negative things that are happening. Everything can be managed; everything has a solution. I believe that God has a plan, a purpose for each person. I make my plans, and if it is God's will, they will be fulfilled. I learned how to face things as an adult. I know I can get ahead. I am confident. Life is just like this sometimes. There can be moments of pain, of storms, of disease, of other difficulties, but as long as I serve God, my soul will go to Him. My body stays.
Marcela	Ecuador	34	I just stay calm. I am very aware then I can change something, and when there's nothing, I can do about it, I let it go. I've faced difficulties in my life, and I have overcome them. I try not to ruminate on them. I had to be strong. I consider the difficulties in my life not to be a big deal; I just learn from them.
Juana	Mexico	26	I believe that God allows us to get things because they are meant for us. And if we don't get them, then it wasn't meant to be. It's not always easy to find strength, but being here [in this country], you have to have a purpose, to know what you want and to want to advance.
Ascención	Guatemala	34	There are just times in this world when you have to suffer.

Name	Home country/ territory	Age	Comment
Camila	Mexico	36	I need to get my children ahead—they have me and no one else. I don't have time to get emotional, because if I'm sad, if I'm crying, then they feel badly. Mothers have to do a lot for their children. We have to work for them, take care of them, and we cannot fall, we cannot collapse. We have to do everything with a stone face.
Jeaneth	El Salvador	30	I just focus on the simplest, most practical solutions. I know that everything that happens. . . everything is temporary, everything has a reason, a "why," and sometimes it is just not worth getting so frustrated by the small things. I want to fight and to get ahead.
Karina	Ecuador	42	Everything that has to happen happens, but you have to hold on and know how to get ahead. You can't stay put; you can't get stuck. You have to get ahead.
Mirelia	Dominican Republic	39	The Bible says that everything works for the good. We must face things and learn from them. We have life, and so we must please God and move forward, try to overcome, try to get our families ahead.
Leticia	Guatemala	33	I try not to put too much importance on things. When I feel stress, I try to relax, to not think about anything. I just tell myself, "Keep going. Do not let yourself fall apart."
Nieve	Ecuador	19	I just try to be positive. Everything will be okay. It will work out. Maybe I'll talk with my husband, and we'll make a plan. I don't worry.
Marisol	Mexico	39	There are times when I get up at dawn and try to pray a lot, to listen to God, so as not to feel anger at everything that has happened to me. I ask for peace and then I become stronger. I listen to Christian recordings that help me focus on overcoming and keeping a positive mind. I believe that, through my faith in God, all things will pass.
Marta	Ecuador	24	I try not to think about it so much. I try not to be too affected. I think everything happens for a reason.

Table B.1   *(continued)*

Name	Home country/ territory	Age	Comment
Ivette	Ecuador	24	I try not to think about it too much. If something difficult happens, I try to take it easy, to find solutions. I try, with my son, to do things in the house to distract us, to release some of that pent up stress. I take it all in stride. Always looking up, don't look back. Let this push me ahead and move forward to build a better future for my children.
Anita	Puerto Rico	39	I try to find a purpose in everything. I can cry and talk to someone who can help me make sense of things. But in the end, I'm going to have a child, a child that I have to fight for.
Mildred	Mexico	33	I think I'm strong. I think the fact that I'm responsible for my children and that they depend on me helps me to be strong. Difficulties will always be there.
Noelia	Mexico	40	I just try to stay positive and seek help when I need it.
Aida	Honduras	26	I just try to handle it, push it from my mind, and let it pass. I don't have any family or friends here, only my children. And so, I have to learn to deal with things on my own.
Lidia	Mexico	25	I try to be a very positive person. Everything happens for a reason. And in negative situations, I try to find the positive. A solution. Getting ahead, pushing ahead, as always.
Meri	Ecuador	26	I believe I am strong, that I can move forward. I always like to be positive, to find the solution and not cause more problems.
Vanessa	Puerto Rico	39	I'm normal, I'm human. I get angry. And when I do, I try not to think about it and try to relax. I'll inhale, exhale, focus on calming my body, and then when I feel more relaxed, I analyze the situation, look at the pros and cons, and make a plan.
Carla	Puerto Rico	21	You can't let one thing stop you. You have to keep going. I just encourage myself, try to push myself harder.

Name	Home country/ territory	Age	Comment
Linette	Puerto Rico	26	I try not to let things overwhelm me. I try not to overthink things. I'm always saying, you know, I'm going through this because God has a plan for me. I try to encourage myself and believe that things will get better. I always have that mindset that's like, well, if you want it to work out, you can't just sit here and wait. You have to do things for yourself.
Gladys	Ecuador	41	I have no other choice. I just have to turn to God and trust that things will be okay. I try not to stress over things that I cannot change. And it works. I feel stronger and stronger over time, to be honest.
Amalia	Peru	37	I don't think things are just destiny—you make your own destiny. You have to live by your own decisions. You have to think about the risks, whether things are worth it, and figure out how to fix it. I have my own will to survive and to move ahead.
Patricia	Ecuador	27	We all have difficulties, and we have to know how to resolve them. To not let them overwhelm us and focus on the here and now. Problems will pass, right?
Nely	Mexico	24	I try to calm down and try to see things from a different perspective. Maybe I'll talk to my husband. I have to be stronger because my parents aren't here with me. I try to recover quickly, knowing everything happens for a reason.
Sonia	Colombia	36	I stay positive and try to calm own. I'll drink some *hierbabuena* [mint] tea and think of my baby, my son. I try to accept the things that happen, however difficult they may be, trusting in God and His will.

Table B.2   Comments Describing the Economic Impacts of COVID-19

Name	Home country/ territory	Age	Comment
Ysabel	Ecuador	19	Because of the pandemic, my partner has not worked at all. We both lost our jobs.
Adelina	Puerto Rico	21	When I first found out I was pregnant, it was, like, mid-pandemic, and a lot of jobs wasn't hiring. I would've been working at the moment if the pandemic wasn't here. It's like you can't apply to a job right now because of the pandemic.
Célia	Ecuador	35	In the time of the pandemic, my husband stopped working, and he is the one who supports the house. I went months without working. Everything stopped suddenly.
Jackelín	Guatemala	40	They lowered my husband's work. There were fewer hours and people did not want to go in, out of fear, you see.
Juana	Mexico	26	Before I was pregnant, I was working cleaning houses. But I got pregnant, and with everything with COVID, they didn't allow me to come in.
Ascención	Guatemala	32	I used to work in the food carts, but I'm out of work right now because of the current pandemic.
Camila	Mexico	36	Right now, with everything going on, it's quite frustrating. For three months we had no work.
Jeaneth	El Salvador	30	My baby's father and I have a shared bank account, but he was let go from work. They only let him work twenty hours a week, and [because he is an immigrant with temporary protected status] he got the state to pay him the other twenty. But many months have passed now, and he hasn't been paid.
Karina	Ecuador	42	I don't have any money. Because of the pregnancy and COVID, I can't work. My partner didn't work for like two months.
Mirelia	Dominican Republic	39	My love, I lost my job. Because of the pandemic, the business where I worked was sold.
Nieve	Ecuador	19	Work has gone down really, really badly. My husband's job canceled a lot of work. We had to take out a loan in my home country so we can manage things here.

Name	Home country/ territory	Age	Comment
Ivette	Ecuador	24	We got the virus and my husband stopped working. The three of us [my husband, my son, and me] were in the house for about a month. There was no money. We had to borrow from our friends, and we're paying it back little by little.
Raquel	Chile	24	When all this started, my husband was instantly unemployed, and I didn't have a job. While he was still out of work, the people we were subletting from kept forcing us to pay, and I couldn't. They wanted to kick us out. Oh, no, that was horrible.
Anita	Puerto Rico	39	When I got to Connecticut, they hadn't closed everything down yet, but then two weeks later they closed, and I couldn't get a job.
Mildred	Mexico	33	Well, since everything started, I spent like three months out of work. I came back in late May, but the work has gone down. I'm just grateful to have a job right now.
Noelia	Mexico	40	Well, when it all really started, my husband had all his jobs canceled. Because he works inside houses, and you couldn't go into houses to work. He was out of work for about two weeks.
Lidia	Mexico	25	I used to work, but when we got here, the virus started, and unfortunately, no, I couldn't continue. I was cleaning houses, and I lost my job. We live on what my husband brings in, and sometimes it's a little tight and we have to borrow.
Meri	Ecuador	26	Because of COVID, I haven't been able to work as I normally would. I wanted to keep working in cleaning, but because of my pregnancy, I was told that it was better not to continue because I was going to be in contact with many people and could get infected with COVID at any time.
Vanessa	Puerto Rico	39	Before COVID, I had three jobs, and things were all right. I was caring for patients at home, and I had time in a factory. But then when cases began rising in Connecticut, I was only allowed to work with one patient. And so now I'm trying to economize.

Table B.2   (continued)

Name	Home country/ territory	Age	Comment
Cintia	Dominican Republic	36	Of course, the pandemic affected my finances. My work stopped for like a month or two. My family had to help me.
Carla	Puerto Rico	21	When COVID happened, the manager cut hours, so it's been a struggle. At first, I was getting sixty hours, sometimes sixty-five. My paycheck was looking, like, around six hundred every week. But then COVID hit, and I'd get half of that, so, like, three hundred every week. I had to talk to my landlord to see if he could help me out with the rent.
Linette	Puerto Rico	26	I had just gotten a job, you know, a couple months before the pandemic started. And then the pandemic hit, and I lost it, I had to go to unemployment. We had to quarantine, and I was so stressed out, I got Bell's palsy. COVID is horrible, horrible. It really takes a toll on you.
Gladys	Ecuador	41	Since all this COVID happened, all my work went down to 50 percent. I still haven't gotten all my clients back.
Jenifer	Guatemala	32	My husband was furloughed from work for a while. We had to use up our little savings.
Amalia	Peru	37	Well, my husband lost work. And because of the pandemic, I don't even dare to look for a job.
Kara	Guatemala	25	With the pandemic, work has gone down a lot. So now it's a struggle to make rent, buy food.
Rosalia	Guatemala	27	At first, I didn't work for like two weeks. And my husband has work some days, other days not. So, because of this disease, we've been late on the rent.
Nely	Mexico	24	At first it was hard, I think for everyone. I stopped working because I have asthma, and they said it was very dangerous for people with asthma and told us not to go in.
Meliza	Mexico	40	Since the pandemic started last March, I haven't been working. Our savings are running out.

Organizations for
Immigration and Health
Policy Reform and Activism

NEW HAVEN ORGANIZATIONS

Unidad Latina en Acción   https://ulanewhaven.org

Semilla Collective   https://www.semillacollective.org/

Junta for Progressive Action   https://www.juntainc.org

Haven Free Clinic   https://www.semillacollective.org/

Apostle Immigrant Services   https://www.apostleimmigrantservices.org

Community Foundation for Greater New Haven   https://www.cfgnh.org

Fair Haven Community Health Care   https://fhchc.org

NATIONAL ORGANIZATIONS

American Immigration Council   https://www.americanimmigration
council.org

Center for Gender and Refugee Studies   https://cgrs.uchastings.edu

Vera Institute   https://www.vera.org

UndocuBlack Network   https://undocublack.org

Detention Watch Network   https://www.detentionwatchnetwork.org

Florence Immigrant and Refugee Rights Project   https://firrp.org

Immigrant Legal Resource Center   https://www.ilrc.org

Immigration Advocates Network   https://www.immigrationadvocates.org

Immigrant Defense Project   https://www.immigrantdefenseproject.org

National Immigration Forum   https://immigrationforum.org

National Immigration Law Center   https://www.nilc.org

National Immigrant Justice Center   https://immigrantjustice.org

National Immigration Forum   https://nipnlg.org

Migration Policy Institute   https://www.migrationpolicy.org

United We Dream   https://unitedwedream.org

Movimiento Cosecha   https://www.lahuelga.com

References

Abraído-Lanza, Ana F., Anahí Viladrich, Karen R. Flórez, Amarilis Céspedes, Alejandra N. Aguirre, and Ana Alicia De La Cruz. 2007. "Commentary: Fatalismo Reconsidered; A Cautionary Note for Health-Related Research and Practice with Latino Populations." *Ethnicity and Disease* 17 (1): 153–58.

Abrego, Leisy J. 2014. *Sacrificing Families: Navigating Laws, Labor, and Love across Borders.* Stanford, CA: Stanford University Press.

Alcoff, Linda Martín. 2000. "Is Latina/o Identity a Racial Identity?" In *Hispanics/Latinos in the U.S.: Ethnicity, Race and Rights,* edited by Jorge Gracia and Pablo DeGreiff, 311–44. London: Routledge.

Allyn, Bobby. 2019. "California Is 1st State To Offer Health Benefits to Adult Undocumented Immigrants." NPR, July 10. www.npr.org/2019/07/10/740147 546/california-first-state-to-offer-health-benefits-to-adult-undocumented-im migrants.

American College of Obstetrics and Gynecology. 2019. "Obstetric Analgesia and Anesthesia." March. www.acog.org/en/clinical/clinical-guidance/practice-bull etin/articles/2019/03/obstetric-analgesia-and-anesthesia.

American Immigration Council. 2020. "Immigrants in Connecticut." American Immigration Council. July 6. www.americanimmigrationcouncil.org/research /immigrants-connecticut.

Anderson, Karen O., Carmen R. Green, and Richard Payne. 2009. "Racial and Ethnic Disparities in Pain: Causes and Consequences of Unequal Care." *Journal of Pain* 10 (12): 1187–1204. https://doi.org/10.1016/j.jpain.2009.10.002.

Andrés-Hyman, Raquel C., Jose Ortiz, Luis M. Añez, Manuel Paris, and Larry Davidson. 2006. "Culture and Clinical Practice: Recommendations for Working with Puerto Ricans and Other Latinas(os) in the United States." *Professional Psychology: Research and Practice* 37 (6): 694–701. https://doi.org/10.1037/0735-7028.37.6.694.

Ansfield, Bench. "Oak Street Connector." A People's History of the Hill. New Haven, CT: Arts Council of Greater New Haven. https://youraudiotour.com/tours/740/stops/3186.

Anzaldúa, Gloria. 2012. *Borderlands/La Frontera: The New Mestiza*. 4th ed. San Francisco, CA: Aunt Lute.

Appel, Allan. 2008. "Ecuadorian Consulate Opens." *New Haven Independent,* September 18. www.newhavenindependent.org/index.php/archives/entry/ecuadorian_consulate_opens.

Artiga, Samantha, and Jennifer Kates. 2020. "Addressing Racial Equity in Vaccine Distribution." Kaiser Family Foundation (blog). December 3. www.kff.org/racial-equity-and-health-policy/issue-brief/addressing-racial-equity-vaccine-distribution.

Atallah, Devin G. 2017. "A Community-Based Qualitative Study of Intergenerational Resilience with Palestinian Refugee Families Facing Structural Violence and Historical Trauma." *Transcultural Psychiatry* 54 (3): 357–83. https://doi.org/10.1177/1363461517706287.

Ayala, César J. 1996. "The Decline of the Plantation Economy and the Puerto Rican Migration of the 1950s." *Latino Studies Journal* 7 (1): 61–90.

Backe, Emma Louise. 2020. "Capacitating Care: Activist Anthropology in Ethnographies of Gender-Based Violence." *Feminist Anthropology* 1 (2): 192–98. https://doi.org/10.1002/fea2.12022.

Bartlett, Judith G., Lucia Madariaga-Vignudo, John D. O'Neil, and Harriet V. Kuhnlein. 2007. "Identifying Indigenous Peoples for Health Research in a Global Context: A Review of Perspectives and Challenges." *International Journal of Circumpolar Health* 66 (4): 287–370. https://doi.org/10.3402/ijch.v66i4.18270.

Bass, Paul. 2007. "Rescue Mission to Fair Haven." *New Haven Independent,* February 13. www.newhavenindependent.org/index.php/archives/entry/rescue_mission_to_fair_haven.

Bassett, Mary T, Jarvis T Chen, and Nancy Krieger. 2020. "The Unequal Toll of COVID-19 Mortality by Age in the United States: Quantifying Racial/Ethnic Disparities." *Harvard Center for Population and Development Studies Working Paper* 19 (3): 1–18.

BBC News. 2020. "Amazon Faces Backlash over Covid-19 Safety Measures," June 17, 2020. www.bbc.com/news/technology-53079624.

———. 2021. "Coronavirus: Pfizer Confirms Fake Versions of Vaccine in Poland and Mexico." April 22. www.bbc.com/news/world-56844149.

Beach, Randall. 2020. "Monarch Butterflies Might Soar Again—with a Little Help from Their Friends." *Connecticut Magazine*. www.connecticutmag.com/the-connecticut-story/beachcombing/monarch-butterflies-might-soar-again-with-a-little-help-from-their-friends/article_96f45fd8-7b75-11ea-a0e2-bb40 54e8bd39. html.

Becker, Marc. 2013. "The Stormy Relations between Rafael Correa and Social Movements in Ecuador." *Latin American Perspectives* 40 (3): 43–62.

Beitsch, Rebecca. 2021. "Budget Package Includes Plan for Pathway to Citizenship, Green Cards for Millions." *The Hill*, August 9. https://thehill.com/policy/national-security/566964-budget-reconciliation-package-includes-pathway-to-citizenship.

Bernard, H. Russell, and Clarence C. Gravlee. 2014. *Handbook of Methods in Cultural Anthropology*. Lanham, MD: Rowman & Littlefield.

Biehl, João Guilherme, Byron Good, and Arthur Kleinman. 2007. "Introduction: Rethinking Subjectivity." In *Subjectivity: Ethnographic Investigations*, edited by João Guilherme Biehl, Byron Good, and Arthur Kleinman. Berkeley: University of California Press.

Bolter, Jessica, Muzaffar Chishti, and Doris Meissner. 2021. "Back on the Table: U.S. Legalization and the Unauthorized Immigrant Groups That Could Factor in the Debate." Washington, DC: Migration Policy Institute. www.migrationpolicy.org/sites/default/files/publications/mpi-rethinking-legalization-2021_final.pdf.

Bonanno, George A. 2004. "Loss, Trauma, and Human Resilience: Have We Underestimated the Human Capacity to Thrive after Extremely Aversive Events?" *American Psychologist* 59 (1): 20–28. https://doi.org/10.1037/000 3-066X.59.1.20.

———. 2012. "Uses and Abuses of the Resilience Construct: Loss, Trauma, and Health-Related Adversities." *Social Science and Medicine* 74 (5): 753–56. https://doi.org/10.1016/j.socscimed.2011.11.022.

Bourgois, Philippe, Seth M Holmes, Kim Sue, and James Quesada. 2017. "Structural Vulnerability: Operationalizing the Concept to Address Health Disparities in Clinical Care." *Academic Medicine* 92 (3): 299–307. https://doi.org/10.1097/ACM.0000000000001294.

Brackeen, Darryl J., Daniel Bland, Maritza Bond, Darcey Cobbs-Lomax, New Haven Health System, Mehul Dalal, Natasha Ray, et al. 2021. "Racism as a Public Health Issue Working Group Recommendations to the New Haven Board of Alders." New Haven, CT: Racism as a Public Health Issue Working Group. www.newhavenarts.org/hubfs/RAPHI% 20% 20report.pdf.

Bradford, W. David, and Anne Mandich. 2015. "Some State Vaccination Laws Contribute to Greater Exemption Rates And Disease Outbreaks in The United States." *Health Affairs* 34 (8): 1383–90. https://doi.org/10.1377/hlthaff.2014 .1428.

Braunstein, Elissa, and Stephanie Seguino. 2018. "The Impact of Economic Policy and Structural Change on Gender Employment Inequality in Latin America, 1990–2010." *Review of Keynesian Economics* 6 (3): 307–32. https://doi.org/10.4337/roke.2018.03.02.

Bridges, Khiara. 2011. *Reproducing Race: An Ethnography of Pregnancy as a Site of Racialization*. Berkeley: University of California Press.

Brindley, Emily. 2021. "Connecticut Is a National Leader in COVID-19 Vaccinations, but Health Officials, Advocates Say the State Has So Far Failed Residents of Color." *Hartford Courant*, February 21. www.courant.com/coronavirus/hc-news-coronavirus-vaccine-rollout-disparities-people-of-color-20210221-ci4rqri7efgoxbz2c7ev3ujmqi-story.html.

Brown, Zachary. 2020. *Holes In the Safety Net*. Washington, DC: Public Citizen. https://mkus3lurbh3lbztg254fzode-wpengine.netdna-ssl.com/wp-content/uploads/Holes-in-the-Safety-Net-1-1.pdf.

Buchanan, Maggie Jo, Philip E. Wolgin, and Claudia Flores. 2021. "The Trump Administration's Family Separation Policy Is Over." Center for American Progress. 2021. www.americanprogress.org/issues/immigration/reports/2021/04/12/497999/trump-administrations-family-separation-policy.

Buchanan, Mary, and Mark Abraham. 2015. "Understanding the Impact of Immigration in Greater New Haven." DataHaven. https://ctdatahaven.org/sites/ctdatahaven/files/ImmgRPT_lores_FINAL_PGS.pdf.

Budiman, Abby. 2020. "Key Findings about U.S. Immigrants." Pew Research Center (blog). August 20. www.pewresearch.org/fact-tank/2020/08/20/key-findings-about-u-s-immigrants.

Bunyavanich, Supinda, Anh Do, and Alfin Vicencio. 2020. "Nasal Gene Expression of Angiotensin-Converting Enzyme 2 in Children and Adults." *JAMA* 323 (23): 2427–29. https://doi.org/10.1001/jama.2020.8707.

Butler, Judith. 1997. "Gender Trouble, Feminist Theory and Psychoanalytic Discourse (1990)." In *Space, Gender, Knowledge: Feminist Readings*, edited by Linda McDowell and Joanne Sharp. New York: Routledge.

Caldwell, Juan Montes and Alicia A. 2021. "Men Looking for Work Drive Surge in Illegal Crossings at the U.S. Border." *Wall Street Journal*, March 24.

Carlesso, Jenna. 2021. "CT Legislature Expands HUSKY to Undocumented Kids." *CT Mirror*, June 10. https://ctmirror.org/2021/06/09/proposal-opening-husky-to-undocumented-children-in-connecticut-wins-final-approval.

Castañeda, Heide. 2019. *Borders of Belonging: Struggle and Solidarity in Mixed-Status Immigrant Families*. Stanford, CA: Stanford University Press.

Castañeda, Heide, Seth M. Holmes, Daniel S. Madrigal, Maria-Elena DeTrinidad Young, Naomi Beyeler, and James Quesada. 2015. "Immigration as a Social Determinant of Health." *Annual Review of Public Health* 36 (1): 375–92. https://doi.org/10.1146/annurev-publhealth-032013-182419.

Castellanos, M. Bianet. 2017. "Rewriting the Mexican Immigrant Narrative:

Situating Indigeneity in Maya Women's Stories." *Latino Studies* 15 (2): 219–41. https://doi.org/10.1057/s41276-017-0057-z.

Chavez, Leo. 1992. *Shadowed Lives: Undocumented Immigrants in American Society*. San Diego, CA: Harcourt Brace.

———. 2013. *The Latino Threat: Constructing Immigrants, Citizens, and the Nation*. Stanford, CA: Stanford University Press.

Chua, Kao-Ping, and Rena M. Conti. 2020. "Despite the Families First Coronavirus Response Act, COVID-19 Evaluation Is Not Necessarily Free." *Health Affairs* blog. April 17. www.healthaffairs.org/do/10.1377/hblog20200413.783118/full.

Clark, Eva, Karla Fredricks, Laila Woc-Colburn, Maria Elena Bottazzi, and Jill Weatherhead. 2020. "Disproportionate Impact of the COVID-19 Pandemic on Immigrant Communities in the United States." *PLoS Neglected Tropical Diseases* 14 (7): e0008484. https://doi.org/10.1371/journal.pntd.0008484.

Clerke, Teena, and Nick Hopwood. 2014. "Ethnography as Collective Research Endeavor." In *Doing Ethnography in Teams: A Case Study of Asymmetries in Collaborative Research*, edited by Teena Clerke and Nick Hopwood, 5–18. Cham, Switzerland: Springer International. https://doi.org/10.1007/978-3-3 19-05618-0_2.

Cohn, D'Vera. 2015. "How U.S. Immigration Laws and Rules Have Changed through History." Pew Research Center (blog). September 30. www.pewresearch.org/fact-tank/2015/09/30/how-u-s-immigration-laws-and-rules-have-changed-through-history.

Cohn, D'Vera, Anna Brown, and Mark Hugo Lopez. 2021. "Black and Hispanic Americans See Their Origins as Central to Who They Are, Less So for White Adults." Washington, DC: Pew Research Center. www.pewresearch.org/social-trends/wp-content/uploads/sites/3/2021/05/ST_2021.05.14_Census-Identity_FINAL.pdf.

Comas-Díaz, L. 2001. "Hispanics, Latinos, or Americanos: The Evolution of Identity." *Cultural Diversity and Ethnic Minority Psychology* 7 (2): 115–20. https://doi.org/10.1037/1099-9809.7.2.115.

Connecticut History. 2020. "When Old Saybrook Was a College Town." Connecticut History (blog). October 7. https://connecticuthistory.org/when-old-saybrook-was-a-college-town.

Connors, Bob. 2012. "Unprecedented Settlement Reached over ICE Raids." *NBC Connecticut*, February 14. www.nbcconnecticut.com/news/local/immigration-ice-settlement-new-haven-illegal/1923252.

Cook, Linda S., Jennifer L. White, Gavin C. E. Stuart, and Anthony M. Magliocco. 2003. "The Reliability of Telephone Interviews Compared with In-Person Interviews Using Memory Aids." *Annals of Epidemiology* 13 (7): 495–501. https://doi.org/10.1016/s1047-2797(03)00039-5.

Corva, Dominic. 2008. "Neoliberal Globalization and the War on Drugs: Transnationalizing Illiberal Governance in the Americas." *Political Geography* 27 (2): 176–93. https://doi.org/10.1016/j.polgeo.2007.07.008.

Craven, Christa and Dána-Ain Davis. 2013. *Feminist Activist Ethnography: Counterpoints to Neoliberalism in North America.* Lanham, MD: Lexington.

Cruz, José Miguel. 2016. "State and Criminal Violence in Latin America." *Crime, Law and Social Change* 66 (4): 375–96. https://doi.org/10.1007/s10611-016-9 631-9.

Davis, Angela. 2014. "Communities of Resistance." Lecture given at Southern Illinois University, Carbondale, February 13. www.youtube.com/watch? v=6s8QCucFADc.

Davis, Dána-Ain. 2013. "Border Crossings: Intimacy and Feminist Activist Ethnography in the Age of Neoliberalism." In *Feminist Activist Ethnography: Counterpoints to Neoliberalism in North America,* 23–38. Lanham, MD: Lexington.

———. 2019a. *Reproductive Injustice: Racism, Pregnancy, and Premature Birth.* New York: New York University Press.

———. 2019b. "Obstetric Racism: The Racial Politics of Pregnancy, Labor, and Birthing." *Medical Anthropology* 38 (7): 560–73. https://doi.org/10.1080/0145 9740.2018.1549389.

Dean, Carolyn J. 2003. "Empathy, Pornography, and Suffering." *Differences: A Journal of Feminist Cultural Studies* 14 (1): 88–124.

De Genova, Nicholas. 2017. *The Borders of" Europe": Autonomy of Migration, Tactics of Bordering.* Durham, NC: Duke University Press.

———. 2002. "Migrant 'Illegality' and Deportability in Everyday Life." *Annual Review of Anthropology* 31 (1): 419–47. https://doi.org/10.1146/annurev.anth ro.31.040402.085432.

De León, Jason. 2015. *The Land of Open Graves: Living and Dying on the Migrant Trail.* Berkeley: University of California Press.

Del Olmo, Frank. 1981. "Latinos by Any Other Name Are Latinos." *Los Angeles Times,* May 1981.

———. 1985. "Latino, Si—Hispanic, No." *Los Angeles Times,* October 1985.

Deng, Francis Mading. 2004. "The Impact of State Failure on Migration." *Mediterranean Quarterly* 15 (4): 16–36. https://doi.org/10.1215/10474552-15-4-16.

Denov, Myriam, Maya Fennig, Marjorie Aude Rabiau, and Meaghan C. Shevell. 2019. "Intergenerational Resilience in Families Affected by War, Displacement, and Migration: 'It Runs in the Family.'" *Journal of Family Social Work* 22 (1): 17–45. https://doi.org/10.1080/10522158.2019.1546810.

de Onís, Catalina (Kathleen). 2017. "What's in an 'x'? An Exchange about the Politics of 'Latinx.'" *Chiricú Journal: Latina/o Literatures, Arts, and Cultures* 1 (2): 78–91.

Díaz, Rafael M. 1998. *Latino Gay Men and HIV: Culture, Sexuality, and Risk Behavior.* New York: Routledge.

Dickerson, Caitlin. 2018. "Hundreds of Immigrant Children Have Been Taken From Parents at U.S. Border." *New York Times*, April 21.

Dowling, Julie A. 2014. *Mexican Americans and the Question of Race*. Austin, TX: University of Texas Press.

Duden, Barbara. 1993. *Disembodying Women: Perspectives on Pregnancy and the Unborn*. Cambridge, MA: Harvard University Press.

Edward, Jean. 2014. "Undocumented Immigrants and Access to Health Care: Making a Case for Policy Reform." *Policy, Politics, and Nursing Practice* 15 (1–2): 5–14. https://doi.org/10.1177/1527154414532694.

Ellis, Nicquel Terry. 2020. "'Stand Back and Stand By': Rhetoric Some Call Racist Has Marked Trump's Entire Presidency." *USA Today*, October 13. www

Erfani, Parsa, Nishant Uppal, Caroline H. Lee, Ranit Mishori, and Katherine R. Peeler. 2020. "COVID-19 Testing and Cases in Immigration Detention Centers, April–August 2020." *JAMA*. October. https://doi.org/10.1001/jama .2020.21473.

Fair Haven Community Health Care. 2021. "History." May 25. https://fhchc.org /about-us/history.

Fassin, Didier. 2012. "That Obscure Object of Global Health." In *Medical Anthropology at the Intersections: Histories, Activisms, and Futures*, edited by Marcia C Inhorn and Emily A. Wentzell, 95–115. Durham, NC: Duke University Press. http: //read.dukeupress.edu/content/9780822395478/978082239 5478.

Fassin, Didier, and Richard Rechtman. 2009. *The Empire of Trauma: An Inquiry into the Condition of Victimhood*. Princeton, NJ: Princeton University Press.

Fazel, Mina, Jeremy Wheeler, and John Danesh. 2005. "Prevalence of Serious Mental Disorder in 7000 Refugees Resettled in Western Countries: A Systematic Review." *Lancet* 365 (9467): 1309–14. https://doi.org/10.1016/S014 0-6736(05)61027-6.

Fears, Darryl. 2003. "The Roots of 'Hispanic.'" *Washington Post*, October 15. www .washingtonpost.com/archive/politics/2003/10/15/the-roots-of-hispanic/3d91 4863-95bc-40f3-9950-ce0c25939046.

Fernández, Johanna. 2020. *The Young Lords: A Radical History*. Chapel Hill: University of North Carolina Press.

Ferreira, Francisco H. G., and Jérémie Gignoux. 2011. "The Measurement of Inequality of Opportunity: Theory and an Application to Latin America." *Review of Income and Wealth* 57 (4): 622–57. https://doi.org/10.1111/j.1475-4 991.2011.00467. x.

Finer, Lawrence B., and Mia R. Zolna. 2016. "Declines in Unintended Pregnancy in the United States, 2008–2011." *New England Journal of Medicine* 374 (9): 843–52. https://doi.org/10.1056/NEJMsa1506575.

Fix, Michael, and Jeffrey Passel. 2002. "The Scope and Impact of Welfare Reform's Immigrant Provisions." Washington, DC: Urban Institute. www.urb

an.org/research/publication/scope-and-impact-welfare-reforms-immigrant
-provisions.

Fortuna, Lisa R, Michelle V Porche, and Margarita Alegria. 2008. "Political
Violence, Psychosocial Trauma, and the Context of Mental Health Services
Use among Immigrant Latinos in the United States." *Ethnicity and Health* 13
(5): 435–63. https://doi.org/10.1080/13557850701837286.

Foucault, Michel. 1977. *Discipline and Punish: The Birth of the Prison.* Translated by Alan Sheridan. New York: Vintage.

———. 1980. *Power/Knowledge: Selected Interviews and Other Writings, 1972–
1977.* New York: Vintage.

Futures without Violence. 2021. "The Facts on Immigrant Women and Domestic
Violence." Futures without Violence. www.futureswithoutviolence.org/userfil
es/file/Children_and_Families/Immigrant.pdf.

Galtung, Johan. 1969. "Violence, Peace, and Peace Research." *Journal of Peace
Research* 6 (3): 167–91.

———. 1975. "Peace: Research, Education, Action." In *Essays in Peace Research,* 1:
317–33. Copenhagen, Denmark: Christian Eljers.

Gálvez, Alyshia. 2011. *Patient Citizens, Immigrant Mothers: Mexican Women,
Public Prenatal Care, and the Birth Weight Paradox.* New Brunswick, NJ:
Rutgers University Press.

García Bedolla, Lisa. 2014. *Latino Politics.* 2nd ed. Malden, MA: Polity Press.

Gezici, Armagan, and Ozge Ozay. 2020. "How Race and Gender Shape COVID-
19 Unemployment Probability." SSRN Scholarly Paper ID 3675022. Rochester,
NY: Social Science Research Network. https://doi.org/10.2139/ssrn.3675022.

Gillette, Howard. 2007. "Review Essay: Urban Renewal Revisited." *Journal of
Urban History* 33 (2): 342–50. https://doi.org/10.1177/0096144206294725.

Ginsburg, Faye D., and Rayna Rapp. 1995. *Conceiving the New World Order: The
Global Politics of Reproduction.* Berkeley: University of California Press.

Golash-Boza, Tanya Maria. 2012. *Immigration Nation: Raids, Detentions, and
Deportations in Post-9/11 America.* 1st ed. Boulder, CO: Paradigm.

Golash-Boza, Tanya, and Pierrette Hondagneu-Sotelo. 2013. "Latino Immigrant
Men and the Deportation Crisis: A Gendered Racial Removal Program."
Latino Studies 11 (3): 271–92. https://doi.org/10.1057/lst.2013.14.

Gomberg-Muñoz, Ruth. 2012. "Inequality in a 'Postracial' Era: Race, Immigration, and Criminalization of Low-Wage Labor." *Du Bois Review: Social Science
Research on Race* 9 (2): 339–53. https://doi.org/10.1017/S1742058X11000579.

Gómez, Laura. 2020. *Inventing Latinos: A New Story of American Racism.* New
York: New Press.

Gonzales, Roberto G. 2016. *Lives in Limbo: Undocumented and Coming of Age
in America.* Oakland: University of California Press.

Gonzales, Roberto G., and Leo R. Chavez. 2012. "'Awakening to a Nightmare':
Abjectivity and Illegality in the Lives of Undocumented 1.5-Generation Latino

Immigrants in the United States." *Current Anthropology* 53 (3): 255–81. https://doi.org/10.1086/665414.

González-Duarte, Columba. 2018. "Resisting Monsanto: Monarch Butterflies and Cyber-actors." In *Resistance to the Neoliberal Agri-food Regime: A Critical Analysis*, edited by Alessandro Bonnano and Steven A. Wolf. London: Routledge.

González-López, Gloria. 2007. "'Nunca He Dejado de Tener Terror': Sexual Violence in the Lives of Mexican Immigrant Women." In *Women and Migration in the U.S.-Mexico Borderlands: A Reader*, edited by Denise A. Segura and Patricia Zavella. Durham, NC: Duke University Press.

Good, Byron J. 2010. "Medical Anthropology and the Problem of Belief." In *A Reader in Medical Anthropology: Theoretical Trajectories, Emergent Realities*, edited by Byron J. Good, Michael M. J. Fischer, Sarah S. Willen, and Mary Jo DelVecchio Good, 15: 64–76. West Sussex, UK: Blackwell.

Goodman, J. David. 2019. "De Blasio Unveils Health Care Plan for Undocumented and Low-Income New Yorkers." *New York Times*, January 8.

Google Trends. 2018a. "'Latino' vs. 'Hispanic' Comparison, 2004–Present," 2018. https://trends.google.com/trends/explore? date=all&q=latino, hispanic.

———. 2018b. "'Latinx', 2004–Present," 2018. https://trends.google.com/trends/explore? date=all&q=latinx.

Gravlee, Clarence C. 2020a. "Racism, Not Genetics, Explains Why Black Americans Are Dying of COVID-19." Scientific American Blog Network. June 7. https://blogs.scientificamerican.com/voices/racism-not-genetics-explains-why-black-americans-are-dying-of-covid-19.

———. 2020b. "Systemic Racism, Chronic Health Inequities, and COVID-19: A Syndemic in the Making?" *American Journal of Human Biology* 32 (e23482): 1–8. https://doi.org/10.1002/ajhb.23482.

Green, Adriana Greci. 2007. "Single Book Reviews." *American Anthropologist* 109 (3): 552–53. https://doi.org/10.1525/aa.2007.109.3.552.

Green, Carmen R., Karen O. Anderson, Tamara A. Baker, Lisa C. Campbell, Sheila Decker, Roger B. Fillingim, Donna A. Kaloukalani, et al. 2003. "The Unequal Burden of Pain: Confronting Racial and Ethnic Disparities in Pain." *Pain Medicine* 4 (3): 277–94. https://doi.org/10.1046/j.1526-4637.2003.03034.x.

Green, Delbert A., and Marcus R. Kronforst. 2019. "Monarch Butterflies Use an Environmentally Sensitive, Internal Timer to Control Overwintering Dynamics." *Molecular Ecology* 28 (16): 3642–55. https://doi.org/10.1111/mec.15178.

Green, Linda. 2011. "The Nobodies: Neoliberalism, Violence, and Migration." *Medical Anthropology* 30 (4): 366–85. https://doi.org/10.1080/01459740.2011.576726.

Grugel, Jean, and Pía Riggirozzi. 2012. "Post-neoliberalism in Latin America:

Rebuilding and Reclaiming the State after Crisis." *Development and Change* 43 (1): 1–21. https://doi.org/10.1111/j.1467-7660.2011.01746. x.

Guest, Greg, Emily Namey, and Mario Chen. 2020. "A Simple Method to Assess and Report Thematic Saturation in Qualitative Research." *PLoS ONE* 15 (5): e0232076. https://doi.org/10.1371/journal.pone.0232076.

Guglielmo, Thomas A. 2004. "Encountering the Color Line in the Everyday: Italians in Interwar Chicago." *Journal of American Ethnic History*, 23 (4): 45–77.

Gurwitt, Rob. 2000. "Death of a Neighborhood." *Mother Jones*, October 2000. www.motherjones.com/politics/2000/09/death-neighborhood.

Gutierrez, Melody. 2021. "California Expands Medi-Cal, Offering Relief to Older Immigrants without Legal Status." *Los Angeles Times*, July 27.

Gzesh, Susan. 2006. "Central Americans and Asylum Policy in the Reagan Era." Migration Policy Institute (blog). April 1. www.migrationpolicy.org/article/central-americans-and-asylum-policy-reagan-era.

Hamel, Liz, Ashley Kirzinger, Lunna Lopes, Audrey Kearney, Grace Sparks, and Molyann Brodie. 2021. "KFF COVID-19 Vaccine Monitor: January 2021; Vaccine Hesitancy." KFF (blog). January 27. www.kff.org/report-section/kff-covid-19-vaccine-monitor-january-2021-vaccine-hesitancy.

Hansen, Helena. 2018. *Addicted to Christ: Remaking Men in Puerto Rican Pentecostal Drug Ministries*. Berkeley: University of California Press.

Haraway, Donna. 1988. "Situated Knowledges: The Science Question in Feminism and the Privilege of Partial Perspective." *Feminist Studies* 14 (3): 575–99. https://doi.org/10.2307/3178066.

Hardy, Bradley L., and Trevon D Logan. 2020. *Racial Economic Inequality amid the COVID-19 Crisis*. Washington, DC: Hamilton Project.

Hardy, Lisa J., and Elizabeth Hulen. 2016. "Anthropologists Address Health Equity: Recognizing Barriers to Care." *Practicing Anthropology* 38 (2): 15–17. https://doi.org/10.17730/0888-4552-38.2.15.

Hass, Giselle Aguilar, Mary Ann Dutton, and Leslye E. Orloff. 2000. "Lifetime Prevalence of Violence against Latina Immigrants: Legal and Policy Implications." *International Review of Victimology* 7 (1–3): 93–113. https://doi.org/10.1177/026975800000700306.

Haverluk, Terrence. 1997. "The Changing Geography of U.S. Hispanics, 1850–1990." *Journal of Geography* 96 (3): 134–45. https://doi.org/10.1080/00221349708978775.

Hayes-Bautista, D. E., and J. Chapa. 1987. "Latino Terminology: Conceptual Bases for Standardized Terminology." *American Journal of Public Health* 77 (1): 61–68. https://doi.org/10.2105/AJPH.77.1.61.

Hennink, Monique M., Bonnie N. Kaiser, and Vincent C. Marconi. 2017. "Code Saturation Versus Meaning Saturation: How Many Interviews Are Enough?" *Qualitative Health Research* 27 (4): 591–608. https://doi.org/10.1177/1049732316665344.

Herman, Judith Lewis. 1997. *Trauma and Recovery*. New York: New York: Basic Books (ebook).

Hernandez, Daniel. 2017. "The Case against 'Latinx.'" *Los Angeles Times*, December 2017. www.latimes.com/opinion/op-ed/la-oe-hernandez-the-case-against-latinx-20171217-story.html.

Hoberman, John. 2005. "The Primitive Pelvis: The Role of Racial Folklore in Obstetrics and Gynecology during the Twentieth Century." In *Body Parts: Critical Explorations in Corporeality*, edited by Christopher E. Forth and Ivan Crozier, 85–104. Lanham, MD: Lexington.

Hoffman, Kelly M., Sophie Trawalter, Jordan R. Axt, and M. Norman Oliver. 2016. "Racial Bias in Pain Assessment and Treatment Recommendations, and False Beliefs about Biological Differences between Blacks and Whites." *Proceedings of the National Academy of Sciences* 113 (16): 4296–4301. https://doi.org/10.1073/pnas.1516047113.

Holahan, Charles J., Rudolf H. Moos, Carole K. Holahan, Penny L. Brennan, and Kathleen K. Schutte. 2005. "Stress Generation, Avoidance Coping, and Depressive Symptoms: A 10-Year Model." *Journal of Consulting and Clinical Psychology* 73 (4): 658–66. https://doi.org/10.1037/0022-006X.73.4.658.

Holmes, Seth M. 2013. *Fresh Fruit, Broken Bodies: Migrant Farmworkers in the United States*. Berkeley: University of California Press.

Holtmann, Catherine, and Tracey Rickards. 2018. "Domestic/Intimate Partner Violence in the Lives of Immigrant Women: A New Brunswick Response." *Canadian Journal of Public Health* 109 (3): 294–302. https://doi.org/10.172 69/s41997-018-0056-3.

Humane Borders. 2022. https://humaneborders.org.

Inhorn, Marcia C. 2012. *The New Arab Man: Emergent Masculinities, Technologies, and Islam in the Middle East*. Princeton, NJ: Princeton University Press.

Instituto Brasileiro de Geografía e Estatística. 2011. "Pequisa Nacional por Amostra de Domicilios." Rio de Janeiro, Brazil. https://biblioteca.ibge.gov.br /visualizacao/livros/liv61566.pdf.

Jackson, Brooks. 2009. "Obama's Health Care Speech." Fact Check (blog). September 10. www.factcheck.org/2009/09/obamas-health-care-speech.

Johnston, Sandy. 2016. "New Haven Needs Less, Not More, Parking." *New Haven Independent*, January 8. www.newhavenindependent.org/index.php/archives /entry/a_lot_more_than_parking.

Kainz, Natalie, and Thomas Breen. 2021. "City Grew 3.3% , Hispanic Community 15% ." *New Haven Independent*, August 12. www.newhavenindependent.org /index.php/archives/entry/census_puerto_rican_flag.

Kaushal, Neeraj, and Robert Kaestner. 2005. "Welfare Reform and Health Insurance of Immigrants." *Health Services Research* 40 (3): 697–722. https://doi .org/10.1111/j.1475-6773.2005.00381. x.

Keene, Jennifer Reid, and Christie D. Batson. 2010. "Under One Roof: A Review of Research on Intergenerational Coresidence and Multigenerational House-holds in the United States." *Sociology Compass* 4 (8): 642–57. https://doi.org/10.1111/j.1751–9020.2010.00306. x.

Keller, Allen, Amy Joscelyne, Megan Granski, and Barry Rosenfeld. 2017. "Pre-migration Trauma Exposure and Mental Health Functioning among Central American Migrants Arriving at the US Border." *PLoS ONE* 12 (1): e0168692–e0168692.

English Language Unity Act of 2017. H.R. 997. www.congress.gov/bill/115th-congress/house-bill/997/text.

Kolko, Jed. 2016. "'Normal America' Is Not a Small Town of White People." FiveThirtyEight. April 28. https://fivethirtyeight.com/features/normal-america-is-not-a-small-town-of-white-people.

Koonings, Kees, and Dirk Kruijt. 2004. *Armed Actors: Organized Violence and State Failure in Latin America*. London: Zed.

Kyriakakis, Stavroula. 2014. "Mexican Immigrant Women Reaching Out: The Role of Informal Networks in the Process of Seeking Help for Intimate Partner Violence." *Violence against Women* 20 (9): 1097–1116. https://doi.org/10.1177/1077801214549640.

Lahelma, Elina, Pirkko Hynninen, Tuija Metso, Tarja Tolonen, Tuula Gordon, and Tarja Palmu. 2006. "Collective Ethnography, Joint Experiences and Individual Pathways." *Nordic Studies in Education* 26 (1): 3–15. https://doi.org/10.18261/ISSN1891–5949–2006–01–02.

Leacock, Eleanor. 1987. "Theory and Ethics in Applied Urban Anthropology." In *Cities of the United States: Studies in Urban Anthropology*, edited by Leith Mullings, 317–36. New York: Columbia University Press.

Lee, Catherine. 2013. *Fictive Kinship: Family Reunification and the Meaning of Race and Nation in American Immigration*. New York: Russell Sage Foundation.

Lee, Sang Yoon (Tim), Minsung Park, and Yongseok Shin. 2021. *Hit Harder, Recover Slower? Unequal Employment Effects of the Covid-19 Shock*. Working Paper 28354. Cambridge, MA: National Bureau of Economic Research. https://doi.org/10.3386/w28354.

Lee, Sonia Song-Ha. 2014. *Building a Latino Civil Rights Movement: Puerto Ricans, African Americans, and the Pursuit of Racial Justice in New York City*. Chapel Hill, NC: University of North Carolina Press.

Leonard, Nicole. 2021. "Fair Haven Launches Door-to-Door campaign To Bring More Equity in COVID-19 Vaccine Rollout." Connecticut Public Radio, March 15. www.ctpublic.org/health/2021–03–15/fair-haven-launches-door-to-door-campaign-to-bring-more-equity-in-covid-19-vaccine-rollout.

Lind, Dara. 2019. "Democratic Debate: Section 1325 Repeal, Julián Castro's Immigration Proposal, Explained." *Vox*, June 26. www.vox.com/2019/6/26/18760665/1325-immigration-castro-democratic-debate.

López, Gustavo. 2015. "Hispanics of Peruvian Origin in the United States, 2013." Pew Research Center's Hispanic Trends Project. September 15. www.pewrese arch.org/hispanic/2015/09/15/hispanics-of-peruvian-origin-in-the-united-st ates-2013.

Lopez, Mark Hugo. 2013. "Hispanic or Latino? Many Don't Care, Except in Texas." Pew Research Center. October 28. www.pewresearch.org/fact-tank/20 13/10/28/in-texas-its-hispanic-por-favor.

Lopez, Mark Hugo, Jeffrey S. Passel, and D'Vera Cohn. 2021. "Key Facts about the Changing U.S. Unauthorized Immigrant Population." Pew Research Center. April 13. www.pewresearch.org/fact-tank/2021/04/13/key-facts-about -the-changing-u-s-unauthorized-immigrant-population.

Lowe, Andrew, Anthony C. Norris, A. Jane Farris, and Duncan R. Babbage. 2018. "Quantifying Thematic Saturation in Qualitative Data Analysis." *Field Methods* 30 (3): 191–207. https://doi.org/10.1177/1525822X17749386.

Lynas, Mark. 2020. "COVID: Top 10 Current Conspiracy Theories." Alliance for Science. April 20, 2020. https://allianceforscience.cornell.edu/blog/2020/04 /covid-top-10-current-conspiracy-theories.

Madden, Kelly L., Deborah Turnbull, Allan M. Cyna, Pamela Adelson, and Chris Wilkinson. 2013. "Pain Relief for Childbirth: The Preferences of Pregnant Women, Midwives and Obstetricians." *Women and Birth* 26 (1): 33–40. https://doi.org/10.1016/j.wombi.2011.12.002.

Magne, Fabien, Alexa Puchi Silva, Bielka Carvajal, and Martin Gotteland. 2017. "The Elevated Rate of Cesarean Section and Its Contribution to Non-commu- nicable Chronic Diseases in Latin America: The Growing Involvement of the Microbiota." *Frontiers in Pediatrics* 5 (192): 1–11. https://doi.org/10.3389/fp ed.2017.00192.

Marable, Manning, and Leith Mullings, eds. 2009. *Let Nobody Turn Us Around: Voices of Resistance, Reform, and Renewal.* 2nd ed. Lanham, MD: Rowman & Littlefield.

Marshall, Thomas Humphrey, and Tom Bottomore. 1987. *Citizenship and Social Class.* London: Pluto.

Martin, Philip L. 2014. "The United States: Benign Neglect toward Immigration." In *Controlling Immigration. A Global Perspective,* edited by James F Hol- lifield, Philip L Martin, and Pia M. Orrenius, 83–99. Stanford, CA: Stanford University Press.

McLemore, Monica R., Molly R. Altman, Norlissa Cooper, Shanell Williams, Larry Rand, and Linda Franck. 2018. "Health Care Experiences of Pregnant, Birthing and Postnatal Women of Color at Risk for Preterm Birth." *Social Science and Medicine* 201 (March): 127–35. https://doi.org/10.1016/j.socscim ed.2018.02.013.

Medina, Jennifer. 2007. "New Haven Welcomes a Booming Population of Immi- grants, Legal or Not." *New York Times,* March.

Mehta, Seema, and Melissa Gomez. 2019. "Where December Democratic Debate Candidates Stand on Immigration." *Los Angeles Times*, December 17. www.lati mes.com/politics/story/2019-12-17/democratic-debate-presidential-candidat es-immigration-policy.

Mendenhall, Emily. 2012. *Syndemic Suffering: Social Distress, Depression, and Diabetes among Mexican Immigrant Women.* New York: Routledge.

Menjívar, Cecilia. 2006. "Liminal Legality: Salvadoran and Guatemalan Immigrants' Lives in the United States." *American Journal of Sociology* 111 (4): 999–1037. https://doi.org/10.1086/499509.

Menjívar, Cecilia, and Leisy Abrego. 2012. "Legal Violence: Immigration Law and the Lives of Central American Immigrants." *American Journal of Sociology* 117 (5): 1380–1421. https://doi.org/10.1086/663575.

Metzl, Jonathan M., and Helena Hansen. 2014. "Structural Competency: Theorizing a New Medical Engagement with Stigma and Inequality." *Social Science and Medicine* 103 (February): 126–33. https://doi.org/10.1016/j.socscimed.20 13.06.032.

Minor, Jes. 2015. "It's Not Just the Confederate Flag: The Example of New Haven." HuffPost. July 6. www.huffpost.com/entry/its-not-just-the-confeder _b_7719112.

MIT Press. 2017. "Immigration and the American Backlash." MIT Press, February 21. https://mitpress.mit.edu/blog/immigration-and-american-backlash.

Monarch Watch. 2022. "Monarch Tagging." Monarch Watch. https://monarchwa tch.org/tagging.

Moriarty, Andrew. 2022. "Restoring Immigration Registry: Priority Bill Spotlight." FWD.Us (blog). July 19. www.fwd.us/news/immigration-registry-bill.

Mullin, Amy. 2005. *Reconceiving Pregnancy and Childcare: Ethics, Experience, and Reproductive Labor.* Cambridge: Cambridge University Press.

National Immigration Law Center. 2016. "Is It Safe to Apply for Health Insurance or Seek Health Care?" National Immigration Law Center. November 30. www.nilc.org/issues/health-care/health-insurance-and-care-rights.

Ndugga, Nambi, Latoya Hill, and Samantha Artiga. 2021. "Latest Data on COVID-19 Vaccinations by Race/Ethnicity." KFF. August 4. www.kff.org/coro navirus-covid-19/issue-brief/latest-data-on-covid-19-vaccinations-race-ethni city.

New American Economy. 2016. "The Contributions of New Americans in Connecticut." New American Economy. http: //research.newamericaneconomy .org/wp-content/uploads/2017/02/nae-ct-report.pdf.

New Haven Independent. 2011. "More Latinos, Fewer Whites and Blacks." *New Haven Independent,* March 2011. www.newhavenindependent.org/index.php /archives/entry/more_latinos_fewer_whites_and_blacks.

New Haven Register. 2020. "See Maps New Haven Uses to Address Coronavirus

Hot Spots; Testing Sites." *New Haven Register,* April 30. www.nhregister.com /news/article/See-maps-of-New-Haven-coronavirus-hot-spots-15236719. php.

Ngai, Mae M. 2014. *Impossible Subjects: Illegal Aliens and the Making of Modern America.* 2nd ed. Princeton, NJ: Princeton University Press.

Noe-Bustamente, Luis, and Antonio Flores. 2019. "Facts on Latinos in America." Pew Research Center's Hispanic Trends Project. September 16. www.pewresea rch.org/hispanic/fact-sheet/latinos-in-the-u-s-fact-sheet.

Nordstrom, Carolyn. 2004. *Shadows of War: Violence, Power, and International Profiteering in the Twenty-First Century.* Berkeley: University of California Press.

Norwitz, Errol R, and Joon Shin Park. 2022. "Overview of the Etiology and Evaluation of Vaginal Bleeding in Pregnancy." UpToDate. www.uptodate.com /contents/overview-of-the-etiology-and-evaluation-of-vaginal-bleeding-in-pr egnancy.

Nostrand, Richard L. 2010. "The Hispano Homeland in 1900." *Annals of the Association of American Geographers* 70 (3): 382–96. https://doi.org/10.1111 /j.1467–8306.1980. tb01321. x.

Obstetric Care Consensus. 2014. "Safe Prevention of the Primary Cesarean Delivery, 1." Washington, DC: American College of Obstetrics and Gynecology. www.acog.org/en/clinical/clinical-guidance/obstetric-care-consensus/articles /2014/03/safe-prevention-of-the-primary-cesarean-delivery.

O'Leary, Mary. 2016. "Undocumented Immigrants Find Opportunity in New Haven." *Washington Times,* October 2016.

Ong, Aihwa, Virginia R. Dominguez, Jonathan Friedman, Nina Glick Schiller, Verena Stolcke, David Y. H. Wu, and Hu Ying. 1996. "Cultural Citizenship as Subject-Making: Immigrants Negotiate Racial and Cultural Boundaries in the United States [and Comments and Reply]." *Current Anthropology* 37 (5): 737–62.

Oquendo, Angel R. 1995. "Re-imagining the Latino/a Race." *Harvard BlackLetter Law Journal* 12. https://doi.org/10.1525/sp.2007.54.1.23.

O'Reilly, Karen. 2015. "Migration Theories: A Critical Overview." In *Routledge Handbook of Immigration and Refugee Studies,* edited by Anna Triandafylli- dou. London: Routledge.

Orson, Diane. 2014. "Central American Migrant Children Arrive in Connecticut." Connecticut Public Radio, July 11. www.wnpr.org/post/central-american-migr ant-children-arrive-connecticut.

Overseas Security Advisory Council (OSAC). 2020. *Ecuador 2020 Crime and Safety Report: Guayaquil.* March 3. www.osac.gov/Content/Report/c1275f7f -6c44–4bd9-bbb8-185b0022497e.

Oxhorn, Philip. 2001. "Desigualdad social, sociedad civil y los límites de la ciu- dadanía en América Latina." *Economía, Sociedad y Territorio* 3 (9): 153–95.

Page, Kathleen R., Maya Venkataramani, Chris Beyrer, and Sarah Polk. 2020.

"Undocumented U.S. Immigrants and Covid-19." *New England Journal of Medicine* 382 (21): e62. https://doi.org/10.1056/NEJMp2005953.

Palmer, David Scott, ed. 1994. *The Shining Path of Peru*. 2nd ed. New York: Palgrave Macmillan. https://doi.org/10.1007/978-1-137-05210-0.

Panter-Brick, Catherine, Anna Goodman, Wietse Tol, and Mark Eggerman. 2011. "Mental Health and Childhood Adversities: A Longitudinal Study in Kabul, Afghanistan." *Journal of the American Academy of Child and Adolescent Psychiatry* 50 (4): 349–63. https://doi.org/10.1016/j.jaac.2010.12.001.

Panter-Brick, Catherine, Marie-Pascale Grimon, Michael Kalin, and Mark Eggerman. 2015. "Trauma Memories, Mental Health, and Resilience: A Prospective Study of Afghan Youth." *Journal of Child Psychology and Psychiatry, and Allied Disciplines* 56 (7): 814–25. https://doi.org/10.1111/jcpp.12350.

Parmet, Wendy E. 2019. "The Trump Administration's New Public Charge Rule: Implications For Health Care and Public Health." *Health Affairs* blog. August 13. www.healthaffairs.org/do/10.1377/hblog20190813.84831/full.

Pattnaik, Anooj, Diwakar Mohan, Sam Chipokosa, Sautso Wachepa, Hans Katengeza, Amos Misomali, and Melissa A. Marx. 2020. "Testing the Validity and Feasibility of Using a Mobile Phone-Based Method to Assess the Strength of Implementation of Family Planning Programs in Malawi." *BMC Health Services Research* 20 (1): 221. https://doi.org/10.1186/s12913-020-5066-1.

Pearce, Jenny. 2010. "Perverse State Formation and Securitized Democracy in Latin America." *Democratization* 17 (2): 286–306. https://doi.org/10.1080/13 510341003588716.

Perreira, Krista M, and India Ornelas. 2013. "Painful Passages: Traumatic Experiences and Post-traumatic Stress among U.S. Immigrant Latino Adolescents and Their Primary Caregivers." *International Migration Review* 47 (4): 976–1005. https://doi.org/10.1111/imre.12050.

Pletcher, Mark J., Stefan G. Kertesz, Michael A. Kohn, and Ralph Gonzales. 2008. "Trends in Opioid Prescribing by Race/Ethnicity for Patients Seeking Care in US Emergency Departments." *JAMA* 299 (1): 70–78. https://doi.org /10.1001/jama.2007.64.

Prendergast, Curt, and Alex Devoid. 2021. "Migrant Deaths: A Crisis Deepens in the Desert." *Arizona Daily Star,* December 2.

Public Citizen. 2013. "NAFTA's Broken Promises 1994–2013: Outcomes of the North American Free Trade Agreement." Public Citizen. https://www.citizen .org/article/naftas-broken-promises-1994–2013-outcomes-of-the-north-ameri can-free-trade-agreement.

Quesada, James. 2011. "*No Soy Welferero:* Undocumented Latino Laborers in the Crosshairs of Legitimation Maneuvers." *Medical Anthropology* 30 (4): 386–408. https://doi.org/10.1080/01459740.2011.576904.

———. 2012. "Illegalization and Embodied Vulnerability in Health." Special issue, part 2. *Social Science and Medicine (1982)* 74 (6): 894–96. https://doi.org/10 .1016/j.socscimed.2011.10.043.

Rabe Thomas, Jacqueline, and Walter Smith-Randolph. 2021. "Help Coming for Undocumented Immigrants Trapped in Connecticut Hospitals." *CT Mirror,* July 21. http: //ctmirror.org/2021/07/21/help-coming-for-undocumented-immigrants-trapped-in-connecticut-hospitals.

Rabin, Rebecca F., Jacky M. Jennings, Jacquelyn C. Campbell, and Megan H. Bair-Merritt. 2009. "Intimate Partner Violence Screening Tools: A Systematic Review." *American Journal of Preventive Medicine* 36 (5): 439–445. e4. https://doi.org/10.1016/j.amepre.2009.01.024.

Raj, A., and J. Silverman. 2002. "Violence against Immigrant Women: The Roles of Culture, Context, and Legal Immigrant Status on Intimate Partner Violence." *Violence against Women* 8 (3): 367–98. https://doi.org/10.1177/107 78010222183107.

Ramos, Paola. 2020. *Finding Latinx: In Search of the Voices Redefining Latino Identity.* New York: Vintage Books.

Ravenstein, Ernest George. 1885. "The Laws of Migration." *Journal of the Statistical Society of London* 48 (2): 167–235.

Rhodes, Scott D., Lilli Mann, Florence M. Simán, Eunyoung Song, Jorge Alonzo, Mario Downs, Emma Lawlor, et al. 2014. "The Impact of Local Immigration Enforcement Policies on the Health of Immigrant Hispanics/Latinos in the United States." *American Journal of Public Health* 105 (2): 329–37. https:// doi.org/10.2105/AJPH.2014.302218.

Rierden, Andi. 1992. "Problems Temper Puerto Ricans' Success." *New York Times,* February 16, 1992.

Roberts, Dorothy E. 1999. *Killing the Black Body: Race, Reproduction, and the Meaning of Liberty.* New York: Vintage.

———. 2002. *Shattered Bonds: The Color of Child Welfare.* New York: Basic Books.

Rodriguez Guzman, Juan, Marco A. Ramos, Michelle Silva, Douglas A. Mata, Hanna Raila, Robert Rohrbaugh, and Andres Barkil-Oteo. 2018. "Training Health Professional Students as Lay Counselors to Treat Depression in a Student-Run Free Clinic." *Journal of Student-Run Clinics* 4 (1). https://stude ntrunfreeclinics.org/journalsrc.org/index.php/jsrc/article/view/61.

Rodríguez-Muñiz, Michael. 2021. *Figures of the Future: Latino Civil Rights and the Politics of Demographic Change.* Princeton, NJ: Princeton University Press.

Roemer, John E. 1998. *Equality of Opportunity.* Cambridge, MA: Harvard University Press.

Rosenberg, Jared. 2002. "Neonatal Death Risk: Effect of Prenatal Care Is Most Evident after Term Birth." *Perspectives on Sexual and Reproductive Health* 34 (5): 270. https://doi.org/10.1363/3427002.

Rosenthal, E. Lee, J. Nell Brownstein, Carl H. Rush, Gail R. Hirsch, Anne M. Willaert, Jacqueline R. Scott, Lisa R. Holderby, and Durrell J. Fox. 2010. "Community Health Workers: Part of The Solution." *Health Affairs* 29 (7): 1338–42. https://doi.org/10.1377/hlthaff.2010.0081.

Rubio-Goldsmith, Raquel, Melissa McCormick, Daniel Martinez, and Inez Duarte. 2006. "The 'Funnel Effect' and Recovered Bodies of Unauthorized Migrants Processed by the Pima County Office of the Medical Examiner, 1990–2005." SSRN Scholarly Paper ID 3040107. Rochester, NY: Social Science Research Network. https://doi.org/10.2139/ssrn.3040107.

Rubio-Hernandez, Sandy P., and Cecilia Ayón. 2016. "*Pobrecitos los Niños:* The Emotional Impact of Anti-immigration Policies on Latino Children." *Children and Youth Services Review* 60 (January): 20–26. https://doi.org/10.1016/j.chi ldyouth.2015.11.013.

Runner, Michael, Mieko Yoshihama, and Steve Novick. 2009. *Intimate Partner Violence in Immigrant and Refugee Communities: Challenges, Promising Practices and Recommendations.* Family Violence Prevention Fund. https:// doi.org/10.1037/e601452012-001.

Rutter, Michael. 2012. "Resilience: Causal Pathways and Social Ecology." In *The Social Ecology of Resilience: A Handbook of Theory and Practice,* edited by Michael Ungar, 33–42. New York: Springer New York. https://doi.org/10.10 07/978-1-4614-0586-3_3.

Salmon, Daniel A, Stephen P Teret, C Raina MacIntyre, David Salisbury, Margaret A Burgess, and Neal A Halsey. 2006. "Compulsory Vaccination and Conscientious or Philosophical Exemptions: Past, Present, and Future." *Lancet* 367 (9508): 436–42. https://doi.org/10.1016/S0140-6736(06)68144-0.

Sanchez, Joseph. 2016. "Obamacare in New Mexico: The New Mexico Health Insurance Exchange; Who or What Influences and Motivates Hispanic Individuals to Enroll?" PhD diss. , University of New Mexico.

Scheper-Hughes, Nancy. 1992. *Death without Weeping: The Violence of Everyday Life in Brazil.* Berkeley: University of California Press.

———. 1994. "Embodied Knowledge: Thinking with the Body in Critical Medical Anthropology." In *Assessing Cultural Anthropology,* edited by Robert Borofsky. New York: McGraw-Hill.

Schmidt, Samantha, and Rebecca Tan. 2020. "The Number of Pregnant Latinas with Covid-19 Is Staggering. And a Warning Sign, Doctors Say." *Washington Post,* August 16.

Schofield, Thomas J, Rand D Conger, and Tricia K Neppl. 2014. "Positive Parenting, Beliefs about Parental Efficacy, and Active Coping: Three Sources of Intergenerational Resilience." *Journal of Family Psychology* 28 (6): 973–78. https://doi.org/10.1037/fam0000024.

Schouler-Ocak, Meryam. 2015. "Introduction: The Relevance of Trauma among Immigrants." In *Trauma and Migration: Cultural Factors in the Diagnosis and Treatment of Traumatised Immigrants*, edited by Meryam Schouler-Ocak, 3–8. Cham, Switzerland: Springer International. https://doi.org/10.10 07/978-3-319-17335-1_1.

Sigona, Nando. 2012. "'I Have Too Much Baggage': The Impacts of Legal Status on the Social Worlds of Irregular Migrants." *Social Anthropology* 20 (1): 50–65. https://doi.org/10.1111/j.1469-8676.2011.00191. x.

Silva, Michelle A., Manuel Paris, and Luis M. Añez. 2017. "CAMINO: Integrating Context in the Mental Health Assessment of Immigrant Latinos." *Professional Psychology: Research and Practice* 48 (6): 453–60. https://doi.org/10.1037/pr 00000170.

Smith, Linda Tuhiwai. 2012. *Decolonizing Methodologies: Research and Indigenous Peoples*. 2nd ed. London: Zed.

Solimano, Andrés. 2004. *Political Violence and Economic Development in Latin America: Issues and Evidence*. Santiago, Chile: United Nations Economic Commission for Latin America and the Caribbean.

Soucheray, Stephanie. 2021. "Biden Details 5-Step COVID Vaccine Plan, Names New Lead for Vaccines." *Center for Infectious Disease Research and Policy*, January 15. www.cidrap.umn.edu/news-perspective/2021/01/biden-details -5-step-covid-vaccine-plan-names-new-lead-vaccines.

Spetz, Joanne, Mark W. Smith, and Sean F. Ennis. 2001. "Physician Incentives and the Timing of Cesarean Sections: Evidence from California." *Medical Care* 39 (6): 536–50.

St. Jean, Yanick, and Joe R Feagin. 2015. *Double Burden: Black Women and Everyday Racism*. New York: Routledge.

Stannard, Ed. 2017. "Demonstrators in New Haven Protest Trump's Enforcement of Immigration Law." *New Haven Register*, January 2017.

Statista Research Department. 2021. "Total Fertility Rate by Ethnicity, U.S. 2019." Statista. May 5. www.statista.com/statistics/226292/us-fertility-rates-by-race -and-ethnicity.

Stewart, Nicholas. 2018. "' Magnificent Cit[ies]' New Haven, Saadiyat Island, And Yale's Global Expansion." *Yale Historical Review* blog. 2018. http: //histor icalreview.yale.edu/sites/default/files/files/Stewart.pdf.

Stolberg, Sheryl Gay. 2020. "Some States Balk After C.D.C. Asks for Personal Data of Those Vaccinated." *New York Times*, December 8. www.

Stone, Lyman. 2018. *How Many Kids Do Women Want?* Institute for Family Studies. June 1. https://ifstudies.org/blog/how-many-kids-do-women-want.

Strocka, Cordula. 2006. "Youth Gangs in Latin America." *SAIS Review of International Affairs* 26 (2): 133–46. https://doi.org/10.1353/sais.2006.0045.

Sullivan, Shane. 2021. "Liquid Gold: False COVID-19 Vaccines Emerge in Latin America." InSight Crime blog. January 18. https://insightcrime.org/news/ana lysis/false-covid-vaccines-emerge.

Tavernise, Sabrina, and Robert Gebeloff. 2021. "A Rise in Hispanic and Asian Population Fuels U.S. Growth, Census Reports." *New York Times,* August 12.

Tedeschi, R. G., and L. G. Calhoun. 1996. "The Posttraumatic Growth Inventory: Measuring the Positive Legacy of Trauma." *Journal of Traumatic Stress* 9 (3): 455–71. https://doi.org/10.1007/BF02103658.

Treitler, Vilna Bashi. 2015. "Social Agency and White Supremacy in Immigration Studies." *Sociology of Race and Ethnicity* 1 (1): 153–65. https://doi.org/10.1177/2332649214560796.

Trumbo, Silas P, Cara B Janusz, Barbara Jauregui, Mike McQuestion, Gabriela Felix, Cuauhtémoc Ruiz-Matus, Jon K Andrus, and Ciro De Quadros. 2013. "Vaccination Legislation in Latin America and the Caribbean." *Journal of Public Health Policy* 34 (1): 82–99. https://doi.org/10.1057/jphp.2012.66.

Tsai, J., J. P. Cerdeña, R. Khazanchi, E. Lindo, J. R. Marcelin, A. Rajagopalan, R. S. Sandoval, A. Westby, and C. C. Gravlee. 2020. "There Is No 'African American Physiology': The Fallacy of Racial Essentialism." *Journal of Internal Medicine* 288 (3): 368–70. https://doi.org/10.1111/joim.13153.

Ungar, Michael. 2011. "The Social Ecology of Resilience: Addressing Contextual and Cultural Ambiguity of a Nascent Construct." *American Journal of Orthopsychiatry* 81 (1): 1. https://psycnet.apa.org/doi/10.1111/j.1939-0025.2010.01067. x.

U.S. Census Bureau. 2010. *Profile of General Population and Housing Characteristics: 2010 Demographic Profile Data.* www.census.gov/library/publications/2012/dec/cph-1. html.

———. 2018. "Hispanic Origin," 2018. www.census.gov/topics/population/hispanic-origin/about.html.

———. 2020. "Hispanic Heritage Month 2020." August 11. www.census.gov/newsroom/facts-for-features/2020/hispanic-heritage-month.html.

———. 2021. "Guilford Town, New Haven County, Connecticut." U.S. Census Bureau QuickFacts. July 1. www.census.gov/quickfacts/guilfordtownnewhavencountyconnecticut.

U.S. Department of Education. 2015. *Resource Guide: Supporting Undocumented Youth.* Washington, DC: U.S. Department of Education. www2. ed.gov/about/overview/focus/supporting-undocumented-youth.pdf.

Vaca, Federico E., Craig L Anderson, and David E Hayes-Bautista. 2011. "The Latino Adolescent Male Mortality Peak Revisited: Attribution of Homicide and Motor Vehicle Crash Death." *Injury Prevention : Journal of the International Society for Child and Adolescent Injury Prevention* 17 (2): 102–7. https://doi.org/10.1136/ip.2010.028886.

Vallejo, Camila. 2021. "Afghan Refugees Arrive in CT, and Resettlement Agency Calls for Assistance." *CT Mirror,* August 20. http: //ctmirror.org/2021/08/20/afghan-refugees-arrive-in-connecticut-as-resettlement-agency-calls-for-assistance.

Van Natta, Meredith. 2019. "First Do No Harm: Medical Legal Violence and Immigrant Health in Coral County, USA." *Social Science and Medicine* 235 (August): 112411. https://doi.org/10.1016/j.socscimed.2019.112411.

Vanthuyne, Karine, Francesca Meloni, Monica Ruiz-Casares, Cécile Rousseau, and Alexandra Ricard-Guay. 2013. "Health Workers' Perceptions of Access to Care for Children and Pregnant Women with Precarious Immigration Status: Health as a Right or a Privilege?" *Social Science and Medicine* 2013 (93): 78–85. https://doi.org/10.1016/j.socscimed.2013.06.008.

Vazquez, Mayra. 2019. "The Housing Choice Voucher (HCV) Program and Upward Mobility: Through a Latino Lens." Washington, DC: Congressional Hispanic Caucus Institute. https://chci.org/wp-content/uploads/2019/04/Pol icy-Brief-Mayra-Vazquez.pdf.

Vera Institute of Justice. 2020. *Profile of the Foreign-Born Population in New Haven, Connecticut.* Brooklyn, NY: Vera Institute of Justice. www.vera.org/do wnloads/publications/publicationsprofile-foreign-born-population-new-hav en.pdf.

Verdery, Ashton M., Emily Smith-Greenaway, Rachel Margolis, and Jonathan Daw. 2020. "Tracking the Reach of COVID-19 Kin Loss with a Bereavement Multiplier Applied to the United States." *Proceedings of the National Academy of Sciences* 117 (30): 17695–701. https://doi.org/10.1073/pnas.2007476117.

Vespa, Jonathan, Lauren Medina, and David M. Armstrong. 2020. *Demographic Turning Points for the United States: Population Projections for 2020 to 2060.* Washington, DC: U.S. Census Bureau. www.census.gov/content/dam/Census /library/publications/2020/demo/p25-1144.pdf.

Villavicencio, Karla Cornejo. 2018. "A Family Separated but Still Together." *New Haven Independent,* November 8. www.newhavenindependent.org/index.php /archives/entry/nelson_article.

Vlahov, David, Micaela H. Coady, Sandro Galea, Danielle C. Ompad, and Jeremiah A. Barondess. 2007. "Pandemic Preparedness and Hard to Reach Populations." *American Journal of Disaster Medicine* 2 (6): 281–83.

Vogt, Wendy A. 2018. *Lives in Transit: Violence and Intimacy on the Migrant Journey.* Oakland: University of California Press. www.ucpress.edu/book/978 0520298552/lives-in-transit.

Vuong, Ocean. 2019. *On Earth We're Briefly Gorgeous.* New York: Penguin.

Vyas, Darshali A., David S. Jones, Audra R. Meadows, Khady Diouf, Nawal M. Nour, and Julianna Schantz-Dunn. 2019. "Challenging the Use of Race in the Vaginal Birth after Cesarean Section Calculator." *Women's Health Issues* 29 (3): 201–4. https://doi.org/10.1016/j.whi.2019.04.007.

Waldstein, Anna. 2017. *Living Well in Los Duplex: Critical Reflections on Medicalization, Migration and Health Sovereignty.* Durham, NC: Carolina Academic Press.

Walia, Harsha. 2021. *Border and Rule: Global Migration, Capitalism, and the Rise of Racist Nationalism*. Chicago: Haymarket.

Wang, Jingyi, Brynmor Lloyd-Evans, Domenico Giacco, Rebecca Forsyth, Cynthia Nebo, Farhana Mann, and Sonia Johnson. 2017. "Social Isolation in Mental Health: A Conceptual and Methodological Review." *Social Psychiatry and Psychiatric Epidemiology* 52 (12): 1451–61. https://doi.org/10.1007/s001 27-017-1446-1.

Warren, David Liles. 1976. "Town-Gown Conflict: Ideology, Class Resentment, and Group Interest, in the Responses to an Elite University." PhD diss., University of Michigan. Available at www.proquest.com/docview/302797276 /citation/AAACCDDE62B04344PQ/1.

Washington, Harriet A. 2019. *A Terrible Thing to Waste: Environmental Racism and Its Assault on the American Mind*. New York: Hachette.

Weathers, F. W., B. T. Litz, T. M. Keane, P. A. Palmieri, B. P. Marx, and P. P. Schnurr. 2013. "The PTSD Checklist for DSM-5 (PCL-5)." National Center for PTSD. www.ptsd.va.gov.

Wertsch, James V. 2007. "National Narratives and the Conservative Nature of Collective Memory." *Neohelicon* 34 (2): 23–33. https://doi.org/10.1007/s11105 9-007-2003-9.

WestRasmus, Emma K., Fernando Pineda-Reyes, Montelle Tamez, and John M. Westfall. 2012. "Promotores de Salud and Community Health Workers: An Annotated Bibliography." *Family and Community Health* 35 (2): 172–82. https://doi.org/10.1097/FCH.0b013e31824991d2.

Wexler, Lisa Marin, Gloria DiFluvio, and Tracey K. Burke. 2009. "Resilience and Marginalized Youth: Making a Case for Personal and Collective Meaning-Making as Part of Resilience Research in Public Health." *Social Science and Medicine* 69 (4): 565–70. https://doi.org/10.1016/j.socscimed.2009.06.022.

White House. 2021. "Remarks by President Biden on the 100 Million Shot Goal." The White House. March 18. www.whitehouse.gov/briefing-room/speeches -remarks/2021/03/18/remarks-by-president-biden-on-the-100-million-shot -goal.

Wiese, Elizabeth Batista-Pinto. 2010. "Culture and Migration: Psychological Trauma in Children and Adolescents." *Traumatology* 16 (4): 142–152.

Willen, Sarah S. 2007. "Toward a Critical Phenomenology of 'Illegality': State Power, Criminalization, and Abjectivity among Undocumented Migrant Workers in Tel Aviv, Israel." *International Migration* 45 (3): 8–38. https://doi .org/10.1111/j.1468-2435.2007.00409. x.

———. 2012a. "How Is Health-Related 'Deservingness' Reckoned? Perspectives from Unauthorized Im/Migrants in Tel Aviv." *Social Science and Medicine* 74 (6): 812–21. https://doi.org/10.1016/j.socscimed.2011.06.033.

———. 2012b. "Migration, 'Illegality,' and Health: Mapping Embodied Vulnerability and Debating Health-Related Deservingness." *Social Science and Medicine* 74 (6): 805–11. https://doi.org/10.1016/j.socscimed.2011.10.041.

———. 2019. "Perhaps, to Flourish." In *Fighting for Dignity: Migrant Lives at Israel's Margins.* Philadelphia: University of Pennsylvania Press.

———. 2022. "Flourishing and Health in Critical Perspective: An Invitation to Interdisciplinary Dialogue." *SSM—Mental Health* 2 (December): 100045. https://doi.org/10.1016/j.ssmmh.2021.100045.

Witmer, A., S. D. Seifer, L. Finocchio, J. Leslie, and E. H. O'Neil. 1995. "Community Health Workers: Integral Members of the Health Care Work Force." *American Journal of Public Health* 85 (8, part 1): 1055–58. https://doi.org/10.2105/AJPH.85.8_Pt_1.1055.

Wucker, Michele. 2007. "A Safe Haven in New Haven." *New York Times.* April 15.

Xi, Joyce. 2013. "A Healthier New Haven." *Yale Scientific Magazine.* May 29. www.yalescientific.org/2013/05/a-healthier-new-haven.

Yale University. 2013. *The Yale Endowment, 2013.* New Haven, CT: Yale University. https://static1.squarespace.com/static/55db7b87e4b0dca22fba2438/t/578e4246e58c629352d758ed/1468940872526/Yale_Endowment_13.pdf.

Yoshikawa, Hirokazu, and Jenya Kholoptseva. 2013. "Unauthorized Immigrant Parents and Their Children's Development: A Summary of the Evidence." Washington, DC: Migration Policy Institute. www.migrationpolicy.org/sites/default/files/publications/COI-Yoshikawa.pdf.

Zahn, Brian. 2018. "Immigrants Shaped New Haven of Today." *New Haven Register,* June 17.

Zhao, Yu, Zixian Zhao, Yujia Wang, Yueqing Zhou, Yu Ma, and Wei Zuo. 2020. "Single-Cell RNA Expression Profiling of ACE2, the Putative Receptor of Wuhan 2019-NCov." *BioRxiv,* January.01.26.919985. https://doi.org/10.1101/2020.01.26.919985.

Index

Abrego, Leisy, 61–62
adaptation, 4, 5, 13–14. *See also* monarch butterfly metaphor
Adelina (interlocutor), 150–51, 153, 154, 185, 190
Ad Hoc Committee on Racial and Ethnic Definitions of 1975, 72
Affordable Care Act, 126, 165
Aida (interlocutor), 60–61, 188
Alejandra (interlocutor), 155
Algonquian-speaking tribes, xi
Almudena (interlocutor), 21, 48–49, 50, 51–52, 53, 75, 135–36, 140, 168, 175
Amalia (interlocutor), 34, 189, 192
American Immigration Council, 193
Anahi (interlocutor), 41–42, 43, 63
Ana Paula (interlocutor), 52–53
"anchor babies," 36, 168
Anita (interlocutor), 188, 191
anti-Latinx prejudice, 35–36
Antoinetta (interlocutor), 55, 146–47, 148
Apostle Immigrant Services, 193
archival research, 15
Argentina, 85; social programs in, 22–23
Ascención (interlocutor), 21–22, 25, 50, 76, 136, 168–69, 186, 190
assimilationism, 9
asylum, application/granting of, 32

asylum court hearings, 29
avoidance coping strategies, 129–30

behavioral health services, as essential services, 171–72
Biden administration, 175–76
Binational Migration Institute, 47
biomarker study, 183
Blackness: Afro-Latino identity, 65–66; anti-Blackness, 68, 70; dark-skinned Latinas treated as, 32–36; erasure of identities of, 14, 66–67; opportunity deprivation in Latin America of African-descended people, 21; reproduction and, 36
Bolívar, Simón, 73
Bolivia, social programs in, 22
bootstrap mentality, 38–39
border crossing: gender-based violence, 45–49; immigration detention conditions, 49–50; migration-related trauma from, 43–44; process of, 28; violence and, 14
Border Protection , Anti-terrorism, and Illegal Immigration Control Act of 2005, 101
Bracero Agreement, 62
Branford neighborhood, interlocutors from, 12
Brazil, racial classification systems in, 35
Bridges, Khiara, 112, 113, 119, 168

220   INDEX

British East India Trading Company, 107
Brown Power political movement, 73
bureaucratic disentitlement, 122–27
Bush administration, 101

Camila (interlocutor), 30, 34, 187, 190
Caribbean, 54–55
Caridad (interlocutor), 42–43, 63–64
Carla (interlocutor), 34, 188, 192
Castro, Julián, 174
Célia (interlocutor), 1–4, 15, 21, 26, 39, 55–57,
    76, 115–21, 142, 150, 157, 160, 185, 190
census data, 15, 72, 77–80, 78–79, 115
Center for Children's Advocacy, 169
Center for Gender and Refugee Studies, 193
Central American migrants, 32, 86–87
chain migration, 76
Chapa, Jorge, 72
Chavez, Leo, 53, 69, 114
children: of immigrants, 13; of interlocutors,
    13
Children's Health Insurance Program
    (CHIP), 172
Chile: interlocutors from, 191; social spending
    programs in, 22. See also Raquel
    (interlocutor)
Chinese Exclusion Act of 1882, 62
Cintia (interlocutor), 34, 120–21, 148, 150,
    192
clinical screenings, 12
clinics and undocumented women, 7
College Bound, 84
Colombia, 85–86, 189
colonial era: gender stereotypes since, 21; vio-
    lence during, 19
Columbus Family Academy, 95
Community Foundation for Greater New
    Haven, 109, 193
community health worker (CHW) programs,
    171–72
conclusion, 179–81
Connecticut Mental Health Center, 184
coping strategies, 40; avoidance coping strat-
    egies, 129–30. See also imperative
    resilience
Córdova, Celestina, 84
Coronavirus Aid, Relief, and Economic Secu-
    rity (CARES) Act, 145
Correa, Rafael, 22
Costa Rica, 67
countries of origin: departure from, 14; dis-
    placement from, 14
COVID-19 pandemic: accommodating

trauma during, 11; attitudes toward vac-
    cination, 158–61; consequences for Latina
    migrant mothers, 15; disparities, 177; eco-
    nomic anxiety during, 39; effects on inter-
    views, 1, 3; embodied experiences of, 15,
    146–49; employment during, 13; exposure
    risks, 15, 177; fears over, xiii, 4; financial
    impacts (economic loss) of, 15; financial
    impacts of, xiv, 4; genetic explanations, 15;
    illness and death of loved ones, 4, 15, 149–
    51; immigration court dates under, 29;
    imperative resilience during, 11–12; indi-
    vidualistic explanations, 15; need to
    reform policies after, 172–73; personal
    impact of, 4; racial disparities, 15; racial
    inequities and, 15; responses to, 5; Semilla
    Collective and, 104; social impacts of, xiv,
    151–58; structural vulnerability and, 15;
    vaccine outreach, 15, 177; zero tolerance
    policies and, 165
criminalization, for skin tone and immigra-
    tion status, 33
criminal justice system, in Latin America,
    40
Cruz, Lee, 85, 91, 94–95, 96–97, 104, 176–77,
    179, 181
Cruz, Nikolas, 70
Cubans, 85, 86
cultural loss of children of immigrants, 13

DACA (Deferred Action for Childhood Arriv-
    als), 29, 31, 39, 175
Davis, Angela, 178
Davis, Dána-Ain, 119
Dean, Carolyn, 11
decolonization, 178
Deferred Action for Childhood Arrivals
    (DACA), 29, 31, 39, 175
DeLauro, Rosa, 77
de León, Jason, 165
Delia (interlocutor), 161
del Olmo, Frank, 73
demographics: census data, 77–80; demo-
    graphic shifts in late 20th century, 85–90;
    early Puerto Rican community, 80–85;
    Latinxs in New Haven today, 90; politici-
    zation of Latinx term, 14–15. See also
    Latinx category
Department of Homeland Security (DHS),
    38–39
deportation, fears over, 30
DeStefano, John, 85, 87, 93, 102, 105
Detention Watch Network, 193

discrimination, experiences of, 35
Dominguez, Virginia R., 28
Dominican Republic, 67, 70, 86; COVID-19
    pandemic and, 147; employment in, 158;
    interlocutors from, 186, 187, 190, 192;
    migrants to New Haven from, 89, 90;
    police as instruments of structural vio-
    lence in, 24. *See also* Antoinetta (interloc-
    utor); Cintia (interlocutor); Delia (inter-
    locutor); Elvira (interlocutor)
Donelson, Tiffany, 159
Dowling, Julie, 71
drugs: Latin American criminalization of
    production and commerce of, 23; US War
    on Drugs, 23
Duden, Barbara, 124

East Haven neighborhood, interlocutors
    from, 12
economic anxiety: during COVID-19 pan-
    demic, 39; of interlocutors, 39–40
economic development, 15; in New Haven,
    104–6
economic precarity and opportunity: in Latin
    America, 21, 57–58; as reasons for migrat-
    ing, 14, 55–59
economic stimulus checks, inability to access
    of, 4
Ecuador, 2, 31; employment in, 2; interlocu-
    tors from, 40, 185, 186, 187, 188, 189, 190,
    191, 192; kidnapping in, 3; migrants to
    New Haven from, 89; poverty in, 4, 21;
    social programs in, 22; violence in, 4. *See
    also* Célia (interlocutor); Gladys (inter-
    locutor); Karina (interlocutor); Maribel
    (interlocutor); Meri (interlocutor); Nieve
    (interlocutor); Susana (interlocutor);
    Teresa (interlocutor); Ysabel
    (interlocutor)
Ecuadorian community, 92
Edinburgh Postnatal Depression Scale, 6
Elmira (interlocutor), 34
El Salvador: employment in, 21; interlocutors
    from, 187, 190; migrants to New Haven
    from, 86; TPS for migrants from, 29. *See
    also* Ysabel (interlocutor)
Elvira (interlocutor), 24, 139–40, 157–58, 186
Elyse (interlocutor), 124–25
embodied experiences of COVID-19, 146–49
Emergency Quota Act of 1921, 62
employment: in Ecuador, 2; exploitable
    laborers, 14; of interlocutors, 13. *See also*
    "illegality" (undocumented status)

English language proficiency, 35
environmental activism, in New Haven,
    94–101
essential services: about, 170–71; behavioral
    health services as, 171–72; food, housing,
    and financial support as, 172–73; immi-
    gration policy and, 174–76; intimate part-
    ner violence and, 173–74
ethics and inequity studies, 6–8
ethnicity, Latinx as race versus, 15, 70–72
ethnographic interviews, reliance on, 6
ethnographic tables, 185–93

Fair Haven Community Health Care
    (FHCHC), 95, 95–96, 109, 193
Fair Haven neighborhood, 78–80, 81, 85,
    87–88, 95; gains to, 15; improvements in,
    97–98; interlocutors from, 12; migrants
    in, xi; Monarch Watch Tagging Program,
    181
Family Academy of Multilingual Exploration
    (FAME), 95
family background in Latin America, 21
family reunification as reason for migrating,
    14, 53–55
FARC (Fuerzas Armadas Revolucionarias de
    Colombia) (Revolutionary Armed Forces
    of Colombia), 86
FHCHC (Fair Haven Community Health
    Care), 95–96
Figures of the Future (Rodríguez-Muñiz), 65
Florence Immigrant and Refugee Rights
    Project, 194
flourishing, 128
food, housing, and financial support as essen-
    tial services, 172–73
Foucault, Michel, 38, 61
Fountain, Megan, 88, 102
Franceschi, Norma, 80–81, 85–87, 90–93,
    95–96, 103, 105, 131–32
"freeloader" label, 36
Friedman, Jonathan, 28
friendships, illegality and, 29–30

Galtung, Johan, 178
Gálvez, Alyshia, 38, 39, 53, 155
gang violence, 23
gender-based violence, 14; border crossing
    and, 45–49; intimate partner violence,
    173–74
gender discrimination, 109
gender diversity, 109
gendered racial removal programs, 101

gender identity: Center for Gender and Refugee Studies, 193; Latina term usage and, 75; shared histories of, 109
gender inequality: in Latin America, 21–22; strategic coupling and, 114, 138
gender-neutral words, 64, 74–75
generational diversity, 109
Gibson, Brehon, Dawn, 108
Ginsburg, Faye, 113
Gladys (interlocutor), 34, 136–38, 189, 192
global disadvantage, strategies in response to, 11
God: faith in, 133; spirituality and, 15
Golash-Boza, Tanya, 101
Gómez, Laura E., 35
González-Duarte, Columba, 142
González-López, Gloria, 24
Good, Byron, 154
Granski, Megan, 6, 32
Gravlee, Clarence C., 145
Guatemala: employment in, 22; gender inequality in, 21–22; interlocutors from, 186, 187, 190, 192; migrants to New Haven from, 86, 88–89. See also Anahi (interlocutor); Ascención (interlocutor); Jackelín (interlocutor); Jenifer (interlocutor); Verónica (interlocutor)
Guilford, 81, 82–83
Gurria, José Ángel, 106

Hamden neighborhood, interlocutors from, 12
Harp, Toni, 77
Hart-Celler Act of 1965, 53–54, 86, 113
Haven Free Clinic, 169, 193
Hayes-Bautista, David E., 72
Head Start programs, 8, 95–96, 127
health: immigration enforcement and, 30; migration-related trauma and, 14, 44; in New Haven, 94–101; racialization of, 15; structural vulnerability and, 15. See also mental health
healthcare access: assistance to, 37–38; DACA and, 39; policies for moving onward and, 165–70. See also Yale–New Haven Health
health inequities, COVID-19 pandemic and, 15
hielera (ice box), 49–50
Hill neighborhood, 79–80, 81, 84, 85
Hispanic Clinic of Connecticut Mental Health Center, 184
Hispanic/Latino: as distinct from Blackness,

66; as ethnicity, 69; terminology note, 72–75
Hoberman, John, 119
Holmes, Seth, 39
home countries: replication of conditions in, 14. See also Latin American governments; specific countries
Hondagneu-Sotelo, Pandierrette, 190
Honduras: interlocutors from, 188; police as instruments of structural violence in, 18, 23. See also Aida (interlocutor); Lidia (interlocutor)
housing, 15; in New Haven, 91–94
Humane Borders, Inc., 43
humitas (steamed corn cakes), 4
Huntington, Samuel P., 69
HUSKY (Connecticut Medicaid), 39, 55, 125–26, 147, 169–70

Illegal Immigration Reform and Immigration Responsibility Act of 1996 (IIRIRA), 164, 173
illegality, production of, 61–62
"illegality" (undocumented status), 14, 28–32; constraints from, 40
Immigrant Defense Project, 194
Immigrant Legal Resource Center, 194
immigration, New Haven and, 101–4
Immigration Act of 1864, 62
Immigration Advocates Network, 194
Immigration and Customs Enforcement (ICE), 103
Immigration and Nationality Act of 1965, 53–54, 86
Immigration Control and Reform Act of 1986, 29
immigration detention conditions: border crossing and, 44, 49–50; under zero tolerance policy, 61
immigration enforcement: critics of, xii; effects on health, 30; legal violence of, 44
immigration policy: color line, 53–54; essential services and, 174–76; exclusionary practices of, 62, 63; restrictiveness of US, 29
immigration reform, 15; as structural intervention, 12
Immigration Reform and Control Act of 1986, 125, 175
immigration status, liminality of, 33
imperative resilience: about, 127–31; defined, 11, 28; intergenerational fortitude, 15, 138–41; of migrant mothers, xiv, 11–12;

pressing onward concept and, 40, 141–43; spirituality, 131–34; strategic coupling, 15, 134–38; techniques of, 15

Inadmissibility on Public Charge Grounds, 38–39

Indigenous peoples: anti-Indigenous racism in Americans, 9, 68; Eansketambawg, xi; erasure of identities of, 14, 66–67; interlocutors, 33, 59; of New Haven, xi; opportunity deprivation in Latin America, 21; social movements in Latin America by, 22, 40, 59

individual subjectivity, neglect of, 14

inequality of opportunity, 21, 40

inequities, COVID-19 pandemic and health, 15

insecurity, of home countries, 13

institutional barriers, to care, 15

Integrated Refugee and Immigrant Services, 77

intergenerational fortitude, 138–41; defined, 15

intergenerational trauma, 3–4, 6, 183

interlocutors: defined, xii; methodology and, 1–3, 12–13, 183–84. *See also specific interlocutors*

intimate partner violence, essential services and, 173–74

intimate relationships, reliance on, 12

Ivette (interlocutor), 160, 188, 191

Jackelín (interlocutor), 30, 34, 45–47, 114–15, 132–34, 149, 150, 153–54, 161, 186, 190

Jamaica: interlocutors from, 186. *See also* Nikki (interlocutor)

Jeaneth (interlocutor), 187, 190

Jenifer (interlocutor), 34, 129–30, 192

Joscelyne, Amy, 6, 32

Juana (interlocutor), 24, 25–26, 76, 140, 150, 171, 186, 190

Junta for Progressive Action, 76, 84–85, 86, 92, 109, 193

Kaiser Family Foundation (KFF), 159

Kara (interlocutor), 192

Karina (interlocutor), 187, 190

Keller, Allen, 6, 32

Lamont, Ned, 170

Latin@ (term), 73

Latina (term), 75

Latina birth, racialization of, 15, 112–15

Latin America: gender inequity, 22; racial

classification systems in, 35; refugees originating from, 32; social programs in, 22; US interventions in, 40

Latin American governments: criminalization of drug production and commerce, 23; criminal violence and, 23, 40; as driver of migration, 14, 19, 25–26, 40

Latin American migrants, medical anthropologists on, xiv

Latin American migration to New Haven, 15, 75–77

Latin American violence, 17–40; about, 14–15, 17–19, 40; "illegality"/undocumented status, 28–32; new violence of Latin America, 19–20; police as instruments of structural violence, 23–25; poverty, 36–40; racism, 32–36; state failure as driver of migration, 14, 19, 25–26, 40, 59; structural vulnerability, 26–28; violence of social inequality, 20–23

Latina motherhood, racialization of, 15

Latinidad: as contradiction, 65–68; embodied expressions of, 33; politicization of, 68–70

Latin Kings, 92, 94

Latino/a (term), 73

Latino/Hispanic. *See* Hispanic/Latino

Latino threat narrative, 69, 77

The Latino Threat (Chavez), 69

Latinx category, 64–110; about, 14, 109–10; census data, 77–80; defined, 64–65; demographic shifts in in Hill neighborhood, 80, 81; in New Haven, 77, 79, 81, 85, 86, 87, 89, 90; late 20th century, 85–90; early Puerto Rican community, 80–85; heterogeneity of, 14; inherent contradictions of, 14, 34–35; Latin American migration to New Haven, 15, 75–77; *Latinidad* as contradiction, 65–68; Latinx as race (vs. ethnicity), 70–72; Latinx defined, 64–65; Latinxs in New Haven today, 90; limitation of, 14–15; in New Haven today, 90; politicization of *Latinidad*, 14–15, 68–70; population politics, 77–80; social movements and New Haven, 91–109; terminology note, 72–75. *See also* New Haven

Latinx community, 81, 83–89; in Connecticut, 83; in Fair Haven neighborhood, 78–80; in Hill neighborhood, 80, 81; in New Haven, 77, 79, 81, 85, 86, 87, 89, 90

Latinxs: defined, xi–xii; European heritage of, 9; gains to Latinx community, 15; in New Haven, xi–xii; terminology note, 73–74

Leacock, Eleanor, 178
Lee, Catherine, 54
Lee, Richard "Dick," 107–8
Lee, Sonia, 66
legal residency, applications for, 38–39; obtaining of legal status, 32
legal violence, 14, 61–62
Leocadia (interlocutor), 34
Leticia (interlocutor), 187
Lidia (interlocutor), 17–19, 23, 25, 34, 188, 191
liminality: of children of immigrants, 13; of immigrants, 33; liminal legality, 29
Linette (interlocutor), 189, 192
Livable City Initiative (LCI), 91
Looney, Martin M., 169–70
low-income mothers, prenatal care programs and, 15
Lucía (interlocutor), 56–57, 58
Lugo, John Jairo, 92

Malcolm X, 110
Manship, Jim, 88, 93, 102–3, 105
Mapuche people, 8, 9
Marable, Manning, 142
Marcelina (interlocutor), 55–56
Maribel (interlocutor), 31, 154–55
Marisol (interlocutor), 54, 141, 187
marriage, status adjustments after, 31–32
Marta (interlocutor), 160, 187
Martin, Trayvon, 70
maternity, 109; shared histories of, 109
Matos, Kica, 86, 88, 90, 92, 101, 110
matrilineal bonds, 12, 15. See also intergenerational fortitude
Me and My Baby program, xiii, 7, 95, 113, 122–27, 170, 171
Medicaid: denial of, 125–26; extended to undocumented, 169, 170; familiarity with, 55; fears of costs, 147–48; sweat equity and, 39
medical anthropologists, on Latin American migrants, xiv
medical anthropology, 4–5
medical registration, name confusion and, 1
Meliza (interlocutor), 34, 155, 192
Menjívar, Cecilia, 61–62
mental health, migration-related trauma and, 14
mental health equity, policies to foster, 11
Meri (interlocutor), 156, 188, 191
mestiza, interlocutors, 33
mestizaje (racial miscegenation), 70
methodology: approach, 4–6; ethics of studying inequity, 6–8; ethnographic tables, 185–92; interlocutors, 1–3, 12–13, 183–84; oral history interviews, 6, 15; overview, 14–16; positionality and, 8–11; terminology note, 72–75
MetroPlus Healthcare program, 170
Mexican Farm Labor Agreement of 1942, 62
Mexican migrant women, nutrition and diet of, 155
Mexico, 67; employment in, 20–21; interlocutors from, 186, 187, 188, 190, 191, 192; migrants to New Haven from, 88–89, 89, 90; police as instruments of structural violence in, 24. See also Almudena (interlocutor); Juana (interlocutor); Lidia (interlocutor); Lucía (interlocutor); Marisol (interlocutor); Meliza (interlocutor); Noelia (interlocutor); Priscila (interlocutor)
migrant mutual aid organizations, 4. See also organizations for immigration and health policy reform and activism; Semilla Collective; Unidad Latina en Acción (ULA)
migrants: migrant labor, 62; social safety net erosion and, 163–65
migration: influences for, 14; Latin American migration to New Haven, 15, 75–77; lawful migration process, 29; migration histories, 5; migration-related trauma, 43–44; monarch butterfly metaphor, 13–14; permanence of, 13; reasons for migrating, 14, 51–61; shared histories of, 109; state failure as driver of, 14, 19, 25–26, 40, 59; theories of, 50–51. See also reasons for migrating; theories of migration; violence of migration
Migration Policy Institute (MPI), 174–75, 194
migration-related trauma: health outcomes and, 44; relocations leading to, 14; surveys of, 6; term usage, 44
Mildred (interlocutor), 34, 188, 191
Mirelia (interlocutor), 187, 190
mixed-status families, 31
monarch butterfly metaphor, xii, xiii–xiv, 13–14, 43, 51, 53, 63, 130–31, 142, 179–81
Morales, Evo, 22
motherhood as racialized, 111–43; about, 15, 111–12, 142–43; attitudes toward, 5; bureaucratic disentitlement, 122–27; imperative resilience, 127–41; Me and My Baby program, 122–27; obstetrical hardiness and risk, 115–21; racialization of Latina birth, 15, 112–15; resilience to resistance, 141–42

Movimiento Cosecha, 194
MPI (Migration Policy Institute), 174–75, 194
Mullings, Leith, 142

National Immigrant Justice Center, 194
National Immigration Forum, 194
National Immigration Law Center, 194
National Immigration Project, 194
Naturalization Act of 1790, 62
Nely (interlocutor), 189, 192
neoliberalism: in Latin America, 21; models
    of citizenship, 38; US promotion of eco-
    nomic policies of, 23
New Haven: economic development in, 104–
    6; environmental activism in, 94–101;
    health and environmental activism in,
    94–101; housing and urban safety in,
    91–94; immigration and, 101–4; indige-
    nous peoples of, xi; interlocutors from,
    12; jobs for Spanish speakers in, xiii;
    Latin American migration to, 15, 75–77;
    Latinxs in, 90; organizations for immigra-
    tion and health policy reform and activ-
    ism, 193; Puerto Ricans in, 81; resettle-
    ment in, 4; urban safety in, 91–94; as
    welcoming city, 91–109; Yale–New Haven
    Health and, 106–9; Yale University and,
    6–7, 106–9
Newsom, Gavin, 170
Nicaragua: migrants to New Haven from, 86;
    TPS for migrants from, 29
ni de aquí, ni de allá (neither from here nor
    from there) feeling, 13–14
Nieve (interlocutor), xii–xiv, 187, 190
Nikki (interlocutor), 31, 32–33, 39, 123, 149–
    50, 156, 161–62, 186
Nixon administration, 72
Noelia (interlocutor), 34, 57–58, 172, 188, 191
Nordstrom, Carolyn, 48

Obama, Barack, 165
obstetrical hardiness and risk, 115–21
On Earth We're Briefly Gorgeous (Vuong), 13
Ong, Aihwa, 28
Operation Bootstrap, 83
oppressive structures, strategic resistance
    and, 11
oral history interviews, 6, 15
organizations for immigration and health
    policy reform and activism, 193–94. See
    also migrant mutual aid organizations
Ornelas, India, 44
Ortiz, Edith, 92

othering: of Latinx, 71–72; of migrant
    women, 36, 64, 69, 112

painful passages, 44. See also migration-
    related trauma
pandemic. See COVID-19 pandemic
Panter-Brick, Catherine, 131
Paraguay, 67
parenting, attitudes toward, 5
patience, of migrant mothers, 14
Patricia (interlocutor), 189
Perreira, Krista M., 44
personal factors, as influences, 14
Personal Responsibility and Work Opportu-
    nity Reconciliation (PRWORA), 164, 173
personal violence, as reasons for migrating,
    14, 59–61
Peru: immigration process from, 29; inter-
    locutors from, 189, 192; militants in, 86.
    See also Caridad (interlocutor)
Pinos, Nelson, 77
police: as instruments of structural violence,
    23–25; migrants attitude toward, 30; rac-
    ist targeting by, 33
policies for moving onward: about, 16, 161–
    63; healthcare access, 165–70; migrants
    and erosion of social safety net, 163–65
policy reform, reparative work and, 8
political drivers, overemphasis on, 14
population politics, 68, 77–80
positionality, 8–11
post-traumatic stress disorder (PTSD), 4, 6,
    44, 48
poverty, 36–40; constraints from, 40; good
    poor/bad poor distinction, 38; of inter-
    locutors, 13; in Latin America, 57–58;
    stress of, 4
power hierarchies: constraints from, 14; of
    healthcare and social welfare, 38
precarity: of migrant mothers, xiv, 4; of
    undocumented, 4
pregnancy: medical support for, 37; racism
    and, 36
prenatal care: deportation fears and inade-
    quate, 30; provision of free, 7; racializa-
    tion of Latina birth and motherhood in,
    15
pressing onward concept: about, xiv, 179–81;
    capacity for, 16, 27, 28; imperative resil-
    ience and, xiv, 141–43; mothering and, 3,
    131, 135; political defiance and, 142;
    resources for, 15. See also imperative resil-
    ience; policies for moving onward

Priscila (interlocutor), 20–21, 37–38, 75–76, 123, 128–30, 134–35
Project Comprehension, 84
promotores de salud (PdS) programs, 171–72
promotor programs, 172
PRWORA (Personal Responsibility and Work Opportunity Reconciliation), 164, 173
PTSD (post-traumatic stress disorder), 6, 44, 48
public aid: citizenship/legal residency and, 38–39; lack of, 12. *See also* social welfare system
Puerto Rican communities, 66, 69, 86, 87; early, 80–85
Puerto Rico, 55; interlocutors from, 185, 188, 189, 190, 191, 192; migrants to New Haven from, 89

Quinnipiac(k), xi, 77
Quinnipiac River, xi

race suicide, 113
racial-based inequities, COVID-19 pandemic and, 15
racial categories: self-identification struggles, 34–35. *See also* Latinx category
racial classification systems, 35
racial disparities, COVID-19 pandemic, 15
racial diversity, *Latinidad* and, 109
racial inequities: COVID-19 pandemic and, 15; in Latin America, 21
racialization: of health, 15; Latinas experience of, 33–34
racialization of Latina birth, 112–15
racialized health, 144–78; about, 15–16, 144–46, 176–78; attitudes toward vaccination, 158–61; embodied experiences of COVID-19, 146–49; essential services, 170–76; illness and death of loved ones, 149–51; policies for moving onward, 161–70; social impacts, 151–58
racial miscegenation (*mestizaje*), 70
racism, 32–36; acknowledging, 15; constraints from, 40; experience of, 32–36; production of, 14
Ramos, Paola, 74–75
Ramos, Rafael, 91–92
rape: border crossing and, 45, 46; fears in Latin America over, 46–47, 49, 60; migrant women's risk of, 44; strategic coupling and, 137; structural violence and, 24, 25
Rapp, Rayna, 113
Raquel (interlocutor), 34, 36–37, 76, 169–71, 191

Ravenstein, Ernest, 50–51
Reagan administration, 29, 86
reasons for migrating: economic precarity and opportunity, 14, 55–59; family reunification, 14, 53–55; personal violence, 14, 59–61; rebellious acts, 14, 51–53
rebellious acts, as reasons for migrating, 14, 51–53
reconquista threat, 69
Registry Act of 1929, 175
relocations, migration-related trauma and, 14
remesas (remittances), 40
remittances (*remesas*), 40
reparative work, 8
reproductive equity, 15; policies to foster, 11
reproductive histories, 5
resilience: costs of, 180; defined, 11, 128; to resistance, 141–42. *See also* imperative resilience
resistance, from resilience to, 141–42
resistencia, defined, 11
resources: access in Latin America, 22; cognitive, 12; community, 40; emotional, 12; investment of, 12; somatic, 12
reunification. *See* family reunification
Rivera, Pete, 86, 104–5
Roberts, Dorothy, 36, 141
Rodriguez, Adriana, xii
Rodríguez-Muñiz, Michael, 65, 68, 77, 115
Roemer, John, 21, 168–69
Rojas, Fátima, 104
Rosalia (interlocutor), 192
Rosenfeld, Barry, 6, 32

Scheper-Hughes, Nancy, 143
Schiller, Nina Glick, 28
Second Star of Jacob Church, 85
self-classification, 34–35
Semilla Collective, 4, 104, 193
Sendero Luminoso (Shining Path), 86
sequir adelante (press onward). *See* pressing onward concept
sexual assaults: fears of, 48; in Latin America, 24, 59; in Peru, 86. *See also* rape
sexual diversity, *Latinidad* and, 109
Sigona, Nando, 53
situational factors, as influences, 14
social adversity, 5
social impacts, of COVID-19, 151–58
social inequality, violence of, 20–23
social programs: failure of in Latin America, 14, 19, 25–26, 40, 59; in Latin America, 22
social reciprocity, 37

social safety net, migrants and erosion of, 163–65
social support: from family, 30; of home countries, 13, 22; as limited, 12, 22
social welfare system: 20th century concerns about, 77; Foucault on social welfare, 38; gaps in, 168; healthcare support as distinguished from, 37; in Latin America, 22, 40; presumption of dependence on, 112; PRWORA, 164; racist attitudes toward, 113; resistance to, 20; retrenchment of, 62; Trump administration's cuts to, 165
sociodemographics, 5
sociopolitical violence, impact of, 19
Sonia (interlocutor), 189
Sonoran Desert, 42–43
South American migrants, 86, 87
Spanish Cultural Association of New Haven, 84
Spanish Empire, 70
Special Supplemental Nutrition Program for Women, Infants, and Children (WIC) office, 8, 162
spirituality, 131–34; defined, 15; reliance on, 12
state failure, as driver of migration, 14, 19, 25–26, 40, 59
status. See undocumented state ("illegality")
stereotypes, 21, 36, 115
Stolcke, Verena, 28
St. Raphael's Hospital, 122
strategic coupling, 28, 134–38; defined, 15
structural disadvantage, strategies in response to, 11
structural interventions, immigration reform, 12
structural reform, connecting sectors for, 12
structural violence, police as instruments of, 23–25
structural vulnerability, 26–28; conditions of, 14; COVID-19 pandemic and, 15; defined, 28; surviving, 14, 40
survival, about, 14. See also racialized health
Susana (interlocutor), 31, 35, 185
sweat equity, 39

temporary protective status (TPS), 29, 175
tenacity, of children of immigrants, 14
Teresa (interlocutor), 26–28, 173
terminology note, 72–75
A Terrible Thing to Waste (Washington), 97
theories of migration, 50–51; push-pull theories, 14

TOLAC (trial of labor after Cesarean), 116–21
TPS (temporary protective status), 29, 175
trauma: accommodating, 11; acknowledging, 15; COVID-19 and, 3; intergenerational trauma, 9–10; migration-related trauma, 43–44, 44; surveys of symptoms of, 6; surviving, 14; traumatic birth experiences, 15
Treaty of Guadalupe-Hidalgo, 65
trial of labor after Cesarean (TOLAC), 116–21
Trump administration: chain migration, 76; hostility of, xiv, 29, 35–36; welfare program cuts by, 38–39, 165; zero tolerance policy of, 61
Tutu, Desmond, 123

UndocuBlack Network, 193
undocumented status ("illegality"), 14, 28–32
undocumented women, clinics and, 7
unemployment, lack of benefit access, 4
Ungar, Michael, 130
Unidad Latina en Acción (ULA), 76–77, 92, 103, 109, 193
uninsured mothers, prenatal care programs and, 15
United States: interventionism by, 23; neoliberal economic policies promotion by, 23
United We Dream, 194
urban safety, 15; in New Haven, 91–94
U.S. Census Bureau, 15, 69
US naturalization, costs of, 29

vaccination: attitudes toward, 15, 158–61; vaccine hesitancy, 15
values, transmission of, 15
Vanessa (interlocutor), 188, 191
van Natta, Meredith, 169
Vera Institute, 193
Verónica (interlocutor), 60
violence: about, 14; criminal violence in Latin America, 23; gender-based violence, 61, 173–74; intimate partner violence, 173–74; migration-related trauma, 4, 43–44; new violence of Latin America, 19–20; personal violence as reasons for migrating, 14, 59–61; of social inequality, 20–23. See also rape; structural violence
violence of migration, 41–63; about, 14, 41–43; border crossing, 45–50; conclusion, 63; migration-related trauma, 43–44; production of illegality, 61–62
Violence against Women Act of 1994, 174
visas, family tourist visas, 2
vulnerability. See structural vulnerability

Vuong, Ocean, 13, 51, 180

Waldstein, Anna, 155
Walia, Harsha, 62
Washington, Harriet A., 97
Waterbury neighborhood, interlocutors from, 12
welfare. *See* social welfare system
West Haven neighborhood, interlocutors from, 12
Whiteness, 9, 54, 69, 70–71
WIC (Special Supplemental Nutrition Program for Women, Infants, and Children) office, 8, 162
Willen, Sarah, 29–30, 37
Wilson, Joe, 165
wisdom, transmission of, 15
Women's Center of Yale–New Haven Health, 6, 7, 26, 112, 119, 127
Worker and Immigrant Rights Advocacy Clinic (WIRAC), 103

xenophobia, forces of, 109

Yaiza (interlocutor), 40
Yale, Elihu, 107
Yale Human Investigation Committee (HIC), 183
Yale–New Haven Health, xiii, 37, 80, 109, 170; bill processing by, 168; New Haven and, 106–9; Women's Center of, 6, 7, 26, 111–12, 118, 127
Yale–New Haven Hospital, 85, 109, 116, 122, 162, 184
Yale School of Public Health, 94
Yale University, 106–7, 109; New Haven and, 6–7, 106–9; reparative work and, 8
Young Lords, 93–94
Ysabel (interlocutor), 21, 35, 49, 59–60, 61, 160–61, 180, 185, 190

zero tolerance policies, 165
Zimmerman, George, 70

Founded in 1893,
UNIVERSITY OF CALIFORNIA PRESS
publishes bold, progressive books and journals
on topics in the arts, humanities, social sciences,
and natural sciences—with a focus on social
justice issues—that inspire thought and action
among readers worldwide.

The UC PRESS FOUNDATION
raises funds to uphold the press's vital role
as an independent, nonprofit publisher, and
receives philanthropic support from a wide
range of individuals and institutions—and from
committed readers like you. To learn more, visit
ucpress.edu/supportus.